ADOLESCENTS: Theoretical and Helping Perspectives

International Series in Social Welfare

Previously Published Books in the Series:
Crane, J.A., *The Evaluation of Social Policies*, 1982
Schuerman, J.R., *Multivariate Analysis in the Human Services*, 1983.
Hollingsworth, J.R., and Hanneman, R., *Centralization and Power in Social Service Delivery Systems*, 1983
Stein, T.J. and Rzepnicki, T., *Decision Making in Child Welfare Services*, 1984
Clarke, R. and Hope, T., *Coping with Burglary*, 1984
Sherman, E., *Working with Older Persons*, 1984

ADOLESCENTS
Theoretical and
Helping
Perspectives

Inger P. Davis
San Diego State University
College of Human Services
School of Social Work

Kluwer-Nijhoff Publishing
a member of the Kluwer Academic Publishers Group
Boston/Dordrecht/Lancaster

Distributors for North America:
KLUWER ACADEMIC PUBLISHERS
190 Old Derby Street
Hingham, Massachusetts 02043, U.S.A.

Distributors outside North America:
KLUWER ACADEMIC PUBLISHERS GROUP
Distribution Centre
P.O. Box 322
3300 AH Dordrecht,
THE NETHERLANDS

Library of Congress Cataloging in Publication Data

Davis, Inger P.
   Adolescents: theoretical and helping perspectives.

   (International series in social welfare)
   Bibliography: p.
   Includes index.
   1. Youth — United States. 2. Adolescent psychology.
3. Interpersonal relations. 4. Youth — Services for — United
States. I. Title. II. Series.
HQ796.D29   1985   305.2′35   84-20175
ISBN 0-89838-165-7

Printed in the United States of America

Contents

Acknowledgments

Appreciation is expressed to William J. Reid, editor of the International Series in Social Welfare for his encouragement and unintrusive and constructive suggestions. The Office of Human Development Services, Department of Health and Human Services provided financial support in the early stages of this project (Child Welfare Teaching Grant, 1979 #8-1092377, 1980 #9-1092376, and 1982 #1-1092377). Elsie Herman, Hope Logan, and Lorraine Newbrough, former colleagues of mine at the School of Social Work, San Diego State University, participated directly in one or more of these grant supported child welfare projects. Their contributions are gratefully acknowledged.

Several graduate seminars made use of early versions of this book, which has been enriched by the students' ideas and practice experiences. Graduate research assistants helped in several phases of this project: Laura Haslam, Sandra A. Parsons, Linda Peterson, and Diana S. Smith deserve special mention. I am grateful for contributions from many other persons, social service agency representatives, practitioners from various disciplines, and, not least, for what I have learned directly from troubled adolescents and their families.

ADOLESCENTS: Theoretical and Helping Perspectives

1 INTRODUCTION

This book deals with ways of helping families cope with the difficulty of raising adolescents. Professional social workers — along with other human service professionals — encounter these families in numerous settings: child welfare and family service agencies, hospitals, schools, community mental health clinics, residential treatment centers, juvenile halls and detention centers, recreational and vocational training organizations, and many others. While families from all walks of life may be found in these settings, families who have suffered the additional stresses of poverty, discrimination, and the consequences of physical and mental illness are commonly overrepresented.

Even under the best of circumstances, the adolescent years often put the strongest family structures to the test — sometimes to the breaking point. A recent national study of over one thousand average, middle-income, two-parent families reviewed the strengths, stresses, and satisfactions of the family life cycle (Olson and McCubbin 1983). As many would expect, families with adolescents were found to experience more stress and lower levels of family adaptability, cohesion, and marital and family satisfaction than any other developmental stage. The families with adolescents who fared best were those with such marital resources as good communication and conflict resolution skills, satisfying sexual relations, and good parent-adolescent communication.

1

Qualities like these are in short supply in many of the families served by the agencies listed above. For a 13-year-old adolescent boy who has experienced 13 separations from parental figures, including two sets of adoptive parents and three sets of foster parents, the fundamental questions of the adolescent separation-individuation process become separation from whom? From what set of parents? For him and thousands of other adolescents, the launching into young adulthood occurs not from a family but from foster homes, residential centers, group homes, or psychiatric hospitals. Compared with the total adolescent population of the United States, the number in out-of-home care is small, but an attempt is made throughout this book to portray the whole gamut of adolescents in families and environments ranging from nurturant to hostile.

A Few Statistics on the Adolescent Population

Close to 40 million teenagers accounted for 17.4 percent of the U.S. population in 1980;[1] ten years earlier they formed an even greater part of the population — 19.6 percent — which was the highest proportionate size of the adolescent population since the 1910 census. The number of adolescents in need of support and services to cope with the developmental tasks of adolescence is unknown. It is known that 42 percent of the 1.768 million children who received services from public agencies in 41 states in the first quarter of 1977 were between 11 and 17 years of age while the remaining 59 percent were preadolescents (Shyne and Schroeder 1978). No later figures are available.

The percentage distribution on the world continents of the world population of 10–19 year olds (as derived from the United Nations' Demographic Yearbook 1981) gives another perspective of the size of the U.S. teenage population which made up only 6.6 percent of the 12 percent on the North American continent. (The figures presented do not include China for which no statistics could be located.)

	Percentage of World Teenage Population, 1981
Africa	9%
North America	12
South America	9
Asia and Oceania	46
Europe	13
Union of Soviet Republics and Ukraine	11

Trends in the Research Literature on Adolescence

Over the last couple of decades many popular and professional assumptions regarding normalcy in adolescent behavior and family interaction have been challenged by large-scale studies of adolescents. Empirical studies have also generated assessment instruments beneficial to work with the individual adolescent as well as the family group. The impact of these developments is noted in the professional literature as a trend toward greater utilization of family-group interventions in dealing with adolescent behavior problems.

Researchers today show a healthy caution in not generalizing from study samples of "clinic" or incarcerated youth to the general adolescent population, and they have gained greater knowledge of variations in healthy family interaction. Even so, it still seems true that adolescent psychology by and large builds on studies carried out with white, middle-class, adolescent males. Only the last few years show an increase in studies of adolescents from varied cultural backgrounds and social classes and of female adolescents.

The social work profession gives priority to improvement of overall services to families marred by poverty, physical and mental illness, discrimination, and other stressful environmental factors. Therefore, gains in knowledge in adolescent psychology are of somewhat limited value to the social worker specializing in work with adolescents from such backgrounds. The need for additional research covering all ethnic, cultural, and socioeconomic groups seems clear. This book is designed to clarify the nature of this need and to give guidance to the direction of such research efforts.

A hopeful development of the last decade is the seeming replacement of turf struggles among disciplines addressing adolescent behavior problems with the view that such problems call for interdisciplinary research efforts and service delivery. This may mark a return to the spirit prevalent at the turn of this century, when education, medicine, and the emerging social work profession joined forces in research efforts as well as in development of services for children and youth in hospitals, schools, clinics, and social agencies. After World War I representatives from the "pure" science disciplines joined these research efforts, and we saw the beginning of what Robert R. Sears calls "the tremulous partnership that always seems to exist when pure and applied science, and the services of scientists, are directed toward fulfilling social rather than purely intellectual needs" (p. 4). The preference for social usefulness of the research product to the field of child and youth development over purely tested theoretical propositions has imposed a multidisciplinary structure on this area of research and practice. Social work has been a continuous partner on such interdisciplinary teams, even though the emphasis in social work generally has been more on service delivery than on research.

While *tremulous* seems an adequate term for the applied and pure research partnership, a much stronger term, such as discordance, is needed to depict the relationship between research and practice. The thirst for knowing versus the compulsion for doing are in a constant battle. In some human service professionals, one or the other force wins out 90 percent of the time, and they can live relatively peaceful lives. In others the two forces appear of almost equal strength; they have to live with the constant tension of moving back and forth between the worlds of practice and research. Richard J. Gelles, whose writings and research on family violence have been helpful to so many from different disciplines, has expressed very well the agonies of shifting gears from research to practice. During a sabbatical year from research spent in the role of clinician in an interdisciplinary outpatient clinic dealing with child abuse cases, Gelles found himself stating publicly that he considered child abusers to be crazy, despite his earlier published statement discrediting psychopathological explanations. Once, having this pointed out to him, he exclaimed: "I don't care what I wrote — these people are nuts!" (Gelles 1983, p. 18).

Turning to research findings used in this book, it needs to be made clear that this is not a review of research chosen for quality of research design and research execution. The aim has been to gather ideas and information about adolescent behavior in association with their families and peers that are of potential usefulness to practitioners, not to present only true and tested empirical evidence. One complication is that information and ideas on this topic are often hidden, if not buried, in studies dealing primarily with some other family or developmental variables.

Some common flaws and limitations of the studies utilized include nonrepresentative samples; one-shot or cross-sectional measurements, as longitudinal studies, are very rare; self-report data from adolescents, which are sometimes in disagreement with parent- or teacher-generated data; and lack of control for intervening variables that may account for observed differences, for example, as found in studies of adolescent experiences in single-parent families, where it is difficult to sort out the impact of the predivorce family interaction, the divorce experience itself, interaction with one parent, or the lowered socio-economic status usually associated with the change from two-parent to one-parent living. Furthermore, many studies are vague about age distribution of samples. Sometimes, only the range from 6 to 15 years is given with no way of knowing of any differences between the preadolescents and the adolescents. At other times, the text or case illustrations indicate that adolescents were indeed included, but there is no way of knowing how many there were. The common concerns about use of clinical samples certainly are present in many of the studies referred to — the sample families and/or adolescents may be worse off than those who do not seek help because they can manage on their own, but they may also be better off than those who are too miserable and too lacking in strength and motivation to seek help. As usual in large-scale survey samples, one is limited to those who respond and who may be quite uncharacteristic from the nonrespondents. An example is Patricia Lutz's (1983) study of adolescent experiences in stepfamilies, which fills a serious gap in knowledge. Via the schools she identified 294 such adolescents; 113 returned signed permission slips and 103 actually completed the questionnaire. Very useful information was obtained: namely, that the greatest source of stress experienced was loyalty conflict, while being part of two households was not considered to be especially stressful, as one would be led to believe from the literature in general. Valuable as this information is one is left with the nagging doubt about what the experiences of stepfamily living were for the 191 nonrespondents.

General Purpose of Book and Sources of Materials Used

This book draws together and discusses findings about the adolescent stage of development, including characteristics of various family and peer interaction patterns, and about outcomes of different modes of intervention used with adolescent clients and their families. Throughout the book attention is given to male and female adolescent experiences and to cultural and ethnic variations. This book integrates information and insight gained from clinical observations with knowledge derived from empircial studies in adolescent development and pathology. The hope is that a unified reference for adolescent behavior and intervention will be helpful to practitioners and students who contemplate expanding their services to adolescents. It is also hoped that the book will provide a fairly comprehensive picture of U.S. social work with adolescents for readers outside the United States. The interventive modes discussed in this book are limited to direct work with adolescents and their families, that is, to interpersonal helping aimed at facilitating problem solving and changes in relationship interactions that promote adolescent developmental task achievement. The counseling role is frequently combined with that of advocate and broker to link the young clients with essential environmental resources. This perspective in no way diminishes the importance of administrative and other social work functions in this field; adolescents are often leery of "establishment" agencies and skeptical of what the adult world is up to, so that the total gestalt of the service setting needs to reflect respect for and sensitivity to the needs of this age group.

Material for the book has been gathered from about 1500 journal articles and about 200 books representing many professional disciplines. While some movement toward greater recognition of this developmental stage is evident in the number of professional journals and specializations within professions, it is startling how widely scattered the information about adolescence is. The author has been systematically gathering materials for at least ten years. It has at times been a discouraging process, often like shifting a ton of sand through a tea sieve only to discover that what looked like nuggets of gold turned out to be false. In this process valuable findings, observations, and ideas no doubt have been discarded since they were not directly relevant to the point at hand. From those readers whose favorite studies or pieces of clinical literature were not included I ask forbearance; I welcome suggestions regarding anything I may have overlooked.

Much of the material included in this book has been tested in teaching graduate social work seminars on troubled adolescents and their families. Six such seminars have been taught, of which two were specifically designed for graduate students who were specializing in child welfare services to adolescents. The latter seminars were supported by Federal Child Welfare Teaching Grants, facilitating production of three monographs (Davis 1979, 1980, and 1982). Parts of these monographs have been incorporated into this book. Case vignettes and other case illustrations have been provided by experienced practitioners, and some have been generated by the graduate seminars. Others are from the author's own clinical experience in work with adolescents and their families in the United States and in Denmark. Cases are used as illustrations of certain ideas or points, not as evidence for theoretical propositions or as accounting for specific interventive techniques. All names, dates, places and other identifying information in the cases have been changed to protect confidentiality.

Plan for the Book

Chapter 2 presents a brief overview of changing perceptions of adolescence over time. It reviews the impact on adolescent behavior of the sexual, physical, and intellectual changes of puberty, with special attention to late maturers and those with physical and intellectual handicaps. It also presents selected adolescent developmental theories from the biological/instinctual, psychodynamic, behavioral, and social-psychological schools of thought.

Havighurst's formulation of the eight adolescent developmental tasks sets the stage for the major thrust of chapter 3 — the adolescent's maturational separation from the family of origin. This process is viewed in the light of findings from four major and numerous small-scale studies of families with adolescents and from reported clinical observations. The dual task of raising autonomous children and meeting parental maturational needs is considered in families with varying degrees of competence in launching adolescents, including parents utilizing what Stierlin has called the binding, expelling, and delegating modes of separation. The adolescent's move out of the family is next considered under the circumstances of divorce, the move from single-parent and remarried families. The chapter is concluded by consideration of the role of siblings in adolescent developmental processes.

Chapter 4 completes part I, which concerns adolescent developmental psychology. The relative importance of the influence of parents and peers is considered in the adolescent's move toward autonomy and identity formation exemplified by four stages: identity achievement, moratorium, foreclosure, and identity diffusion. Relations with peers of the opposite sex, teenage pregnancy, abortion, parenthood, and marriage are considered, followed by the interplay between vocational commitment and the all-too-few job opportunities for the young. The chapter closes by reviewing gender, social class, and cultural variations in adolescent development.

Part II deals with services and interventions to adolescents whose behavior is troublesome to themselves, their families, or the community. Chapter 5 presents supportive services available to adolescents living with their biological families that are provided by the school, medical care, community mental health services, and other private and public agencies and organizations. Special attention is given to the under- and over-representations of various minority adolescents in these services. This chapter concludes with a brief overview of adolescents and the legal system. Chapter 6 continues the account of services to adolescents, profiling services for those who must be or are separated from their families. Four types of out-of-home care are presented: family foster care, adoption, residential treatment and psychiatric hospital care, and community group homes. The final section deals with some aspects of parental involvement in the lives of adolescents in out-of-home care.

Chapter 7 focuses on how human service professionals help adolescents and their families, that is, the interventive methods. The chapter opens with a recapitulation of a number of theoretical frameworks presented in part I as a foundation for assessment and intervention planning. The empirical basis for which interventive modes have been found useful with specific types of adolescent behavior problems is summarized, followed by the pros and cons of family-group treatment, peer-group interventions, and counseling of the adolescent on an individual basis.

Chapter 8 presents interventions with selected groups of adolescents in need of services. The groups include teenagers from divorced and remarried families and adolescents in out-of-home care and adoptive homes. Finally, the dynamics and treatment of runaway youths are discussed. Many other groups of adolescents deserve attention, such as those with learning disabilities, those struggling with depressive and suicidal thoughts, those coping with eating disorders and psychiatric illnesses, those trying to overcome addictions to alcohol or chemical substances, and those who start down the road of juvenile delinquency. The plight and needs of these adolescents are touched upon at various points, but a full analysis and discussion of these topics awaits another book.

Note

1. According to the U.S. Department of Commerce (1982), the 10–19 year olds numbered 39.5 million in 1980, while the total U.S. population counted 226.5 million persons.

I ADOLESCENT DEVELOPMENT AND PSYCHOSOCIAL TASKS

2 HISTORY, FACTS, AND THEORIES

Is the concept of adolescence universally and uniformly defined and understood across cultures and time? What do we know about the adolescent stage of psychosocial development, and how empirically grounded is this knowledge? These and other philosophical and theoretical questions are addressed in this chapter to provide a foundation for discussions in later chapters of assessment and interventions with adolescent clients and their families.

Adolescence, the developmental period between childhood and adulthood, spans the years from 12–13 to the early 20s. It is a complex period of human growth that leaves many parents, teachers, and counselors perplexed and startled by rapid changes in mood and behavior. The complexity is reflected in a multitude of definitions and theories about adolescence. Some theorists argue that adolescence is not a distinct stage of development but rather an ongoing, gradual, growth process with no characteristic behaviors distinguishing adolescents from children or adults. Others, the stage theorists, maintain that adolescence is a distinct stage, beginning with pubescence, that is, the bodily changes of sexual maturation, and ending at a somewhat ill-defined point of achievement of adult status and roles.

The word *adolescence,* derived from the Latin verb *adolescere* — to grow up — appeared for the first time in the 15th century (Muuss 1982, p. 8). At times the terms *adolescence* and *youth* are used interchangeably; however, *youth* has a broader connotation than *adolescence* and is often used to express an attitude or state of mind rather than a designation of the period between childhood and adulthood. Furthermore, the term *youth* often conveys something positive, while *adolescence* can convey something negative. To have one's appearance or behavior referred to as youthful is experienced as flattering; few, if any, welcome being called adolescent.

A Few Historical Pointers

Adolescent psychology as a scientific discipline began with the research of G. Stanley Hall. His two-volume textbook, published in 1904, views adolescence from the perspectives of physiology, anthropology, sociology, sex, crime, religion, and education. Prior to Hall no theorist dealt exclusively with adolescence, but writings based on personal experiences, historical accounts, and philosophical and religious thinking about the nature of man give us impressions of how young persons were viewed and treated through history. A brief review will trace major changes in such views and the concomitant societal reactions.

An early Greek view is exemplified in Aristotle's (384-322 B.C.) division of human development into three distinct seven-year stages: The first, infancy (from birth to 7), depicts the child as animal-like, but with potential for higher development than animals; a second stage is boyhood (from 7 to puberty), followed by young manhood (from puberty to 21), in which the young man by deliberate and voluntary choices develops habits that then later form the right kind of character for maturity. As the person passes through these stages, the three-layered soul-life develops from the lowest level, which is centered on biological needs, to perception, to the highest level, which includes the ability to think and reason. During young manhood education was considered needed to increase the ability for abstract thinking through the study of topics such as mathematics, astronomy, and theory of music. Greek civilization thus presupposed a substantive difference between childhood and adult life in that the transition between the two was made through the means of education. This Aristotelian view, however, was lost and not rediscovered until the Middle Ages (Muuss 1982, pp. 13-14).

Gillis (1974) in his study of youth in preindustrial Germany and England observed that childhood was not seen as coming to an end with puberty, but with leaving home or lowering the dependence on parents. As early as the age of 7 children left home and moved into other households as servants or apprentices. By the age of 14 the majority was living in this state of semi-dependence. Complete independence was reached when the youth could afford to marry by the mid- or late 20s. Thus the preindustrial European concept of youth as a long transition from complete dependence to independence implies some acceptance of a distinctive period of youth, but one quite different from the present-day concept of adolescence.

Ariès (1962), in his historical study of family life in the Middle Ages, similarly found no distinction between child and adolescent; these words were used interchangeably. Children were regarded as only quantitatively different from adults; they wore adult-style clothes, and painters portrayed children as small-scale adults. They were thought to be born with innate abilities and ideas that were not qualitatively different from those of the adults, with whom they were mixed as soon as they could do without their mothers, usually around the age of 7. Abilities were then thought to be primarily hereditary by nature.

As stated by Muuss (1982), the British philosopher John Locke (1632–1704), the father of empiricism, challenged the belief that ideas are innate. He proposed that the mind of the newborn is like a blank piece of paper (tabula rasa), and that ideas and knowledge can come only from the experience of observing objects around us and from the internal operations of the mind stemming from these sensory observations. Mental activity, first slowly developing during childhood then increasing during adolescence, was seen as culminating in a fully developed rational faculty by the end of adolescence. Thus Locke saw the child as different from the adult in being without mental faculties and the adolescent as different in being in the process of attaining them. From Locke's perspective experiences offered a child are strong determinants of its development. His theory favors nurture over nature, and the emphasis on the importance of the environment combined with his urgings that human nature be systematically observed and studied make Locke a forerunner of 20th century behaviorism and learning theory.

A second philosoher presented by Muuss (1982) as contributing to the acceptance of the unique nature of childhood and youth was Jean Jacque Rousseau (1712–1778), who proposed that healthy human development, a natural preplanned process, takes place only when the child is freed from the limitations and strict discipline of the adult world and allowed to engage in play and other activities natural to a child. He urged parents and teachers to be sensitive to and focused on the child's feelings and thinking in order to allow nature to take its course. Meanwhile, Rousseau's own five children were brought up in a children's institution. Theories often seem to fit the circumstances of others so much better than our own.

Rousseau introduced a theory of saltatory development, in which major spurts in the developmental process take place at certain times. His four stages of development are marked by the emergence of distinct new functions. During infancy (from birth to 4 or 5) the child is animal-like in its physical needs and undifferentiated feelings; in the savage stage (from 5 or 6 to 12) the faculty of sense dominates; the age of reason (from 12 to 15) is marked by growth in the ability to reason, in self-consciousness, and in physical strength; and adolescence (from 15 to 20) is the time when emotional maturation results in a shift from selfishness to consideration of others.

Education of the Young — Past and Present

Today it is difficult to imagine a society without compulsory education for all; the learning needs of the individual and society's dependence on skilled and professionally trained persons compel such education. During the Middle Ages, however, when children were not differentiated from adults, educational institutions served only those with special yearnings for learning, regardless of age. Schools and other seats of learning were populated by men of all ages, boys mixed with men. Only as the special nature and needs of children and youth were recognized was schooling seized upon as a means of developing the mind and guiding a basically sinful human nature in its spiritual and moral development.

During the 16th and 17th centuries, growing proportions of male adolescents received formal schooling, often in boarding schools. This privilege was bestowed primarily on middle- and upper-class youth; children of working-class and poor families largely remained in the work place. Girls were excluded from schools regardless of their class; apart from domestic apprenticeship, girls were given hardly any education (Ariès 1962, pp. 330–333).

Public, tax-supported education first developed in Germany and the Scandinavian countries during the 19th century. Public education was popular in the United States at an early time. Massachusetts, for example, made free high school education compulsory in 1827 (Sears 1975, p. 7), and compulsory tax support to schools was offered in several states by the 1830s. However, the commitment to public education was not universal; by 1900 only two-thirds of the states offered compulsory public education (Sommerville 1982, p. 195).

As schooling became compulsory for all it was discovered in several places that many children were incapable of learning. In France, for example, where compulsory education started late (in 1882), the Paris school board hired Binet and Simon in 1904 to develop tests that would help the board decide which children should be excluded from school altogether, which needed a special kind of schooling, and which could profit from normal schooling (Sears 1975, p. 10).

In the United States, the schools were faced not only with the physically handicapped, developmentally disabled, and incorrigible children, but also with many children of immigrant families of various cultures and languages. The demands for alternative educational programs were great, and by the early 1900s almost 200 major cities in the United States had such programs. They were, however, almost immediately criticized for stigmatizing the pupils, for having an overrepresentation of the poor and ethnic minority children, and for isolating rather than educating these children (Cullinan, Epstein, and Lloyd 1983, p. 18).

Gillis (1974) has called adolescence a phenomenon of the middle class, which monopolized it until the turn of the century when secondary education gradually became available to the laboring population. In 1890 only 5–6 percent of the 14- to 17-year-olds attended high school in the United States; this percentage increased to 33 percent by 1920, 70 percent by 1940, and over 80 percent by the 1960s (Elder 1980, pp. 12–13). It was only as legislation set limits for the use of minors in industry (1917) and as so-called mother's pensions made it possible for widowed families to survive that some of the poor and working-class adolescents became able to take advantage of free public education.

Concentrating an ever-increasing percentage of the youth cohorts in high schools has had many consequences. It has offered greater opportunity for peer association, development of youth cultures and fads, intermingling of poor and rich, and — albeit slowly — integration of minority and majority youth. Major 20th century studies of the high school population, thoughtfully reviewed by Elder (1980), make clear the inequality of access to education beyond high school and to job opportunities (status deprivation) and increasing age segregation.

This cursory review of changes in attitudes and perceptions of youth over the centuries leaves out numerous crucial events and factors. Examples are the treatment of physically and mentally handicapped children and youth as demonically possessed; the witchhunts of those challenging the beliefs of the day (Joan of Arc was 19 years old when she was burned at the stake in Rouen in 1431); and the atrocious working conditions of the numerous children and adolescents who in some places accounted for substantial portions of the labor force in coal mines and industries in the Old as well as the New World. Also not covered is the topic of humanitarian efforts under private and public auspices that during the first two decades of this century led to protective legislation and establishment of welfare and to social and judicial organizations designed to address the needs of adolescents and to cope with the growing problems of juvenile delinquency (Gillis 1974, pp. 133–35; Sears 1975, p. 8). Further explorations of these matters would take us too far afield here. In subsequent chapters a historical view will be taken when it will add to present-day understanding of the topic at hand.

Physical Growth

Sexual Maturation and Bodily Growth

The renown British scholar of adolescent growth and development, J.M. Tanner (1980) pointed out that pubertal, sex-specific, physiological changes have not altered in perhaps thousands of years. The biological growth of girls takes place two years earlier than that of boys, and some boys complete their total growth process before other boys of the same age have started theirs. The sequence of biological events has also remained stable, but these events now occur at a younger chronological age.

We tend to think about puberty as a fairly sudden biological event, while in fact the reproductive system starts its development at conception. Puberty is distinguished from the rest of the biological life cycle by its magnitude and rate of change (Petersen and Taylor 1980). The bodily growth spurt and sexual maturation are brought about by the sex hormones (androgens and estrogens) and other hormones. Boys as well as girls produce both kinds of sex hormones, but more androgen is produced by the male reproductive glands, the testes, than by the female. Conversely, more estrogens are produced by the female glands, the ovaries, than by the male.

Tanner's maturational scales (1980, p. 188; also reprinted in Johnston 1979; and in U.S. Dept. HEW 1980) give the average values for British boys and girls of height spurt and development of secondary sex characteristics, that is, development of pubic hair, accelerated growth, and onset of menarche in girls. Tanner notes that the North American averages are within two or three months of the British averages. The first sign of puberty in girls is the appearance of "breast-buds" between the ages of 8 and 13, and puberty is completed within three years. Menarche, the first menstrual period, normally occurs toward the end of this period after the peak of height spurt. The age of onset of menarche ranges from 10 to 16 1/2 years. Puberty in boys starts two years later than in girls; pubic hair appears between the ages of 10 and 15, and penis growth starts between 11 and 14 1/2, with the first ejaculation of seminal fluid taking place about a year after the start of accelerated penis growth.

According to Tanner's study findings, rapid acceleration of skeletal and muscular growth begins in boys around 13 years of age, peaking at about 14. On an average girls start at 11 years of age, peaking at 12. The bodily growth involves almost all bodily dimensions, but not to an equal degree.

Fears that this growth process will never come to an end are commonly experienced by adolescents, who awkwardly try to hide their growing feet and hands. Very little is known about what actually triggers the start and the termination of pubertal growth (Petersen and Taylor 1980). One reason for this is the difficulty of obtaining accurate measures of bodily changes about which many young adolescents feel embarrased and anxious. Anne C. Petersen and her coresearchers (Petersen, Tobin-Richards, and Boxer 1983) present evidence that adolescents' self-reports about pubertal changes are reliable and valid so that more intrusive measures can be avoided for some purposes. This research team also studied possible associations between pubertal changes and psychosocial factors among randomly selected 6th graders from two suburban, middle- to upper-class school districts. Pubertal, cognitive, and psychosocial status were observed over a 3-year period. The findings suggest no relation of puberty to cognitive functioning. However, for boys, a strong and statistically significant linear association was found between pubertal maturation and positive body image and feelings of attractiveness, with facial hair as the strongest factor among the pubertal change items. For girls the strongest association between self-perception and pubertal status (early, intermediary or late maturers) was found among those of intermediary status while late maturers ranked second. Except for breast development, early maturation of all other pubertal indices were less positively experienced by girls. This finding is in accord with that of an earlier study, that girls who menstruate early have very negative feelings about themselves (Petersen 1983).

Physical Illnesses and Handicaps

The many endocrinologic and physical changes of puberty make adolescents vulnerable to a number of medical disorders, of which most are endocrinologic in nature. Commonly occurring illnesses are: growth disorders, acne, obesity, anorexia nervosa, anemia, venereal diseases, hyperthyroidism, diabetes, hypertension, asthma, and mononucleosis (Daniel 1977; Shearin and Jones 1979). As medical advances have prolonged life expectancies of children with congenital or postnatal handicaps, increasing numbers of victims of blindness, deafness, spina bifida, cerebral palsy, and rheumatoid arthritis are found in the adolescent age range.

The impact of illness and disability on the adolescent's psychosocial development depends on many factors. Among them are the onset and severity of the handicap; the premorbid psychosocial development, in the case of postnatal handicaps caused by sudden illness or accidents; the extent to which the handicap arouses pity, shock, overprotection, or ridicule from persons with whom the adolescent interacts; and the degree of support from family, peers, and professionals. The adolescent's reaction may range from withdrawal, negative self-image, a sense of powerlessness, impulsive aggression, and preoccuption with death to overly ambitious goals, which sometimes are reached against all odds. Over one-fourth of the 400 men and women in the Goertzel and Goertzel (1962) study, *Cradles of Eminence,* had physical handicaps that seemed to have been determining factors in the drive for achievement.

Empirical findings on handicapped adolescents are meager and often inconclusive. Chess and Fernandez (1980), for example, review some studies on deafness that support and some that refute the commonly held assumption that deafness is associated with four personality characteristics, impulsivity, hyperactivity, rigidity, and suspiciousness. They spot weaknesses in research methodology (paper-and-pencil tests and routine qustionnaires) as one source of inconclusiveness of the reviewed findings. Their own longitudinal interview study of 171 deaf rubella adolescents and 34 normal controls showed that by age 14 or 15, 75 percent of the adolescents whose sole handicap was deafness did not exhibit impulsive, hyperactive, rigid and suspicious behaviors, as compared with 94 percent of the controls. However, only 32 percent of the deaf adolescents with multiple handicaps showed none of the four behaviors. Self-abuse in the form of hitting, pinching, scratching, and biting of self during emotional tantrums remained constant for the multi-handicapped group, but it gradually subsided over the childhood years for the deaf-only adolescents. The researchers underscore that this differentiation in interaction with the environment has obvious implications for the handicapped adolescents' educational and other development.

Johnson (1981) similarly points to inconclusive findings regarding juvenile diabetes. Some studies show diabetics to have below-average school performance, while others indicate as good a school performance as nondiabetics. Other data reviewed by Johnson suggest that by age 12 to 15 many diabetics are capable of taking responsibility for management of their disease (injections and controlled sugar intake), and some are perhaps overly optimistic in planning careers and future marriage considering the possible serious physical conditions that may develop and the hereditary nature of the illness. Johnson views many studies' findings as uninterpretable because of poor research methodology, particularly in regard to measurement techniques.

Lefebvre (1983) sees adolescence as the time when a disabled youngster fully grasps for the first time the social implications of physical inadequacy in regard to career options, athletic activities, and sexual appeal. She notes that boys generally find functional disabilities (such as orthopedic impairment) more incapacitating, while girls find it harder to accept cosmetic defects. Many factors enter into how the adolescent copes with a chronic disability. The study of Myers, Friedman, and Weiner (1970) of 25 early adolescent girls with scoliosis (curvature of the spine) found that positive coping in accepting the need to wear a brace was related to intellectual understanding of scoliosis and corrective bracing, optimistic views of outcome with a definite termination time, and ongoing support from family and medical staff. Sixteen of the girls adjusted well to wearing the brace, while seven had interfering behavioral symptoms and two girls refused the brace altogether. Negative coping was associated with limitations in intellectual understanding of the condition and treatment; denial of the deformity; excessive dependence on the mother, leading to conflict with her; marital conflicts and other parental problems that diminished the support given to the daughter; and the long duration for wearing the brace, which at first had to be worn 24 hours a day.

Lefebvre (1983) notes similar discrepancies in adolescent reactions. Some keep competing with their nonhandicapped peers and often suffer loneliness, defeat, and rejection in the process; others quit school and "retreat into a wheel chair" or other passivity. Variations in psychosocial reactions to disability were noted in a large-scale survey of cerebral palsy and spina bifida teenagers in Great Britain (Anderson and Clarke 1982). While more than half of these disabled adolescents showed no overt signs of psychological problems, the incidence of such problems as depression, lack of self-confidence, fearfulness and anxiety was three to four times more frequent among the disabled teenagers than among a small control group of nonhandicapped. Negative psychological reactions were not limited to the severely handicapped, as might have been expected, but also found among adolescents with relatively mild disabilities.

In the past, adolescent illnesses and handicaps have been attended to by either pediatricians or medical doctors specializing in adult medicine. Little knowledge existed of the psychological and interpersonal effects of these physical ills at the adolescent stage of development. The last couple of decades have brought about what seems a healthy move toward comprehensive adolescent care by teams of human service professionals and the development of adolescent medicine as a specialty that takes into account the interplay of physical, psychological, and environmental factors in onset and management of illness and handicapping conditions. This development is not limited to the North American continent; three international adolescent medicine symposia with representatives from many countries have already taken place, the last in Jerusalem in 1983.

Concomitant expansion has taken place in helpful, interdisciplinary, professional literature, to which justice is not done here. A few examples of texts are Anderson and Clarke 1982; Coates, Petersen, and Perry 1982; Daniel 1977; and Gallagher, Heald, and Garell 1976. In spite of these helpful developments it still appears that the unknowns outstrip the knowns with respect to explaining the wide gap between early and late biological maturation and the interplay between adolescent maturational processes and physical illness and handicaps. Progress has been made in describing many of the consequences of such conditions, but we still do not fully understand the widely discrepant coping responses of two young men, 17 and 18 years of age, described and compared by Adams and Lindeman (1974). They had similar accidents and subsequent quadriplegia, similar rehabilitation and medical care, and similar preaccident resources and background. Yet one was able to adjust his life goals to the fact that he would never be able to walk again, to complete college, and to gain employment as a teacher; the other never accepted his disability, vacillated between depression and becoming angry and demanding, and made no educational or vocational progress. In their analysis of the two cases, Adams and Lindemann point out that in cases of permanent loss of basic sensory-motor capacities, the ability to move from the "sick" role to the feeling of being "different" becomes crucial. Feeling sick is tied up with expectations of becoming better. Acceptance by the disabled person that he or she is no longer sick but different creates the foundation for a new self-image. If, as was the case for the young man who did not succeed in rehabilitation, the self-image is inexorably tied up with physical prowess, a new self-image cannot emerge (Adams and Lindemann 1974, pp 130–37).

Cognitive Development

Cognitive development of adolescents is demonstrably different from that of children, particularly with respect to problem-solving, vocabulary knowledge, and numerical reasoning. How may this difference be explained, and what are the crucial variables operating in cognitive performance? Some answers may be found in the many theories about cognitive development that burst forth during the 1970s. The grandfather of these theories is the Swiss psychologist Jean Piaget (1896–1980), whose ideas have slowly influenced thinking in the United States. Reasons for this slowness may be the extreme complexity of Piaget's theory, combined with language, philosophical, and methodological barriers. Piaget and his coworkers in Geneva have engaged primarily in qualitative studies of children's thought processes in which the children themselves were asked to explain how they arrived at answers to presented experimental tasks. Recent, more quantitatively oriented research has been critical of some of Piaget's ideas (Keating 1980). However, even Piaget's critics recognize his crucial contributions to the creation of the field of cognitive psychology.

Piaget's theory focuses on logical thinking, structure of thought processes, and the interaction between biological and environmental influences on cognitive functioning. He sees the ability to engage in formal operational thought, developing around age 11 or 12, as the crowning of the evolutionary process that starts at birth. This process leads from the sensorimotor phase (infancy to age 2) to the preoperative phase (from age 2 to 7), in which the child's intuitive thinking is directly dependent on sensory experiences. In the concrete operations phase (from age 7 to 11), the child is capable of limited logical thinking, namely, dealing with concepts that are reality based. What is new in the final, formal operation phase (reached around age 14 or 15) is the capacity for abstract thinking, that is, reasoning about concepts that are independent of concrete stimuli or situations. The concepts may simply be verbally or symbolically expressed. The adolescent's increased ability to conceptualize and engage in propositional thinking also includes "second-degree" thinking, that is, reflection about one's own thinking. These developments have obvious implications for the adolescent's educational and other needs and functioning.

Piaget's notion that adolescence is the last phase of intellectual development has been questioned. Douvan and Gold (1966) conclude in their review of developmental research that most people continued to improve in general intellectual functioning during and beyond adolescence. Some studies report that intellectual ability peaks in the early 20s, with slight variations for specific abilities, and Arlin (1975, as quoted by Muuss 1982) presents some empirical evidence that an additional fifth "problem-finding" stage in adulthood may constitute reasoning beyond the formal operation thought processes of the fourth stage.

In any event, Piaget's work has stimulated expansion of the concept of cognitive development to include Lawrence Kohlberg's cognitive-developmental approach to adolescent morality and the concept of social cognition, which attempts to integrate various social and cognitive phenomena (Muuss 1982). Social cognition research includes Robert Selman's theory of role-taking and David Elkind's theory of adolescent egocentrism, that is, the inability to differentiate between one's own point of view and that of others

(Muuss 1982, chapters 11, 12, and 13). These latest theoretical developments on moral thinking, role-taking behavior, and egocentrism may hold great promise as frameworks for human service interventions with adolescent clients. It is not known if such application has yet taken place.

Prior to adolescence boys and girls do not differ in cognitive functioning. However, sex differences on three cognitive abilities appear during adolescence: males score higher than females on tests of mathematical and spatial ability, and females, on the average, score higher on tests of verbal ability. Petersen and Wittig (1979) suggest that it is more likely that the differences are related to interactions of brain organization, endocrine influences, and educational and socialization experiences rather than solely sociocultural or biological factors. However, this proposed interactional, integrated hypothesis for sex-related differences in cognitive functioning still awaits full empirical testing.

Gifted Adolescents

Another differential on the normal curve of intelligence is the high-scoring gifted adolescent at one end and the mentally retarded at the opposite end. Gifted adolescents are not usually thought of as a group in need of attention by human service professionals, and most of them are not. It is the author's impression — based on clinical observations only — that quite a number of highly gifted adolescents can be found in mental health and social service caseloads. For some of them the bright mind may create additional frustration; others appear able to capitalize on the one individual asset they have and use their superior intellect to achieve in school work and to counterbalance defeats and humiliations in other areas of their lives. Facts are meager about who are the gifted, what becomes of them, and what their lifelong achievements and satisfactions are. Robert Hogan (1980) observes that the literature on gifted adolescents is characterized by a curious conceptual barrenness. He notes difficulties in defining giftedness, which covers more than high intelligence, and the inconclusiveness of the relatively few empirical studies on gifted adolescents. With respect to the enrichment and acceleration programs that many school systems provide to promote development of unusual talents, Hogan reports that the intended rapid assimilation of knowledge has taken place, but these programs do not foster the hoped for increase in imagination and synthesis. On the other hand, they do not seem to be doing any harm either, even though some students participating in accelerated programs tend to have a higher incidence of troubled social relationships than do nonaccelerated youth (Hogan 1980,

p. 556). It is as if the sheer existence of the normal curve of intelligence has never been comfortably integrated into the culture and social philosophy of the United States. Perhaps the heterogeneity of the population accounts for it. In any event a good deal of mental gymnastics is needed to fit together the social philosophies of the dicta "all men are created equal," "rugged individualism," and "survival of the fittest." There is food for formal operational thought beyond the adolescent stage of development!

Mentally Handicapped

Youth of low intellectual functioning — the mentally retarded — have long demanded the attention of human service professionals and policy makers, but such attention has been reluctantly and sporadically given. Intellectual subnormality has many definitions. The World Health Organization (WHO) subdivides "mental subnormality" into (a) mental retardation, signifying below normal functioning caused by environmental factors and without pathology of the central nervous system, and (b) mental deficiency, resulting from pathology. Goldberg (1983) considers this distinction unfortunate in that it perpetuates the false notion of curable and incurable mental retardation. In Scandinavia and other European countries, the term *oligophrenia* is used to denote a permanent brain-damaged condition acquired before or during birth or in early childhood that is characterized by deficient social and emotional development. As reported by Goldberg (1983), the American Psychiatric Association's diagnostic and statistical manual of mental disorders (DSM-III) considers mental functioning to be subaverage when a person obtains an IQ of 70 or below on an individually administered IQ test and concurrently manifests deficient or impaired adaptive behavior relative to chronological age and cultural norms. The term *mental retardation* is used only for conditions developed before age 18. Decreased intellectual functioning appearing after that time is referred to as *dementia* (organic mental disorder). The DSM-III classifies mental retardation according to IQ levels: *mild* ranging from 50–70, *moderate* from 35–49, *severe* from 20–34, and *profound* below 20. Close to 3 percent of the general population score below 70 on standard IQ tests; however, only about 1 percent are recorded as mentally retarded, since many mildly retarded go unnoticed and blend into the general population, often in socially marginal positions (Goldberg 1983, pp. 387–90).

Causes of mental retardation include chromosome abnormalities; interuterine damage from infections, rubella, chemical and drug use, smoking, and malnutrition of the mother; birth trauma; head injuries and diseases during childhood; and environmental and psychosocial disadvantages. Progress has been made in identifying causes of specific kinds of mental retardation, especially of the more severe forms, where genetic, medical, or traumatic factors prevail. Yet in many cases etiological factors are still unknown (Dahl 1980).

Even more so than for the physically handicapped, adolescence brings added stress and rejection to the mental retardates and their families. They develop the same secondary sexual characteristics and drives as their intellectually normal counterparts. They seek and need the companionship of peers, become vulnerable to sexual exploitation by peers and adults, and at times are easily talked into carrying out delinquent acts as the price for acceptance without comprehension of the consequences. As other adolescents, the mentally retarded yearn for a job, for economic and other independence from parents, and for a future family of their own. Even though their thinking capacity rarely goes beyond the preoperational or concrete stages of development (to use Piaget's terms), the young retardate often is aware of not measuring up in school, where he or she often is "socially promoted" to the next grade, or of losing one job after another. The temptation to turn to the parents for ongoing protection is great, and the parents in turn, in their own chronic sorrow and worry about the future of their vulnerable child, have a strong need to overprotect and thus prevent optimal development of social functioning (Daniel 1977).

Even in countries like Denmark, with a highly developed service system providing living conditions and opportunities for the retarded at almost the same level as for the rest of the population, it is often difficult to persuade parents that they are not serving the best interest of their adolescent son or daughter by allowing him or her to remain in the parental home. Oddly enough, in a few cases, the disability pension to which the mental retardate is entitled at age 15 as an incentive to independent living becomes a hindrance when that pension is a substantial item on the family's budget (Dahl 1980). Perfect solutions are not easily come by.

This discussion of the impact of biological and intellectual factors on adolescent development concludes with the summary by Rutter (1980) of his review of primarily British studies. Rutter determined that congenital/genetic influences play a role in the timing of onset of puberty, in intellectual developmental and predisposition to psychiatric and learning disorders, and in criminality. Chromosomal anomalies are linked with some forms of mental retardation and predispositions to aggression and delinquent behavior. These factors are often overlooked as having little practical implication. It is true, as Rutter states, that nothing can be done to alter an individual's genetic makeup after birth, but it is often environmental influences and expectations linked with body size that make adolescence especially stressful for early and later maturers and that determine if disabling physical and mental conditions actually become handicaps in the emotional and social development of children and youth.

Twentieth Century Adolescent Developmental Theories: An Overview

G. Stanley Hall, referred to at the opening of this chapter, observed the biological and intellectual changes at adolescence to be so rapid and comprehensive that he refers to adolescence as a "new birth" through which the qualities of body and soul merge in a manner different from childhood developmental processes (1904, p. xiii). A central idea in his biogenetic psychology is the "recapitulation" theory. It states that the evolutionary history of the human race is linked to the genetic structure and nature of the human being; thus each individual passes through stages similar to mankind's development from savagery, to barbary, to civilization. Like Rousseau, Hall advises parents and teachers not to interfere with these natural and inevitable processes and to wait out periods of unacceptable behavior that will disappear automatically when the stage is completed. This developmental perspective is not uncommon even today; in the author's parent-counseling experience, some fathers (more often than mothers) express the belief that "he is just going through a stage; he'll outgrow it no matter what we do," usually meaning that there is no need to waste time and money seeking counseling.

Another strong and lasting influence of Hall's theory is the notion that conflict is an inescapable component of adolescent development, which can only be successfully completed through "storm and stress." Anthropological studies — notably Margaret Mead's *Coming of Age in Samoa* (1928) — uncovered societies in which adolescence was passed through without major upheavals. These observations and findings of other later empirical studies in the United States (discussed below) have seriously challenged the narrow biogenetic focus of Hall's theory as well as the postulated saltatory and conflictive nature of adolescent development.

Psychoanalytic Theory

Another stage theory with focus on inborn, instinctual drives is Sigmund Freud's psychoanalytic theory. The author will assume the reader's basic knowledge of Freud's theory of psychosexual development during the oral, anal, phallic, and latency age libidinal stages; of his tripartite topographical model of the conscious-preconscious-unconscious mind; the tripartite personality structure of id-ego-superego; and of the gradual shaping and development of mechanisms of defense utilized by the ego to keep a tolerable peace and to control anxiety stirred by id-superego struggles and by conflicts between internal, instinctual drives and environmental, external demands (see Muuss 1982 for elaboration). Sigmund Freud's theories differ from Hall's biogenetic theory in the importance Freud ascribes to parental influences in the preschool years and to cultural and environmental factors in the development of the superego.

Sigmund Freud's theory of psychosexual development is clearly centered on preadolescence; ideas scattered throughout his writings add up to a composite picture of adolescence as a period in which the pleasure of discharge is added to the fore-pleasure of prepubertal sexuality, and the sex drive takes on the added aim of reproduction. Preservation of the human species demands that the adolescent make a shift from the parents as sex-drive objects (fantasied, repressed, or partially real as these object relations may be) to a person of the opposite sex outside the nuclear family of creation. Apparently Freud's contribution to adolescent psychology was limited to pubertal sexuality.[1] Klumpner (1978, p. 68), in his review of Freud's writings on adolescence, found only one reference to application of psychoanalytic structural theory in the comment that the weakness of the adolescent ego is physiologically caused. Freud rarely used the word adolescence, but used the word puberty instead. This was perhaps another reflection of his emphasis on the biological aspects of this developmental stage. Klumpner (1978) concludes his review by stating that Freud repeatedly pointed out that adolescence is an inevitable consequence of the changes of inner biological forces that preserve the human species, and that it is the difficulty in accepting our basic animal nature that makes us continue to look elsewhere for explanations.

Psychoanalytic theory was expanded to greater coverage of adolescence by Sigmund Freud's daughter, Anna, through her books *The Ego and the Mechanisms of Defense,* written in 1946, and *Normality and Pathology in Childhood: Assessments of Development* (1965). She describes two defense mechanisms of having special relevance to adolescence, namely asceticism and intellectualization. Even in normal development these defenses become very strong in order to control the increased drive activity of puberty and as a result of the growth in reasoning ability. In extreme cases asceticism may not only deprive the adolescent of gratification of sexual and other bodily needs but may also lead to intense religiosity. In such cases, or when "intellectualization overruns the whole field of mental life" and is not just applied to instinctual processes, it becomes difficult to decide how much of the behavior is transitional and how much may be pathological (A. Freud 1946, p. 189). One consequence of the strength of the defenses at puberty is increased resistance to psychoanalysis, which many analysts consider contraindicated for this age group.

Ausubel's Integrated Psychology of Adolescent Development

Numerous other writers and researchers from the fields of sociology, law, anthropology, and behavioral psychology have shed light on one aspect or another of adolescent development and behavior during the first half of this century. As often happens when multitudes of theories, ideas, facts, myths, and speculations begin to crowd vision and comprehension, a person comes along with the self-assigned Herculean task of bringing some order out of chaos, of integrating the bits and pieces into a neat comprehensive picture. Such a person is David P. Ausubel, whose 1954 text *Theory and Problems of Adolescent Development* (and its 1977 edition) is a major source of information and insight for the human service practitioner. Ausubel points out that the collapse of Hall's biogenetic theory brought disrepute to attempts to develop systematic theoretical frameworks in the field of adolescent psychology. Two specific unfortunate consequences are pinpointed; first, an undue emphasis on amassing objective data on every conceivable aspect of adolescence without organizing hypotheses to draw meaning from the empirical data; second, the findings of anthropological studies, which demolished Hall's theory, were overgeneralized to the point of denying that adolescence is a distinct phase with principles of its own.

The central thesis of Ausubel's integrated, comprehensive theory is that adolescence is a distinct developmental phase with changes that are biological as well as social in origin. These changes are discontinuous of preceding biosocial conditions of growth and status of the child and require extensive reorganization of the personality structure. This reorganization contains uniform elements across cultures because of common psychological reactions associated with sexual maturation and sex roles combined with new personality traits, changed status, and adult roles in the community. Thus, Ausubel distinguishes between universal psychological problems and psychosocial problems that are conditioned by specific socioeconomic factors and by modes of regulation and attitudes of specific social and cultural orders (Ausubel 1954, p. xii, xiv).

Since the mid-1950s, Ausubel's integrated psychology of adolescent development, along with other theories, has served as a workable framework for human service professionals. To be briefly presented here are the following theories: Neo-Freudianism, Behavior Theory, Social Psychology, and Ecology.

Neo-Freudianism

Peter Blos has expanded on psychoanalytic concepts relevant to the adolescent stage in a number of ways. He sees this stage as the second individuation process (1967), the first being the child's separation from the symbiotic bond with its mother and emergence as an autonomous toddler by the end of the third year of life. The young child is now able to differentiate self from mother, from whose physical presence the child gains relative independence through internalization of the mother, referred to as object representation or imago (Blos 1979, pp 483–84). Similarly, during adolescence the youngster, by relinquishing dependence on the internalized, infantile parental objects, emerges as an independent member of the adult world. For this internal, second individuation process to take place, it is necessary and normal for the adolescent to regress to the preoedipal autonomy struggle between parent and child and to rework once more the oedipal conflict reawakened by the upsurge of sexual drive. These regressive behaviors are exemplified in battles over cleanliness, dress, in moods of despair, narcissism, withdrawal, seductive behavior toward the parent of the opposite sex, and rivalrous criticisms of the same-sex parent. Without these regressive steps, it is assumed that the progression in personality restructuring that leads to emotional maturity cannot take place. The regressive behaviors and the anxiety they provoke make up the "storm and stress" of adolescent turmoil that psychoanalysts equate with normal adolescent development.

Blos (1962 and 1979) carefully spells out how the individuation process progresses over four phases: early adolescence, when the youngster begins to turn away from the parents as love objects; adolescence proper, characterized by the adolescent's search for new object relations (outside the family) combined with a mood of mourning (for the loss of ties with the parents); late adolescence, a period of consolidation with growing autonomy and establishment of personal and sexual identity; and finally, postadolescence, the period in which the young adult makes commitments through occupational choice, courtship, and marriage. Failure to complete the second individuation process may lead to continuous rebelliousness, acting-out, moodiness, negativism, and psychopathology. At times, one observes what Blos calls "derailment of the individuation process," when parental dependence is shed without accompanying reorganization of psychic structure. In such a case, a youngster may make behavioral and social role choices in direct opposition to the parents' wishes and make a permanent break with the parents (as reported by Muuss 1982, pp. 99–103).

Blos enjoys high esteem inside and outside psychoanalytic circles for his contributions to adolescent psychology, and he is one of the few psychoanalysts who has addressed the shortcomings of psychoanalytic theory in general in neglecting female development, to which he gives some attention in his 1979 book and full attention in the 1981 article, "Modifications in the Traditional Psychoanalytic Theory of Female Adolescent Development." However, Blos has also been criticized, particularly for lack of clarity in his theory of regression as an obligatory part of the individuation process. That is, he does not specify under what circumstances and to what extent regression takes place, nor does he specify which part of the personality system undergoes regression (Adelson and Doehrman 1980, p. 101). Blos's writings are not considered easy reading; an excellent introduction to them is Muuss's review and discussion (1982, chapter 5).

Erik Erikson. The neo-Freudian psychologist who has gained the greatest acceptance and popularity is Erik H. Erikson (1950, 1959, 1968, 1975), who has expanded and modified the classical Freudian theory of psychosexual development. Erikson's well-known theory of eight stages of ego identity development covers the total life cycle. It views the ego as an active force in the acquisition of personal identity, and it recognizes that the way in which each stage-specific developmental task (or crisis) is resolved is partly dependent on the culture and historical circumstances of the individual.

Adolescence, by Erikson called a *psychosocial moratorium,* is the fifth of the eight life stages listed here along with the positive or negative possible outcome of each stage-specific developmental task:

Psychosocial Stage	*Positive vs. Negative Outcome*
1. Infancy	Trust vs. Mistrust
2. Early Childhood	Autonomy vs. Shame, Doubt
3. Play Age	Initiative vs. Guilt
4. School Age	Industry vs. Inferiority
5. Adolescence	Identity vs. Identity Diffusion
6. Young Adult	Intimacy vs. Isolation
7. Adulthood	Generativity vs. Self-Absorption
8. Mature Age	Integrity vs. Disgust, Despair

Each developmental task has its time of ascendancy, precipitated by the individual's readiness and the pressures of society and occurring in the same sequence for all people. The phases are epigenetically interrelated in that task achievement or crisis resolution at each stage is dependent on the timing and nature of resolutions of previous stages and consequently will impact outcomes of later developmental stages. In other words, positive resolutions become part of the ego and enhance further development, while an unresolved developmental conflict or a negative resolution may manifest itself in psychopathology and hamper psychological maturation.

Erikson sees identity formation as a lifelong process; like a "good conscience," a sense of identity is never gained once and for all. It is constantly lost and must be regained as we confront new challenges throughout the life cycle. However, it is at adolescence that the central, phase-specific task is that of identity achievement.

Identity is one of the fundamental psychological concepts that "everybody understands," but it is in fact an extremely complex idea. Erikson explains it in several ways. Subjectively, identity is experienced as feeling at home in one's body, as feeling assured of recognition by those who count, and in knowing where one is going. A positive identity includes a sense of sameness over time, a continuity of what one has been and what one is about to become. It is a sense of sameness in different situations and with different persons, a sense of wholeness, and congruence between how one perceives oneself and how one is interpreted by others. Identity also involves a world view that contains a niche uniquely made for you, however small; it is retained and regained through disciplined devotion and fidelity to self and chosen values.

Erikson states that identity is not merely the sum total of previous identifications. At one point he calls it a configuration of constitutional givens, libidinal needs, capacities, significant identifications, effective defenses, and consistent roles (1975, p. 190). At other times Erikson describes identity indirectly by spelling out manifestations of its opposite — identity diffusion. Diffused is the youngster who is unable to make simultaneous commitments to the many choices confronting the adolescent with regard to occupation, physical intimacy, values, and definition of self. He notes that the identity diffused sometimes seek out the psychiatrist, priest, judge, or recruitment officers to be given a place to wait things out. The avoidance of choices results in isolation and an inner void in which the pull toward regression may become irresistible (1975, pp. 318–24).

Erikson mentions that weakness of a person's identity is often revealed in the subsequent developmental stage "young adulthood" with the stage-specific conflict of intimacy vs. isolation. Without a fairly strong sense of identity, no true engagement in friendship or enduring sexual relations can take place, and the search for such relations becomes "desperate attempts at delineating the fuzzy lines of identity by mutual narcissistic mirroring: to fall in love then often means to fall into one's mirror image, hurting oneself and damaging the mirror" (1975, p. 320).

An extreme case of identity diffusion is the choice of a negative identity that perversely unfolds from past identifications and roles that have been presented to the child as most undesirable and dangerous but also most true and real. A child who consistently is given the explicit and implicit message, "you are no good," may eventually believe it. When a positive identity is ruled out as unattainable, the negative is better than none. In the words of one adolescent girl, quoted by Erikson, "At least in the gutter I am a genius" (1975, p. 327). Some parents of adolescents opting for a negative identity are morbidly ambitious or actually superior in their particular fields. Work with such adolescents requires endless patience, the ability to recognize and accept the negative identity as a psychological necessity, and also the ability to convey to the adolescent that there is more to him or her than negatives.

To build his theory, Erikson has drawn upon many cases from his psychoanalytic practice and from his anthropological and biographical studies, and he has inspired many researchers from the fields of clinical and developmental psychology to operationalize the concept of identity. The outcome of some of these empirical efforts will be presented in chapter 4.

Psychoanalytic and neo-Freudian theory unquestionably have had a strong influence on social work practice throughout this century in the United States. It seems that this approach held center stage over the influence from the social and behavioral sciences, especially during the period from the late 1920s to the mid-1950s when several voices clamored to "put the *social* back into social work." The writings of Anna and Sigmund Freud, Blos, and Erikson dominated human behavior syllabi in most schools of social work along with those of many other psychoanalytically oriented scholars and practitioners, such as Irene M. Josselyn's *The Adolescent and His World,* first published in 1952. A slowly developing trend of incorporating cultural and other social influences in the view of man is exemplified in Erikson's writings and in the strongly used report on "Normal Adolescence," published by the Group for the Advancement of Psychiatry in 1968, and in expansion of the reading lists for what then became the "Human Behavior in the Social Environment" courses to include writings from the fields of sociology and behavioral psychology.

The psychoanalytic school of thought has not been nearly as influential among human service professionals on the European continent; Great Britain may fall somewhere in between. Two British authors, Dunham and Jones (1980), for example, mention only one analytically oriented model, namely Erikson's, among the five theoretical frameworks they identify as having been useful to social workers dealing with adolescents. The four other models are (1) the constitutional (biological) model; (2) Bandura's social learning model; (3) Maslow's hierarchical needs model; and (4) the stress model (to be discussed later in connection with ecology).

There are several reasons for the diminished influence of psychoanalytic theory in the field of adolescence. One is its hypotheses of relations between endocrine and psychological changes in early adolescence. Such relations, according to Petersen and Taylor (1980), simply have not been supported empirically and remain assertions of belief. These researchers acknowledge enormous conceptual difficulties in articulation of interrelationships between the three interacting systems — biological, sociocultural, and psychological. They make a convincing case that a mediated- (as opposed to a direct-) effects model is needed to allow study of the psychological impact of puberty as a complex chain of intervening variables from the three systems. Progress has been made in biological research, but studies on psyche/soma relations of puberty remain in a preliminary stage. They speculate that this puzzling fact may be associated with the anxiety that pubescent youth often arouses in many adults.

Empirical Studies Challenging "Storm and Stress" Theory. Another reason for psychoanalytic theory's decreased influence is the accumulated evidence from large-scale studies of the 1960s and 1970s against the psychoanalytic position that storm and stress is an obligatory aspect of normal adolescent development. The difficulty in distinguishing between adolescent turmoil and true psychiatric illness has been addressed by Anna Freud as well as Peter Blos, and yet growing concern was voiced that true psychiatric disturbances remained untreated in being passed over as mere transitory pubertal reactions. To clarify this distinction, Oldham (1978; Oldham, Looney, and Blotcky 1980) reviewed several longitudinal studies of patient and nonpatient adolescents. Some of the major studies reviewed were: Douvan and Adelson's (1966) study of 3,000 teenage boys and girls, the Modal Adolescent Project by Offer (1967, 1969) and Offer et al. (1965), and Masterson and Washburne's (1966, 1967, 1968) study at the Payne Whitney Clinic in New York, where 101, 12- to 18-year-old boys and girls seen in the clinic were compared with a matched sample of nonpatient teenagers. Oldham's synthesis of the findings of these and other studies includes the statements that most adolescents maintain psychic equilibrium while struggling with the developmental tasks; that adolescent development is generally associated with successful family adjustment; that turmoil is normatively manifest in mild forms of depression and minor disagreements with authority figures; that apart from mild depressions and anxiety, symptoms at adolescence are often indicative of psychiatric illness warranting treatment; and that difficulties in distinguishing between psychiatric illness and adolescent reaction have more to do with obscurities in the psychiatric diagnostic system than with the presence or absence of turmoil (Oldham 1980, pp. 277–78).

According to Oldham, major reasons for continuation of the turmoil mythology have been inappropriate generalizations from samples of deviant adolescents; the generation-gap myth, which simply has not been established in samples of normative adolescents; popular literature about adolescent struggles; and attitudes of mental health professionals, who themselves, according to some studies referred to by Oldham, are likely to come from somewhat dysfunctional families, where adolescent turmoil may have been considered normal.

Other reviewers, such as Coleman (1979) and Ellis (1979), essentially arrive at the same conclusions as Oldham. It appears that neither the classical nor the empirical theory of adolescent development is universal; if indeed they represent two different populations, the two theories may be complementary and not contradictory. However, a safer conclusion may be that the evidence is not in yet. Nagging questions linger as to the quality of the evidence we do have. We know from general observation of adolescents around us and from clinical work with individual youngsters that behavioral vacillation is common, and in some we see quite disturbed reactions coexisting with seemingly healthy growth and achievement on other developmental lines. Thus sampling of the behavior of each member of a study sample becomes very tricky, be it a study sample of a nonclinic or a clinic population. Repeated behavior measures may add to the validity of the picture we are trying to draw; however, the longer the time span we allow for repeated measures, the more we introduce "maturation over time" as an intervening variable, which is always a particularly disturbing factor in periods of great change.[2] To put these complexities in simple terms: what we see depends on where and when we are looking. Adelson and Doehrman (1980) have expressed this idea in another, better way. They say that the person exposed to a steady diet of the psychological journal *Child Development* forms a picture of the adolescent as "engaged in an implacable expansion of intellectual and moral capacity," while the faithful reader of the annual volume *Adolescent Psychiatry* sees the youngster as "miraculously holding on to his sanity, but doing so only by undertaking prodigies of defense" (p. 105).

Coleman (1979, 1980) has taken his inquiry a step further in probing into the developmental processes of those adolescents who exhibit only signs of stress. His study of 800 British boys and girls between 11 and 17 years of age indicates that attitudes to all relationships (parental, heterosexual, friendship, groups) change as a function of age, and concerns about different issues reach a peak at different stages of adolescence (thus supporting Blos's ideas). Those who successfully cope do so by dealing with one issue at a time. Coleman's "focal theory" of adolescent development, formulated as a result of his study, states that because the adolescent developmental tasks come into focus at different times, the demands for adaptation in behavior rarely occur all at one time. Those who have more than one issue to deal with at a time are more likely to have problems. Coleman mentions, as an example, that the youngster who matures physically at a normal time can adjust to this before pressures from parents and teachers are brought to bear, whereas the late maturer is more likely to have to cope with simultaneously occurring pressures over a wider area of behaviors (1979, p. 633).

While Coleman's analysis makes sense, it is, as he himself suggests, only one possible way of conceptualizing adolescent development. The human service practitioner more often than not works with adolescents who clearly have multiple issues to cope with at any one time. The paramount question for the practitioner seems to be to find out why several issues are simultaneously present, and to find what is the etiology and meaning of each issue in the context of that particular youngster's life situation. Is the issue clustering a result of extraneous, more or less accidental events, or does it reflect in whole or in part some limitations in that adolescent's coping mechanisms?

Behavior Theory

We now turn to the question of what behavioral theories contribute to our understanding of adolescence. These theories have generated several interventive frameworks such as life and social skills training programs, which will be discussed in later chapters. Several behavioral interventions appear particularly helpful to adolescents, but it is probably correct to say that they are often ignored by many human service professionals. Adverse reactions to Watson's experimentation with Little Albert (Achenbach 1982, pp. 317–18) and other early stimulus-response experiments have proven hard to extinguish. They linger on but do not seem to fit most present-day behavioral theories and practices.

As far as adolescent development is concerned, behavioral theories have little to offer for obvious and intrinsic reasons. In this theoretical perspective, children, youth, and adults are not seen as qualitatively different. The multiple behavioral schools of thought that have emanated from the original stimulus-response theories all share the basic tenet that behavior is primarily environmentally determined rather than a result of internal traits or predispositions. In other words, adolescence is not considered a distinct stage with predetermined, universal, age-related tasks of development. Easily observed differences in the behavior of children and adolescents are ascribed not to internal qualities or traits but to differences in sociocultural expectations of them and to a shift from the child's reliance on parents and teachers as behavior models to the adolescent's increasing imitation of peers and capacity for self-reinforcement.

As spokesmen for one of the behavioral schools of thought — social learning theory — A. Bandura and R.H. Walters have given specific attention to the adolescent period (as reported by Muuss 1982, chapter 14). Their study of antisocial aggression in adolescent males (1959) made substantial contributions to knowledge of parental factors in the socialization processes of aggressive boys. Bandura's formulation of social learning theory has added several new concepts to behavioral theory, which in its classical form saw behavior simply as conditioned, learned responses to environmental stimuli. B.F. Skinner expanded on this idea in conceptualizing how behavior is maintained and changed. His operant conditioning approach sees behavior as linked to its antecedents as well as its consequences. A behavior's rate is increased by some consequences (reinforcers) and decreased when punished by others. However, in Bandura's view operant conditioning does not explain how new behavior is initially acquired. He maintains that new behaviors are learned only through observation and imitation of somebody who is modelling that behavior. In addition, Bandura stresses the continuous reciprocal interaction between the environmental, behavioral, and personal determinants. On the latter point, Bandura takes issue with Skinner, who asserts that, apart from genetic influences, human behavior is controlled by environmental contingencies. Bandura claims (1977, p. 203) that the environment is not an autonomous force — it is regulated, just as behaviors are, by its own contingencies, of which human behavior is one. Bandura, in a humorous vein, sums up this debate on reciprocal determinism by stating that in "the regress of prior causes, for every chicken discovered by a unidirectional environmentalist, a social learning theorist can identify a prior egg" (1977, p. 203).

Bandura's formulation of social learning theory also introduces the new concepts of vicarious reinforcement (learning from observed positive and negative consequences of a model's behavior) and self-reinforcement, a factor that takes on increased importance as an adolescent becomes able to better judge and reward his or her own behavior and to no longer depend solely on parents and other adults for reinforcement.

The self-reinforcement idea has led to current research by Bandura and his collaborators on self-efficacy as a framework for conceptualizing how the individual copes with stress. Bandura assumes that in order to judge one's capacity for coping, information from four different sources must be drawn upon.

1. The performance mode, that is, how similar situations were in fact handled in the past
2. Vicarious information from observing the success or failure of others
3. Social persuasion, that is, undermining or boosting the sense of efficacy by others. The undermining is easier to achieve than boosting since "[p]eople convinced of their inefficacy are unlikely to try challenging activities so they fail to develop their competencies and thus validate their inefficacy" (as quoted in Moore, 1981, p. 100).
4. The person's perception of his or her physiology and its vulnerability (physical arousal in stress situations)

The concept of self-efficacy appears of particular importance during the adolescent years. The choices that have to be made with respect to the many new roles adolescents are expected to take on can be experienced either as added stress beyond the individual's coping capacity or as a challenge from which self-efficacy may be built. This certainly underscores the importance of the expectations and demands adult society puts on adolescents, and it raises questions as to how clear are the messages sent, how carefully matched is social persuasion to the performance mode, and are we providing vicarious information sources that will boost rather than undermine the adolescent self-efficacy potentials. These questions are as crucial from a social policy perspective as they are for therapeutic considerations (Schwartz 1983).

Social Psychology. Like Bandura, the social psychologist Kurt Lewin (1936) views behavior as a function of the person-environment interaction. Lewin's psychology views the environment as including not only the physical, psychological, and social context of the individual, but also the person's perception of that environment. This totality of factors determining the individual's behavior at any given time is called the psychological life space or psychological field, within which the person has varying freedom of movement, depending on what the person is allowed and what the person's abilities permit. As the child grows older more life space becomes accessible. At adolescence, however, the boundaries of the life space become unclear. Lewin speaks of the adolescent being in a marginal position, excluded from many spheres of the child's life space and not yet allowed in most of the adult's life space. The adolescent does not fully belong in either group, and it is not clear which new regions he or she is supposed to enter. Venturing into life space that is not yet open (such as the family car) leads to conflict, while holding back may generate comments such as "at your age you ought to be able to do such-and-such on your own; don't just stand there like a three-year-old and expect to be told."

Figuratively, the adolescent's life space can be seen as the overlap between two circles representing the psychological fields of children and of adults (Lewin 1939, as presented by Muuss 1982); the greater the differences between the two, the smaller the overlap, and the harder it is to pass from the child's to the adult's life space. The smaller the overlap, the greater the rate of change, and the greater the newness of the regions entered into. In one sense the overlap belongs to both circles, that is, the adolescent is simultaneously a child and an adult. In another sense, the overlap stands apart from both circles; the adolescent belongs in neither the child's nor the adult's world. In the United States the adolescent's life space, the "overlap," affords plenty of room on which to stand and move about — with some variations within socioeconomic classes and ethnic groups. In other cultures and countries with different values and resources, the adolescent life space is much more narrowly defined. In some countries it is nonexistent, that is, you are considered a child one day and an adult the next.

In addition to these external, cultural givens, the adolescent's life space contains a body image that changes with biological maturation, along with growing perceptive capacities expanding the life space from proximate to long-term past and future perspectives and allowing greater comprehension of the reality-unreality dimension. By *unreality*, Lewin means such mental factors as dreams, hopes, fears, and fantasies; while the child is not fully capable of distinguishing between these and reality, the adolescent becomes increasingly capable of sorting facts from fiction.

Knowing the attracting and repulsing forces of the adolescent psychological field characteristic of specific cultures makes it possible to compute the probability that certain adolescent behaviors will occur as a result of the disequilibrium and uncertainty of the marginal situation. These behaviors include internal emotional tension and conflict, aggressive and/or withdrawn behavior, role conflicts, and "lack of social anchorage" except in the peer group (Muuss 1982, p. 150). Lewin makes it clear, however, that computed abstract averages, even when drawn from large numbers of individuals, obscure rather than clarify the dynamics of a specific individual's behavior. This dynamic is a unique constellation of mutually interdependent forces within each individual's psychological field, and one of the major field variables is the person's own perception of the field. At times this subjective perception seems to be a stronger force than the objective fact to which it is attached.

Lewin's field theory and his many empirical experimentations (not least his comparison of behavior in autocratic and democratic groups) have been quite influential — perhaps more so in Northern Europe than in the United States. Human service professionals from many disciplines have gained fuller understanding of their adolescent clients in viewing and assessing them from Lewin's "marginal position" framework. As does general system theory, Lewin's field theory guides assessment more than intervention. It has also inspired many of Lewin's former students to expand on and empirically test his spatial theoretical constructs in the fields of child development and ecological psychology (Sears 1975, pp. 52–54).

Ecological Theory

A recent example of ecological theory is Urie Bronfenbrenner's expansion and differentiation of Lewin's psychological field concept into a hierarchy of the interconnected ecological micro-, meso-, and exosystems — one nested inside the other, and all three systems overarched by the macrosystem. The focus of Bronfenbrenner's (1979) book, *The Ecology of Human Development. Experiments by Nature and Design,* is psychological growth within the context of these ecological systems, and he defines human development as lasting changes in the manner in which a person perceives and deals with the environment. Even though he does not apply his ecological model specifically to the adolescent age level, the model is briefly presented here because it is useful for understanding the complexities of the adolescent's ecological world.

Bronfenbrenner sees the ecological environment as reaching far beyond the immediate settings or *microsystems*, such as the home, classroom, or work place, in which the person interacts face-to-face with others. The ecological environment extends to the linkages between these immediate settings, which form the *mesosystem.* This system is nested within the even more distant *exosystem*, in which the person may not even be an active participant though he is still quite affected by it. An example is the reverberation between events in the parent's or spouse's work place and the family home microsystem. Bronfenbrenner's model gives equal importance to its basic unit of analysis the *dyadic,* a two-person system, and the larger interpersonal structures of triads, tetrads, and so forth. He spells out (1979, p. 5) that a dyad's capacity to serve as a nurturing context for human development is linked with the availability and participation of third parties, be they individual human beings or neighborhood conditions and/or health and social services. The supportiveness of these wider settings (exosystems) in turn varies within cultures and in accordance with the overall social policies in a given nation. Each culture, subculture, or nation appears to have a blueprint for how all these settings are interconnected, called the *macrosystem*. A hospital ward in one culture may keep family involvement with the sick at a minimum by limited, rigidly controlled visiting hours, while other cultures with different beliefs about what makes people sick or well allow the whole family to enter the ward with the patient.

Public policies, ideologies, and belief systems of cultures and religious and ethnic groups are but a few examples of macrosystem forces that affect the development of human beings by determining the general conditions of their lives. A force often overlooked in developmental research as well as in practice interventions is the dimension of time (Elder 1980; Bronfenbrenner and Crouter 1983). Are we dealing with a cohort of youngsters who hit adolescence when war is declared, when economic dislocation is extreme causing family structures to crumble and reshape in connection with increased maternal employment and easier access to divorce, when resources have become plentiful because of discovery of new oil or metal deposits or scientific breakthroughs? Such events and developments can make the ecological worlds of cohorts close in birth years drastically different. And, as Bronfenbrenner notes, the trajectories started by historical and environmental events take on a momentum of their own and affect subsequent development. Bronfenbrenner and Crouter (1983), using what they call an outmoded metaphor, compare development to a moving train. It is possible to move back and forth through the cars, but the main destination is where the train is going, since in "most countries there are few places where one can change tracks. America probably presents more possibilities in this regard than many other societies, but even here, many transfers are forced rather than free, especially those leading to unwelcome destinations (p. 401)."

Perhaps adolescence is a period with more "train" options than most other times of our lives, and it seems for certain to be a time when the urge to jump on or off becomes powerful, if not uncontrollable. Rare is the child welfare or youth worker who cannot recall anxious moments transporting youngsters to or from "unwelcome destinations" or who has not been confronted by the adopted adolescent who is pushing backward in the cars to find out how he or she got on the train with a one-way ticket in the first place. Until recently we have stopped the search at the train station — the adoption agency; now we share a little more about how and why the adolescent was taken to the station. Intentionally or unintentionally we sometimes become strong forces in the ecological worlds of our clients.

So far this book has highlighted the biological-instinctual, psychodynamic, behavioral, and social psychological schools of thought as they reflect on adolescent development. Important theorists have been left out; some of them will be introduced in later chapters as called for by the subject matter at hand. Our expectations of change, assessment, and intervention planning and processes are necessarily tied up with the practitioner's view of man as drawn from the various theoretical frameworks to which one is explicitly or implicitly committed. What we think flavors what we do; and the more we consciously take stock of what we know and believe the better informed our practice will be. That is the reason for the fairly extensive presentation of the various theoretical viewpoints of adolescent development.

Summary

This chapter opened with a review of changing perceptions of adolescence over time; then followed accounts of how adolescent physical and cognitive development impact the overall maturation of adolescents at the ends and the middle of the normal curve. While pubertal changes occur in predictable order, they vary greatly in regard to onset and tempo between boys and girls and within groups of boys and girls. Finally central ideas from stage and continuity theories on adolescent psychological development were introduced.

The conclusions arrived at by Michael Rutter (1980) in his extensive review of adolescent development, which included many more British studies than this review, seem to pertain to this chapter as well. He states that most adolescents are not as socially alienated or psychologically disturbed as might be expected, considering the marked changes in physical growth and hormonal production impacting the adolescent's assertiveness, emotions, and sex drive. Rutter sees three reasons why we do not see more disturbance: first, the changes also include increased coping capacities in form of greater cognitive and social skills and greater capacity for emotional appreciation and understanding of others; second, the psychological patterns and functioning shaped by developmental crises of earlier years have readied most teenagers for the adolescent crises; and, finally, the changes do not occur all at once but are extended over a five- to six-year period, and successful coping with the first challenges provides confidence and skills to deal with the later ones.

The next chapter will turn from the focus on theoretical perspectives to the specific psychosocial tasks to be completed by the young before they, in their own view and the view of others, have gained status and recognition as adults.

Notes

1. At least one case offered Sigmund Freud an opportunity to expand on his contributions to adolescent psychology. "Little Hans" returned to Freud's office 14 years after Freud engaged in his one and only case of child analysis, which was carried out primarily through sessions with Hans's father. The reader may recall that 5-year old Hans refused to go outdoors for fear of being bitten by horses. Freud interpreted this phobic reaction as displacement of Hans's fear of what his father might do to him if he found out how much Hans wanted to keep his mother to himself. In spite of the mother's threat that she would have the doctor remove Hans's "widdler" if he kept playing with it, Hans went with his father to Freud's office once, where he turned down his father's and Freud's explanation of why he was afraid of horses by calling it a lot of nonsense. Stafford-Clark (1966), from which this information is taken, offers the simpler explanation that Hans's interest in sexual development of other people and his subsequent fear of horses were parallel developments with no consequential link between them other than Freud's interpretation. In any event, Hans's interest in "widdlers" and his horse phobia subsided, and on his return visit at age 19 he had no memory of either or of his childhood visit to Freud's office. Freud used the case to demonstrate that childhood sexuality indeed exists and is not merely a product of deductions from adults' retrospective analyses or dreams. He drew no conclusions from Hans's apparent healthy and normal development throughout his childhood and adolescence, at the end of which he chose his father's profession of music (Stafford-Clark 1966, pp. 171–175).

2. For an excellent review of longitudinal studies relevant to adolescent development and analysis of research methodologies for longitudinal research, see N. Livson and H. Peskin 1980, "Perspectives on Adolescence from Longitudinal Research," in *Handbook of Adolescent Psychology,* edited by J. Adelson (New York: John Wiley and Sons), chapter 2, pp. 47–98).

3 DEVELOPMENTAL TASKS OF ADOLESCENCE IN RELATION TO THE FAMILY

This chapter spells out the overall psychosocial tasks the adolescent must engage in to achieve adult societal and psychological status. Most of the chapter is devoted to the topic of the parent-adolescent separation process, which forms an essential knowledge base for the human service professional attempting to help troubled adolescents and their families. This individuation process is viewed from a temporal, life stage perspective, and it is studied in terms of how it is played out in two-parent families, under the special circumstances of divorce, in single-parent families, in stepfamilies, and in relations marred by violence. Finally, in keeping with a system theory perspective, sibling relations are briefly discussed.

The Havighurst Formulation of Developmental Tasks

Quoted in many psychology textbooks and used by many practitioners as a guide for assessment of the developmental status of specific adolescent clients, Robert Havighurst's listing of adolescent tasks was first published in 1951 (third edition, 1972) in his book on developmental tasks and education. The eight major tasks to be achieved by adolescents between 12 and 18 years of age are the following:

1. Accept one's physique and use one's body effectively
2. Achieve new relations with peers of both sexes
3. Achieve masculine or feminine sex roles
4. Achieve emotional independence from parents and other adults
5. Prepare for an occupation
6. Prepare for marriage and family life
7. Desire and achieve socially responsible behavior
8. Acquire conscious values and an ethical system to guide behavior

Havighurst defines a developmental task as being midway between an individual need and a social demand as expressed in skills, knowledge, functions, and attitudes. Each phase in life has a new set of tasks appearing in a certain sequence, and failure or success in achieving the tasks impact task function at the next developmental phase. Many of these tasks have what Havighurst calls a "teachable moment"; if that moment is missed it becomes much more difficult to master the task at a later time. His developmental model has much in common with Erikson's epigenetic model and has obvious consequences for educational planning in the importance of gearing the educational demands to the optimal "teachable moments."

The elements of the eight tasks are biological, psychological, and cultural; Mother Nature's primarily biologically based tasks are uniform across cultures (1, 2, and 3), while great variations may be found from society to society in the culturally based developmental tasks (5, 7, and 8). The U.S. President and Chairman Mao may not easily agree on a definition of "socially acceptable behavior." Neither may we find much overlap between the "ethical system to guide behavior" arrived at by youngsters growing up under the influence of Eastern religious/philosophical thought and that of our Western, heterogeneous culture. And variations, at least in timing of tasks, are apt to be found among countries requiring that all citizens of a certain age submit to military service and countries with a more or less voluntary service by the young men only.

Perhaps very little agreement exists in any society about the ideal composite outcome of the adolescent developmental tasks. If one were to ask several people to describe a young autonomous adult who went through the adolescent developmental loops with flying colors and how he or she managed to do it, one probably would end up with several different answers. Different pictures may be drawn for the young men and the young women. Answers may vary depending on the state of the economy, the threat of war,

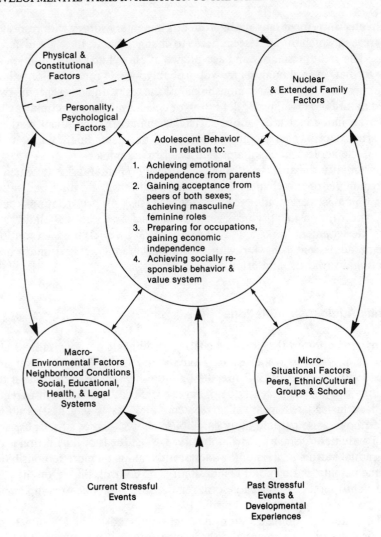

Figure 3-1. Ecological Diagram of Adolescent Behavior

and so forth. Perhaps most of all they will depend on the age of the persons asked. Fluidity and changeability of norms and expectations of adolescent achievements may well be a societal strength, particularly if they incorporate the opinions of the young themselves.

Greater agreement may result from our imaginary survey with respect to the areas in which the adolescent needs to change, that is, the eight different tasks. The great popularity and acceptance of Havighurst's formulation attests to that, even though many will probably vary in their opinions about the upper time limit for accomplishment of the tasks. In any event, the two-faced nature of Havighurst's definition of developmental tasks (midway between an individual need and a societal demand) fits the social worker's need for concepts that facilitate assessment, understanding, and intervention of the adolescent client's psychosocial functioning.

To simplify the analysis of adolescent developmental tasks presented in the remainder of this chapter, Havighurst's eight tasks are discussed within three domains: parent-adolescent interaction (task 4), peer relations (tasks 2, 3, and 6), and identity achievement, defined as vocational choice and moral development (tasks 5, 7, and 8). Figure 3-1 depicts the interrelationship of adolescent behavior with personality, family, micro and macro situational variables, and prior life experiences.[1]

Family-Adolescent Relations

As touched upon in the previous chapter, findings from longitudinal and other family studies (reported by Douvan and Gold 1966; Dunham and Jones 1980; Oldham 1978; Rutter 1980, and others)[2] give evidence that the great majority of adolescents do not have severe conflicts with their parents, but have instead temporary disagreements and day-to-day hassles about curfew hours, use of the family car, house chores, choice of friends, and social activities (Olson and McCubbin 1983). The focus of this section is on the gradual mutual process of the adolescent's taking on more responsibility and the parents' letting go of responsibility and control, that is, on the process of shifting the parent-adolescent relationship from one of complementarity to one of symmetry (Baumrind 1980).

The increase in joint decision making, characteristic of a symmetrical relationship, involves potential disagreements on the substance and timing of the adolescent's expanding autonomy. Conflicts are assumed to be inevitable and healthy since their absence may indicate extreme cases of alienation or domination. The question is, are the conflicts resolved so that the parent-adolescent bonds are strengthened or do they escalate into crises surrounding the relationship like a fog and perhaps leading to serious disruption of the parent-adolescent interaction (Catron and Catron 1983). Professional as well as popular literature generally seems to emphasize the negative, painful aspect of pulling away and letting go rather than the positives of the emergent new relationship and bonding between parent and child, which holds great potential for enrichment of life for both generations. Youniss (1983) puts it aptly by saying that there is a middle ground of reconciliation "between giving up self for the family and abandoning the family for self" (p. 97).

Family-Life Cycle Perspective on Parent-Adolescent Separation

Since the late 1950s the idea has slowly taken hold that the family itself changes as it passes through predictable stages. This family life cycle concept has impacted practice theory along with two other, perhaps related, developments. The first is the application of system theory to family phenomena, and the second, acknowledgement that psychological growth and development occur in individual human beings beyond the formative preschool years and the second individuation process of adolescence. Granted, a life stage, family system perspective may reaffirm a popular notion that it is hard to escape from what runs in the family even after emancipation, but the overall consequence of the above theoretical shifts appears to be a more hopeful stance, prompting practitioners to look for strength rather than pathology.[3]

Contributions to the development of the concept of family life cycle have come from adult developmental psychology, family sociology, social work, and other family therapy fields. An early social work writer, Frances Scherz (1964 and 1971) emphasized three universal tasks — emotional separation versus interdependence, intimacy versus distance, and self- versus other-responsibility — that any family as a system is confronted with and that parallel the developmental tasks of individual family members. These three repetitive tasks recur throughout the family life cycle at the age-specific transitions of the individuals in interplay with the family unit's perception of its task at that specific phase. As psychological tasks rarely are fully achieved by all at all stages, the adolescent's psychological tasks may trigger or reawaken conflict in the parent who has not completed the similar phase-specific tasks. The parents need to offer one another mutual support in order to avoid entangling the adolescent in their own individual or inter-marital conflicts; some parents are unable to manage this maturational stress and accuse each other of failure in child-rearing, or they may collude in attacking the adolescent in order to preserve the marriage.

Rhodes (1977) later translated *cogwheeling* — mutual interdependence of individual and family developmental tasks — within a system theory framework into a typology of seven life cycle stages, two of which address the teenage and early adult years. These stages are: achievement of intimacy in the dyadic relationship on the basis of a realistic (as opposed to an idealized) perception of the spouse; rearing of preschool children; individuation of all family members as parents and school-aged children develop roles and responsibilities outside the family; rearing of teenaged children permitting increased psychological independence of the children; regrouping of the family to allow the young to leave home; rediscovery of the marital relationship after children have left; arrival of grandchildren and development of mutual aid systems spanning the three-generation family.

Carter and McGoldrick's (1980) book even more strongly emphasizes a system theory approach in that the family is clearly defined as more than the sum of its parts, namely, as an emotional system of at least three generations passing through identifiable and predictable phases.

The existence and predictability of developmental phases have long been recognized by practice wisdom; it is only recently that empirical support has been established. Olson and McCubbin's (1983) study of what makes families work found major differences across the seven family life cycle stages, among various family members, and in the predictability of associations among family types and other family variables across these stages. A stratified, randomly selected sample of 1,140 middle-class married couples and families from 31 states was selected from seven life cycle stages, with 261 families in stage 4 (families with adolescents between ages 13 and 18) and 191 families from stage 5 (launching families with adolescents age 19 or older). Independent measures of family variables were obtained from the fathers, mothers, and adolescents. Some of the established differences among stages may actually be associated with characteristics of these particular families, who were formed at different points in historical time. A longitudinal rather than the cross-sectional sample used would have put the family life cycle theory to a harder test, as the researchers point out.

Significant and startling differences were found among the individual family members' perceptions of family dynamics, with the largest discrepancy found between parents and adolescents. Adolescents also reported much lower levels than did their parents of family cohesion and adaptability — the two major dimensions on which the families were compared. General levels of cohesion and adaptability dropped to the lowest point at the Adolescent and Launching stages, with some recovery in the two later stages. Similarly, the highest levels of stress and the lowest levels of marital and family satisfaction were found at the Adolescent stage. The high level of stress was associated not only with changes in adolescent behavior, but also with the parents' added responsibilities in caring for their aging parents, increased financial strains, and the parents' struggle with their own developmental needs exemplified by the fathers changing jobs and mothers entering the work force.

The theoretical frameworks utilized by Olson and McCubbin, as well as by many of the authors in the Carter and McGoldrick book, draw heavily on the writings of two family sociologists, Reuben Hill and Evelyn Duvall. Starting their work in the late 1940s, they have made two major contributions, namely, the three-generational definition of the family system (Hill 1970) and Duvall's classic eight-stage life cycle schema (1957, fifth edition 1977). An independent but similar six stage typology has emerged from the field of family therapy, first formulated by Jay Haley in 1973. Carter and McGoldrick's (1980) schema incorporates ideas from all these sources. Of their six stages, two are relevant to the current discussion. First is "The Family with Adolescents" with the task of increasing the flexibilities of family boundaries to allow room for the adolescent's decreasing dependency needs. Family changes necessary to proceed to the next developmental stage are: shifting of the parent-adolescent relationship, refocus on marital and career issues of the parents, and a beginning concern for the older generation. Second is the stage of "Launching Children and Moving On" with the required shifts of: renegotiation of the dyadic marital system, development of adult-to-adult parent-child relations, relationship realignment allowing inclusion of in-laws and grandchildren, and dealing with disability or death of the parents' parents.

Movement from one stage to the next does not always automatically occur by normative developmental events — as sometimes is implied in family sociological literature (Carter and McGoldrick 1980). A family therapy view is that if the interacting family structure does not meet the developmental needs of one or more of its members, behavioral symptoms develop, and the family becomes incapable of moving on to the next stage; it is derailed from the family life cycle. As Haley (1973) has stated it, the therapist's task then is to help the family become "unstuck" so that the developmental processes again can take their course. The findings of the Olson and McCubbin study essentially support the sociological view of more or less automatic progression in that these normal, study families successfully coped with stage transitions even though considerable stress was experienced (particularly at the adolescent and launching stages as noted). Very few families relied on community or therapeutic resources to make the stage transitions. Haley, and many other family therapists, may be equally right, however, since their observations have been made of families who were not able to make the transitions on their own. Further implications for therapy with families of adolescents of the developmental stress over time (horizontal) and vertical stress in the three-generational family system are discussed in chapter 7.

This section on time perspectives on adolescence concludes with a reference to what Lipsitz in 1977 called the myth that all teenagers constitute a homogeneous group. A few years earlier Jerome Kagan (1972, p. 91) proposed that changes occurring about the age of 12 (around puberty), particularly in the development of cognitive competence, justify designation of a separate developmental stage called early adolescence, covering the period from age 12 to 16. Lipsitz's (1977, p. 161) extensive review provides ample evidence that this age period has been neglected by researchers and service providers. For example, of the several major studies reviewed for information about the family of early adolescents, not a single project dealt exclusively with this period. Without specific attention to early adolescence, says Lipsitz, one is left with the option of gleaning factors from studies of the late adolescent that can be assumed to be of significance.

Notable exceptions to the exclusion of early adolescence are the emergence of the *Journal of Early Adolescence* and studies by John Hill (1980) and by Offer, Ostrow, and Howard (1981) on adolescent self-concept. However, the topic still does not appear to have moved to center stage.[4] Hopefully, future research will clarify the extent to which differences exist between early and late adolescence and the areas of adolescent functioning and relationships in which age does make a difference.

Normal, Two-Parent Families

Empirical Studies. The Olson and McCubbin (1983) study was preceded by a couple of major studies exploring what makes healthy families. The first of them, *The Silent Majority* by Westley and Epstein (1969) identified several family variables associated with the mental health of adolescent children. Data gathered by questionnaires, interviews, and psychological testing of the middle- or upper-class, English, Protestant families of 100 college freshmen in Montreal revealed that the emotional health of children is closely related to the quality of the relationship between parents. Couples with happy and healthy children felt emotionally close, met each other's needs, encouraged positive self-images in each other, were clear about their identities, and saw their children as distinct from themselves. Other predictors of positive child mental health were balanced division of labor and acceptance of parental roles. When both parents fully accepted the parental roles, none of the children was disturbed, as against only one healthy child in 11 families where both parents rejected roles. Of five power patterns (family-dominant, father-led, equalitarian, mother-led, and mother-dominant) the father-led family, in which parents discussed decision making, fared best in having the largest proportion of emotionally healthy children. Twenty years later, Epstein (Epstein and Bishop 1981) suggested that other power-pattern associations may be found today.

The Timberlawn Studies. Over the last couple of decades, Jerry M. Lewis and his coworkers at the Timberlawn Psychiatric Research Foundation in Dallas, Texas, have engaged in ongoing research on healthy and dysfunctional families with adolescents. Their efforts were originally prompted by a desire to find out how family factors impact treatment outcomes of disturbed, hospitalized adolescents. A long-term treatment outcome study (Gossett et al. 1983) required a control group of families with nonhospitalized adolescents in which a subgroup of especially responsive and effective families were identified. This led to the Healthy Family Project (Lewis et al. 1976). The study samples consisted almost exclusively of white, middle- and upper-middle-class, biologically intact, two-parent families with adolescents. Replication with a cross-ethnic (white, black, and Mexican-American) sample of lower-income families was planned, but so far funding has only permitted completion of replication with a sample of working-class black families (Lewis and Looney 1983). As several of the study samples are small, many findings await replication in general, as the researchers repeatedly warn.

These books and a related theoretical analysis by W. Robert Beavers (1977) contain a wealth of material on adolescent-family relations. A few major samples are presented here. The clinical and the volunteer control group families were located on a continuum of family competence, a central concept meaning "the quality of possessing attributes necessary or helpful to achieve or accomplish given tasks" (Lewis and Looney 1983, p. 4). Beyond the basic task of assuring physical survival of family members, throughout the family life cycle there are two overarching tasks of rearing autonomous children and supporting the stabilization and maturation of the parents' personalities. In addition to these two cardinal tasks (originally conceptualized by Talcott Parsons), each family phase has the specific task of providing each family member with the optimal balance of separateness and attachment required for attainment of individual developmental goals. *Separateness* refers to the ability to experience oneself as a differentiated person, autonomously functioning and responsible for one's own life. *Attachment* refers to the ability to relate as well as to make commitments and the ability for intimacy. At the adolescent stage the child's need for separateness increases and attachment to parents decreases, while the parents may need to turn to one another to fill the resultant void in having their own attachment needs met.

It is not known how a representative sample of all U.S. families would distribute itself on the four levels of competence as defined in the Timberlawn studies. The researchers estimate that the top competence level of *optimal families* may represent between 5 and 25 percent of the general population; clinical practitioners experience these families only under conditions of extreme external stress. These families achieve both cardinal tasks; they are characterized by a parental marriage with sharing of power and intimacy achieved. The shared decision-making process comes about naturally rather than being deliberately planned. As parents, the couple is authoritative but not authoritarian; they are in charge but without rigid rules that apply at all times. To use the Beavers's phraseology of child-rearing styles, the parents are "growers" rather than "controllers" (Lewis and Looney 1983, p. 15). Even though others are important to the parents, no other relationships or competing parent-child coalitions are found in optimal families. These families are also characterized by high levels of autonomy along with high levels of closeness. Problems are usually solved efficiently by negotiation, and if a compromise cannot be reached, the parents decide. Emphatic responses and affectionate messages are common; the family mood is one of warmth, humour, and optimism. When tensions, disagreements, and family losses occur — which of course they do — the optimal families appear to know how to cope. The interactional pattern at this competence level is uniquely suited to development of adolescent autonomy as well as parental maturation. However, only longitudinal studies can ascertain if this family pattern is superior at other life cycle stages. It may not be; the Olson and McCubbin (1983) study found that different clusters of family variables and different family types operate at optimal levels over the family life cycle. One additional question relating to optimal parents in the Timberlawn studies calls for further investigation, namely, the finding that many of these parents described their own family-of-origin as dysfunctional.

The second level of competence is represented by the *competent but pained* families, which raise autonomous children but fail to provide sufficient parental support. The parental marriage has not achieved satisfactory levels of intimacy, and it is usually the mother that bears the brunt of this pain. She feels lonely, is often overweight and sour, blames the husband but also acknowledges that he is a good provider and father. The fathers, usually career-oriented loners, see their wives as good mothers but hard to get close to or love. The parental coalition is strained with a rigid division of power — the wife making decisions relating to the children, the husband about finances.

The parents share their love for the children, but because of the missed closeness in the marriage one partner often tries to replace it with closeness to a friend, a child, or a parent, thus creating competing coalitions. Family communications are clear and respectful, but expression of feelings is restricted. Problem solving is effective. Overall these families, in spite of the significant weaknesses, have healthy children who cannot be distinguished from those growing up in optimal families.

The third group on the Timberlawn Competence Continuum is *dysfunctional families*, which are characterized by rigidity and either in a state of chronic chaos or having a dominant-submissive parental structure. This and the fourth group, *severely dysfunctional families,* essentially fail in achieving both cardinal tasks of the family. In the opinion of the Timberlawn research team, the former group is the rule and the latter the exception in the caseloads of human service professionals.

In the dominant-submissive family, one or the other of the parents strongly controls the family, with the submissive spouse in the role of a child. Sometimes this marital pattern is complementary, satisfying to both parties, but most of the time (in both clinical and research volunteer samples) there is open conflict. The powerless, submissive parent often forms coalitions with one or more of the children whose symptomatic behavior goes beyond the control of the strong parent. The emotional mood of the family is either hostility or depression with little expression of feelings. There is no shared problem solving as decision making is made by the dominant parent. Blaming is common, and there is little encouragement to take responsibility for one's own behavior. Children in these families are at risk for significant psychopathology, ranging from severe neuroses to psychotic episodes. In spite of the unhealthy and restrictive family atmosphere, children often have difficulties separating from the family.

The chronically conflicted type of dysfunctional families evolves from unresolvable parental conflict. The parents were never able to solve the power issue in their relationship, avoiding any closeness. The atmosphere in the family created by the parents' ongoing tug-of-war is one of accusation, manipulation, blaming, and great distance between family members. Self-centeredness prevails, and problem solving is ineffective as any issue or problem simply evokes another round of fighting. Children sometimes respond by running away or reaching outside the family in other ways to connect with other groups.

The *severely dysfunctional families* often contain several members with severe and chronic psychopathology. Two types are discernible: the dominant-submissive family with a dominant paranoid/psychotic parent creating a family environment "that blurs self-boundaries, distorts reality, and fosters persistent symbiotic attachments'' (Lewis and Looney 1983, p. 24), and the chaotic family with no one of sufficient strength to create a stable family structure. The chaotic family is adrift in a fused existence allowing no individuation or autonomy. Usually there is very little contact with persons outside the family. Severe thought disturbances are common among children from these families; if the adolescent is brought for treatment the diagnosis is often severe borderline disturbance or schizophrenia.

Lewis and Looney, whose summary of the four patterns of families on the continuum of family competence has been paraphrased above, point out that the underlying, enduring family structure pinpoints the family's location on the continuum, the scale ranging from clear structure and flexible operations in optimal families, to clear structure with rigid operations in dysfunctional families, to unclear structure and disorganized operations in the severely dysfunctional families. The movement is from flexibility to rigidity to chaos. They also point out that external stress or developmental challenges may result in family functioning patterns that temporarily move the family to lower than usual competence levels on the continuum. The Beavers System includes the developmental individuation/separation continuum to a larger extent than the Olson Circumplex Model, which may make the Beavers System more clinically useful (Beavers and Voeller 1983).

There are many parallels between the Circumplex Model (of Olson and his research team) and the Timberlawn Continuum of Family Competence. Olson et al. operate with three major types of families: balanced, mid-range, and extreme. The Circumplex model is developed from the two dimensions of cohesion and adaptability: *cohesion* (composed of emotional and attachment variables) is measured on a scale ranging from disengaged, to separated, to connected, to enmeshed; *adaptability* is measured on a scale from rigid, to structured, to flexible, to chaotic. Obviously the healthier families would fall in the middle ranges of the two scales. Thus balanced families are those scoring in the central ranges on either dimension; mid-range families score in the central range on one of the dimensions and the extreme range on the other; extreme families score in the extreme ends of both scales. Thus, the Circumplex balanced families appear to correspond to the Timberlawn optimal families, mid-range to competent but pained, and extreme to the dysfunctional and severely dysfunctional. Olson and McCubbin give a clarification similar to Lewis and Looney, namely, that it should not be assumed that the balanced family system is always operating in the balanced (mid) ranges. "Being balanced means a family system can experience the extremes on the dimensions when appropriate, but they do not typically function at these extremes for long periods of time . . . both extremes are tolerated and expected. . . . Conversely extreme family types tend to function only at the extremes and members are not expected or able to change their behaviors. As a result, the more balanced family types have a larger behavior repertoire and are more able to change compared to extreme family types" (p. 59).

All empirical studies reported in this section confirm the importance of the quality of the parental relationship for the psychological health of the family system. Additional support is found in a much smaller study by Teyber (1983), which explored the effects of the parental coalition on the emancipation of male adolescents from the family. College freshmen from homes where the parents had not been able to establish a marital coalition as the strongest alliance in the families with subsequent primary cross-generational alliances between the mother and son, experienced more difficulty in separating from the parent (as evidenced in academic failure) than did their successful counterparts from homes characterized by a primary marital alliance. These latter parents may have found it easier to encourage the emancipation of their sons than the parents with cross-generational bonding; for them emancipation is a much more serious emotional loss. Even though the study samples were carefully matched on intellectual ability, the researcher warns that future research is needed to include additional measures of emancipation difficulties other than academic failure, and other samples are needed to further confirm this preliminary finding.

A third major national study addressing parent-adolescent relations is the ongoing Modal Adolescent Research Project at Michael Reese Hospital in Chicago under the leadership of Daniel Offer (1981). The latest report from this project deals with the adolescent self-concept as measured by five topical scales — psychological, social, sexual, familial, and coping self — constituting the Offer Self-Image Questionnaire (OSIQ). Findings are based on responses by thousands of teenagers representing early and late adolescents, boys and girls. While the OSIQ has great strength in having been cross-validated in large samples of youth, its use of self-report measures gives reason for some caution in interpreting findings as totally valid measures of self-concept because of the social desirability tendency of self-report measures to produce inflated answers. Major findings relating to the familial self (feelings and attitudes toward parents) are that the overwhelming majority of normal adolescents (in regular schools) have positive feelings about their parents and that they do not perceive any major problems between themselves and the parents. Close to 90 percent of them think that their parents are satisfied with them most of the time and that they will continue to be a source of pride in the future. The adolescents see their parents as having a good relationship with each other. Seven out of ten say they have a say in family decision making and feel that the parents are patient and reasonable with them. No major differences were found between the sexes, age groupings (13–15 vs. 16–18), or nationalities, indicating consistency of positive feelings about the family among normal teenagers.[5] While a well-functioning family does not assure mental health, keeping everything else constant, "the family will contribute relatively more to the positive development of adolescents than any other psychosocial variable" (p. 65).

Juvenile delinquents and psychiatrically disturbed teenagers have significantly different views of their families than normal or physically ill adolescents, with delinquents holding more negative views than any other group. Only six out of ten delinquents or disturbed adolescents feel their parents are satisfied with them as against close to nine out of ten normals. The two former groups do not see themselves as being an integral part of a cohesive family structure. They feel more often that their parents are ashamed of them and will not be proud of them in the future. The physically ill adolescents have attitudes very similar to the normal group.

Some Clinical Observations.   Clinical professional literature abounds with cases illustrating mostly family situations with problematic parent-adolescent relations. M.V. Bloom (1980) identifies the five-stage separation process as an ambivalent push-and-pull experience for parents and teenagers and lists the variables affecting this process as: individual readiness for independence, cognitive influences, nature of the parent-child relationship, past parent-adolescent experiences in separations, and cultural influences. He illustrates his theoretical points with several extensively reported cases from his own practice.

Patterns of maturational time distortions are presented by Toews, Martin, and Prosen (1981). The first pattern involves parents who try to retard their child's move toward autonomy at the same time the adolescent attempts to speed up the life cycle progression. A second pattern occurs when parents as well as the adolescent try to delay maturation. The third occurs when parents and adolescent collude to accelerate their life cycles. Finally, in the fourth pattern the parents try to accelerate the separation process, while the adolescent is fearful of independence and attempts to delay maturation. Their case illustrations demonstrate therapeutic efforts to synchronize the parents' and the adolescents' maturational processes. A British example of the fourth pattern is also presented by Kraemer (1982).

Ausubel (Ausubel et al. 1977) classifies parent-youth conflicts into two broad categories. One is the prognostically hopeful group in which the disturbance is clearly a transitory phenomenon linked to parental ambivalence, peer group influence, or the adolescent's distortions about emancipation. In the second, unfavorable group, the disturbance in the emancipation process is rooted in parent-child relationship conflicts predating adolescence. Three types of such parent-adolescent relationship disturbances are: the dominant, self-assertive child who has been harshly rejected; the overvalued child suffering rejection in later childhood or adolescence; and the "over-dominated and overmotivated child who rebels openly against parental dominance" (p. 212). Ausubel's retrospective comparison of 20 cases of parent-youth conflict indicated that while childhood conflict had been present in all cases, the 10 nonimproved families showed significantly less favorable parental attitudes prior to adolescence than did the improved group. In the latter group, parents also showed ability to change their attitudes toward their young adult children for the better in the postadolescent period.

Perhaps the best known conceptual framework about parent-adolescent separation is Helm Stierlin's (1973, 1981, and Stierlin et al. 1980) transactional modes of binding, delegating, and expelling. The central idea is that the centripetal force of the need to be close counteracts with the centrifugal force of the need to be separate. Strong families attain a balance that allows simultaneous closeness and individuation. This balance is easily upset at times of transition — such as adolescence. But in healthy (optimal, balanced) families, "loving fights" characterize the shift of the parent-adolescent relationships from complementarity to symmetry. The outcome depends on which transactional mode has dominated the relationship prior to the maturational phase. "When age-appropriate transactional modes are out of phase, too intense, or inappropriately mixed with other modes, the negotiation of a mutual individuation and separation between parent and child is impeded" (1981, p. 35).

Stierlin distinguishes between the three transactional modes of binding, delegating, and expelling, each here summarized from Stierlin's 1981 formulation (chapter 4): In the *binding mode* the parent-adolescent interaction keeps the adolescent "tied to the parental orbit and locked into the 'family ghetto' " (1981, p. XIV). Centripetal forces win. The binding may operate in the affective area, with the parent infantalizing the adolescent who reciprocates by undue regression. Or, at the cognitive level, the parent interferes with the child's self-determination and self-awareness. The bindee becomes unsure of inner signposts, perceptions of self and others, and of his or her basic feelings. Finally, binding may occur through exploitation of loyalty to the family/parents by installing excessive guilt over any attempt to break away.

In the *delegating mode* the centripetal and centrifugal forces appear of equal strength, and the parents are unable to settle for either; they need to bind the children, but also to send them away. The parents subject the children to their own ambivalence by sending them out of the family orbit as parental delegates on a long leash of loyalty that will pull the child back after the mission has been fulfilled. The "delegate" child may experience two kinds of conflicts: loyalty conflicts (as when pitted by one parent against the other) or mission conflicts, occurring when the parent sends the child on incompatible missions.

In the *expelling mode* the parent instigates a premature separation in order to cope with his or her own developmental crisis. The adolescent is in the way. The parents are so busy and preoccupied with their own affairs that the children are considered and treated as expendable. They are prematurely pushed out of the home and seek company with peer groups or other adults. The expelling of the child may appear much like the expelling phase of the delegate mode. The difference is that there is no centripetal leash. The overriding force is the parents' wish to make the expulsion stick.

These three unhappy modes of parent-adolescent separation clearly fit into the dysfunctional and severely dysfunctional families on the Timber-lawn Continuum of Family Competence, with an occasional spill-over into the competent but pained families. They also bring back to the minds of mental health and child welfare practitioners the memories of former and current client families who unfortunately seem to fit these patterns precisely. And the professional social work literature, even though slightly different vocabularies are used, provides numerous illustrations of Stierlin's transactional modes. Rhodes (1977), referred to earlier in this section, elaborates on how parental anxiety, stirred by the adolescent's striving for autonomy, may lead to premature expulsion of the youngster from the family group (as is sometimes seen in requests for immediate out-of-home placements of adolescents) or to binding the adolescent even further to the family group and thereby preventing normal separation and psychological and social maturity from occurring. In the latter kind of family, the adolescent has been triangled into the marital relationship as the mother's confidant, parental surrogate, or mediator (p. 308). A permanent place is assured the adolescent in the family but at great psychological costs. In extreme cases, separation is simply postponed until the biological death of one or both parents.

Parent-Adolescent Relations Affected by Divorce and in Single-Parent and Blended Families

So far the discussion on parent-adolescent relations has focused on the two-parent families. Today this so-called normal family situation is just one of several family compositions. The steadily growing U.S. divorce rate — the highest in the world — is linked with increased rate of single-parent families from 11 percent in 1970 to 22 percent in 1983. In 1975 about 79 percent of all families were headed by a married couple, 18 percent by a mother alone, and 2 to 3 percent by a father alone (Rawlings 1984).

Paradoxically, as the traditional biological family form is adapting and new family compositions and styles develop, children's need for continuity and stability in parental relationships has been more strongly voiced than ever before (Goldstein, Freud, and Solnit 1973, 1979), and permanency planning for children who have to be removed from their homes becomes the mandated principle, if not always the practice, in the child welfare field (as discussed in chapter 5). One senses that these changes are somehow interrelated; however, that topic is left for demographers and family sociologists to sort out in future studies.

A central and persistent concern is the influence on child and adolescent psychological development of these family changes. Early studies have established associations between broken homes and conduct disorders and delinquency, teenage pregnancy, unmarried motherhood, difficulty in infant care, and subsequent marital breakdown. Rutter (1980) from whom this summarization is taken, maintains that many of these disturbances were present prior to family disruption, and while the actual separation of family members itself may add to the stress, conflictual relationships in the family and long-standing family disharmony appear to be the more important variables. Rutter also points out that adverse effects in children are not irreversible if they later live in harmonious homes, which happens to some, while the atmosphere in other homes remains as turbulent as ever after divorce. Furthermore, reactions to family disruption are stronger where children had prior psychiatric or delinquent problems. Finally, adolescent disturbances do not ordinarily represent a "sleeper" effect to family disruption in earlier years (Rutter 1980, pp. 149-150).

The following sections take a closer look at some of the studies relevant to adolescents experiencing divorce and living in single-parent or blended families. One needs to keep in mind, however, that almost all studies in this field have examined families or adolescents in clinical settings, and caution might be called for in interpreting findings of even well-designed early studies as being valid today. The stigma commonly associated with divorce in the past may have been an important intervening variable. While this stigma has not disappeared entirely, replication of 10- to 20-year-old studies may not produce the same findings today in respect to psychological impact on the child and adolescent development.

Adolescents and Parental Divorce. The sample of 60 families of the frequently quoted study by Wallerstein and Kelly (1974, 1979, and 1980) was established by offering counseling to previously well-adjusted children of divorcing families. The setting was the Community Mental Health Center of Marin County, where relatively stable middle-class life is the common experience, so that the findings were not confounded with the effects of poverty, crime, and social breakdown. The sample families had 131 children between the ages of 3 and 19, of which 21 were adolescents. The families were seen by five experienced clinicians trained in work with children and parents. Counseling covered a six-week initial period, and there were follow-up interviews after 12 and 18 months. Five-year follow-up interviews were held with 58 of the original 60 families.

The initial emotional consequences of divorce were bitterly painful for almost all the children. The researchers expected the adolescents to experience less overt distress than the younger children, but most of them expressed great anger at the parents for breaking up the family at a point critical to them. The anger was compounded by shame, embarrassment, considerable sadness, and a sense of loss and betrayal. However, the pain of divorce for adolescents did not appear to be the result of any feeling of responsibility for the parents' divorce as it did among the younger children, who to varying degrees felt they caused the divorce. Adolescents in loyalty conflicts experienced much guilt when in fantasy or reality they aligned themselves with one parent, with resentment at both parents being the inevitable result. They also worried about their own future as marital partners, and had unrealistic concerns about future financial support from the parents.

However, for most of these adolescents the reactions were time limited; within a year they appeared able to move on with their developmental agendas. The researchers concluded that the youngsters who appeared to do best were those able to distance themselves at the height of the conflict. While they appeared somewhat self-centered and insensitive in doing so, it became clear at follow-up that denial and withdrawal had been used constructively to deal with the initial blow and had enabled them to be supportive at a later time. The researchers point to the importance of the particular, individual parent-child relationship built prior to and at the time of the divorce for the disruptive or growth-producing consequences for each individual adolescent. Where the divorce was preceded by long-standing difficulties, the adolescents experienced greater developmental troubles.

At the five-year follow-up, Wallerstein and Kelly (1979 and 1980) found that 34 percent of the total sample of youngsters did very well, as evidenced in good adjustment in school and play and in relations with peers and within the family. Twenty-nine percent of them had resumed appropriate developmental progress, but from time to time they experienced sadness and resentment against one or both parents. The remaining 37 percent unfortunately were suffering from moderate to severe depressions, sexual promiscuity, delinquency, and other behavioral disturbances. On the other hand, the parents surveyed felt that their situations had improved considerably in spite of the stresses they dealt with. The researchers concluded that as a group the children and adolescents did not experience a similar improvement in mental health following the marital dissolution.

Without appropriate comparison groups or a representative sample of all divorced families with children, it is difficult to conclude how characteristic the negative findings of the Wallerstein and Kelly study are of divorced children and adolescents in general. It is possible that the 60 families who volunteered represent the more troubled ones among divorced families. Schwartzberg (1980), in his study of 30 adolescents coping with parental divorce and brought for psychiatric consultation, similarly found that severe depression was present in at least one-third of the cases and to some extent in all. This researcher identified three types of adolescents: those with exacerbation of preexisting psychopathology requiring hospitalizations, those experiencing temporary regression with later resumption of age-appropriate adolescent development, and those who attempted prematurely to master the adolescent task of separation-individuation.

Gudrun Brun (1978) in her psychiatric evaluations of 500 Danish children between ages 3 and 16 from 322 families found 43 percent of the children to suffer from psychiatric disturbances. The evaluations were requested by the court for determination of custody. It was difficult to separate preexisting disorders from temporary reactions to the divorce experience itself. Of the total group of children, she estimated that 28 percent were traumatized by the divorce, 44 percent did not appear affected, and the remaining 28 percent seemed to improve in their more stable environments after the divorce. The stressful effects of divorce in this study were significantly greater for latency age children than for the preschoolers and adolescents.

Despite this evidence of emotional disturbances, divorce children and adolescents do not appear to be overrepresented within clinic populations. Of 2,351 consecutive child psychiatry patients (University of California, Los Angeles) about half had married parents, a little over 44 percent represented children of divorce, and close to 6 percent had a widowed parent (Schoettle and Cantwell 1980), which is equivalent to the general population. The 12- to 18-year-olds accounted for even percentages of the two major samples. The major significant differences found between young people from intact and divorced homes were that physical problems and mental retardation were more frequent in the former group and problems of behavior and social relationships, family conflict, learning, and school problems were more frequent in the divorced group. Controlling for age, sex, and ethnicity, only minor variations were found between the two groups.

The findings of the reported studies notwithstanding, it appears that empirical evidence is still meager as far as the impact of divorce on parent-adolescent separation process is concerned. Perhaps the one hopeful conclusion that can be drawn at this time is that the pervasive view of former days that divorce spells only disastrous and negative consequences for children is tempered with evidence that divorce is experienced positively by some adolescents. Wallerstein and Kelly as early as 1974 identified the potential of divorce as a stimulant of development that, if it does not come prematurely (that is, before the normal detachment has begun to take place) facilitates the growth toward independence. Additional examples will be given below from studies exploring the impact on adolescent maturation of divorce as well as being a member of a single-parent household.

Adolescents Living with a Separated/Divorced Parent. Twenty-two percent of all children under age 18 in the United States live in single-parent families — close to 13 million with their mothers, and 1.2 million with their fathers (Saluter, 1983). Separation and divorce are the major contributors to single-parent families, even though the proportion of children with never-married mothers is increasing and now exceeds the proportion of children with widowed mothers (Bilge and Kaufman 1983; Hogan, Buehler, and Robinson 1983; Rawlings, 1984). The two latter groups are as yet barely mentioned in the professional literature especially as far as adolescents are concerned.

Very few studies, theoretical analyses, or clinical analyses deal specifically with adolescents in families of separation and divorce, and rarely is any distinction made between adolescents who move from a two-parent to a single-parent household as a result of marital dissolution and those who spend most of their childhood years with a divorced parent. As already noted in reference to Rutter's (1980) conclusions regarding broken families, associations between dysfunctional child behavior and family structure can be interpreted many ways depending on the nature of study samples and the extent to which possible intervening variables have been controlled for. Thus findings of higher levels of juvenile delinquency, school failure, and faulty sex-role identification in children/adolescents from one-parent families have been seriously questioned by thorough reviews of research methodology (Blechman 1982; Cashion 1982; Herzog and Sudia 1973). Examples of positive aspects of growing up in a single-parent family are also found in the literature, such as greater independence and other maturational advantages of "growing up a little faster" (Weiss 1979).

A powerful intervening variable is the economic hardship of single-parent families, particularly in those headed by females. Quoting 1980 U.S. Bureau of the Census statistics, Hogan et al. (1983) state that in the 1979 population, female-headed families accounted for 48 percent of all families below the poverty level. Almost one-third of all female-headed families were below the poverty level. As Cashion (1982) points out, lower school performance as well as juvenile delinquency have been found to be associated with poverty, so it is unclear what the relative contributions are of poverty and family structure.

The economic status variables also were influential in a study comparing custodial mothers and fathers (Ambert 1982). Twenty such mothers and seven fathers were interviewed about the behaviors expressed toward them by their children ranging from 3 to 18 years old. The average annual income for the fathers (exempting one who was a millionaire) was $50,000. For ten of the mothers it was $33,000; while out of ten mothers of lower socioeconomic status (SES), none earned above $12,000 a year. None of the fathers experienced any major problems with their children in contrast to the mothers, of whom half reported such problems. Seven of the low-SES mothers reported serious problems, and only two were positive. The mothers with higher education and reasonable financial means reported more pleasure with their children and in turn had children appearing more pleased with their mothers and themselves. The low-SES mothers were often the scapegoats of the children's frustrations. The researchers noted one woman whose "14-year-old pregnant daughter kept telling her that she 'didn't want to grow old to become like me, a woman men do not want.' She compared her mother unfavorably with her father, who was living with another woman and contributing nothing to his children's existence" (Ambert 1982, p. 81). The researcher's exploratory findings were that the custodial fathers experienced the greatest satisfaction with parenting, high-SES custodial mothers had moderate satisfaction, and the low-SES mothers had the least. Another exploratory study comparing divorced single fathers and mothers (Defrain and Eirick 1981) arrived at an opposite conclusion, finding hardly any differences between males and females. Their mean incomes, however, were very similar; the fathers' mean income was $15,700 (a range of $5,000–$27,000) while the mothers' was $12,500 (a range of $3,700–$28,000). No final conclusions can be drawn from these exploratory studies; however, the economic status factor appears to be very powerful as a stress factor in single-mother families and presumably also in the mother-adolescent relationship.

The generally expected lower self-esteem among adolescents in divorced and single-parent homes has been explored in a couple of studies. Parish and Taylor (1979), for example, found lower self-concepts among adolescents who had lost their fathers through divorce than among those from intact families. They speculate that the lower self-concept may not be linked directly to the divorce as such, but with subsequent lowered socioeconomic conditions, the necessity of the mothers to work outside the home, and the need for the mothers to function as sole parents. A later study by Parish (1981) of over 1,400 college students did not confirm the finding of lower self-evaluation of students from divorced homes. What was found was significantly lower evaluations of both fathers and mothers in divorced families as opposed to intact families or from homes where the father had died. The researcher speculated that the problems associated with divorce may drive a wedge not only between the parents but also between parents and children who in a stigmatizing way hold their parents responsible.

Wallerstein and Kelly's five-year follow-up (1980) also sheds some light on the question of self-esteem. They found that high self-esteem in all the children, but particularly in the older boys, was associated with a good father-child relationship sustained by regular visitations. On the other hand, Raschke and Raschke (1979) found no significant differences in self-concept scores of children from intact, single-parent, reconstituted, or other types of families studied. Neither did they find any differences with respect to sex, age, and ethnicity of the 289 third-, sixth-, and eighth-grade children examined. One significant finding was an association between low self-concept scores and reported higher levels of family conflict.

To add to the perplexities, a very recent study by Slater, Stewart, and Linn (1983) identified significant differences among male and female adolescents with regard to family disruption. In a sample of 217 New Orleans public high school students, males from divorced/separated homes had the highest overall self-esteem scores of the four groups. Similarly, the greatest conflict in the homes was experienced by females from disrupted families and males from intact families. For the males, the divorce experience appears to have promoted a more positive self-concept and a better perception of the family atmosphere than that experienced by males from intact homes. The females from the disrupted homes, on the other hand, felt greater conflict in the home and had a lower self-concept. Since most disrupted homes are female-headed households, the researchers speculate that as the father moves out the male adolescent may assume the man-of-the-house role with accompanying opportunity for growth that may lead to higher self-evaluation. Adolescent girls living with their divorced/separated mothers do not seem to experience a similar growth-producing home situation. On the contrary, Blechman (1982) refers to studies indicating that adolescent girls raised by single mothers may develop unconventional heterosexual behaviors and expectations that may make them less prepared for conventional marriage. However, she also points to indications that girls raised by single working mothers may be better prepared for careers than girls raised by homemaker mothers.

Adolescents who in the past have been the focus of family problems may be particularly vulnerable to experiencing divorce and subsequent single-parenting as a barrier in achieving their developmental tasks (Beal 1980). Because of the parents' increased emotional needs at the time of family dissolution, fathers may tend to seek emotional support from their daughters and adolescent sons "may find themselves propelled into a spouse-like or peer relationship with their mothers" (p. 254). If blurring of these generational boundaries continues and leads to lasting symmetrical emotional bonds between parents and adolescents, the adolescent is prevented from age-appropriate separation from the family and may experience difficulties in later establishment of his or her own nuclear family.

To sum up, the variables that appear to determine the impact of divorce and subsequent single-parenting are: the quality of the parent-adolescent relationship and age-appropriateness and quality of the child's general psychosocial development prior to the marital dissolution; (as summarized by Sprenkle and Cyrus 1983) the quality of relations between the child and the custodial parent and between the ex-spouses, particularly the degree of continued conflict between them; the general psychological adjustment of the parents; the relationship between the child and the noncustodial parent; financial resources; and achievement on the part of the child of some sense of control over the divorce situation.

Almost all these variables are family interactional; thus a family system perspective is called for. A trend toward such a view — away from a narrow unidirectional parent-child perspective — is apparent in the recommended guidelines presented by the Committee on the Family of the Group for the Advancement of Psychiatry (1983) to the courts for custody determinations. Similarly, Constance R. Ahrons (1980, 1983) calls for a redefinition of the deficit concept of the divorce family to a more constructive concept of the binuclear family existing in two households. Consequences of these recent trends will be discussed in chapter 8.

Adolescents in Remarried Families. Parental remarriage presents adolescents with the challenge of becoming part of or contributing to the making of a new, coherent family group at the time when the adolescent's developmental task is to relinquish the role of a child. It is a challenge for most, and it becomes a challenge even for stepfamilies of long standing. Although applications by remarried families to social service agencies are highest during the first year of marriage, many reapplications are made as the children reach adolescence (Wald 1981).

Despite the facts that there are already 35 million adult stepparents in the United States and that one child out of every five is a stepchild (Visher and Visher 1983), one is struck by the absence of major longitudinal studies that provide knowledge about life cycle processes in the remarried family and about its impact on child and adolescent development. However, recent important and primarily clinically based works (Visher and Visher 1979; McGoldrick and Carter 1980; Wald 1981; Sager et al. 1983) have started conceptualization of these processes and identification of variables to be covered empirically. All these writers agree that the remarried family has an intrinsically different organizational structure than the nuclear family, which cannot serve as a model for what the stepfamily ought to become. The "REM" family, as Sagar et al. call it, is simply a different creature.

There are many differences from the nuclear family as described by the above literature that all have to come to terms with in the process of merging two single-parent families into a blended family. For example, parent-child bonds predate the new marital parental relationship, which often means that the crucial primacy of parental boundaries is slow to develop leaving the field wide open for flourishing cross-generational alliances that may be especially strong in the case of a long period of single-parenthood. There are now two sets of in-laws and grandparents and there are possible shifts in the birth order of children, who are often members of two households (the stepfamily and that of the other bio parent). There are assymmetrical legal ties in that all members of the nuclear family are legally related while there are no such ties between stepparent and stepchild and among stepsiblings (Wald 1981). Finally, stepfamilies have experienced important losses in the dissolution of the first marriage and there may be unhealed divorce process wounds. Everyday hassles in the early phase of the remarried family center around adjustment to different preexisting lifestyles in relation to eating habits, use of alcohol and drugs, division of labor, attitudes toward obligations, household rules, expression of emotions, and settling of disagreements (Johnson 1980).

For adolescents the integration process appears particularly difficult in the area of discipline. According to Lutz (1983), because adolescence is a time of testing, rebelling, and seeking autonomy, discipline is not responded to positively to begin with and it is more difficult for the teenager who may have enjoyed added responsibilities and freedom during the single-parent stage to return to what is perceived as childlike obedience. Remarried families who have been successful in integrating adolescents from previous marriages stress the importance of being very clear and open about role relationships and family ground rules, acknowledgement by the stepparent of the special relationship between the biological parent and the adolescent, a joint stance by the parents, and regularly scheduled family meetings for all members to discuss running of the household (Whiteside 1982).

Divided loyalties toward the parents may also be harder for adolescents than for younger children to deal with. The parent-child relationship has existed longer, and during the single-parenthood period parents tend to lean more on the older child. Sometimes one or the other of the bioparents demands undivided loyalty; at other times the adolescent's own emotions lead to loyalty conflicts. Their impact on the stepfamily is "hostility to the new relationship, negative comparison of stepparent to parent of same sex, anxiety and guilt if the child likes the stepparent, acting out against the REM parent, anger at recognition of REM since the hope for reconciliation of the parents is now even more remote" (Sager et al. 1983, p. 32).

As the incest taboo is not operating in stepfamilies, the likelihood for sexual attraction between stepparent and step adolescent and between stepsiblings represents an added stress for the remarried families that sometimes results in actual sexual abuse, particularly among stepfathers and stepdaughters (Sager et al. 1983, pp. 293-310). Visher and Visher (1979) report that stepfathers may be especially vulnerable to their attractive stepdaughters when things are not going well in the marital relationship. Furthermore, adolescents are more aware of the sexual relationship of the newly married couple than that of their counterparts in the nuclear family, where many parents are thought of as asexual. Visher and Visher (1983) suggest, on the basis of clinical observations, that the greatest conflict for teenage girls is to come to terms with their mother's sexuality. When an adolescent girls starts running away, using drugs, excessively dating or acting-out, the sexual relationships in the family may be askew and in need of close examination.

It needs to be kept in mind that the extent to which the above stresses are experienced by all or some remarried families is largely unknown since the observations are primarily made from clinical populations. Lutz (1983) surveyed 103 adolescents between ages 12 and 18 living in stepfamilies to find out what they experienced as stressful. An earlier study by Duberman (1975) investigated the same topic but relied on reports from the adults in the stepfamilies. Of the 11 potential stress factors identified by Lutz from the professional literature, the respondents ranked divided loyalties and discipline issues as the most stressful. The one item receiving the highest stress score of all was "Experiencing one natural parent talking negatively about the other natural parent" (p. 371). The finding of discipline as a high stress issue is in accord with findings of other studies, of which some have identified this issue to be the top area of difficulty. Lutz notes, however, that it is not known if teenagers in stepfamilies find discipline issues more stressful than those living in nuclear families.

Other significant findings reveal that adolescents who had lived in a stepfamily for more than two years experienced less stress than those in newly established stepfamilies. There was more stress in families with stepsiblings than in those without and study results indicated more stress in stepfamilies formed after the death of one of the biological parents rather than after divorce. The last finding is inconsistent with Duberman's finding that remarriages after widowhood achieved higher integration as blended families than did families formed by divorce. Lutz speculates that remarriage after divorce may be more stressful to adults, whereas adolescents find living in a remarried family more stressful after the death of a biological parent. An unexpected significant finding showed that less than one-third of these adolescents experienced living in two households as stressful; it appears that it may be more stressful for a teenager to not visit with the noncustodial parent than it is to move back and forth between two households. Stepfather/stepson relationships were experienced as less stressful than stepfather/stepdaughter relations, which is contrary to the finding of no sex difference in stepfather relations in the Duberman (1975) study. The latter study identified the stepmother/stepdaughter relationship as the most difficult. Overall the females in the Lutz study had higher stress scores than the males.

The sample adolescents in the Lutz study did not perceive social attitudes related to their stepfamily status as stressful, and Lutz wonders if stepfamily life may not be as stressful as the literature conveys. It could also be that the 103 adolescents who responded to the questionnaire out of the 294 identified stepfamily teenagers were the ones who had integrated more easily into stepfamily living.

In any event, the above discussions indicate that adolescents in divorce situations — in single-parent and remarried families — may be less likely to separate from their parents through a "loving fight" than their counterparts in optimal or competent but pained intact families. It remains to be seen, however, if they are more vulnerable than those from dysfunctional families to the binding, delegating, or expelling modes of parent-adolescent separation. Strong cross-generational relations are commonly noted; McGoldrick and Carter (1980) list six key triangles in remarried families, of which four involve parent-child relations. Sager et al. (1983) identify children's roles as messengers as one force impinging on the REM family; if the biological parents are not on speaking terms, the adolescent may be delegated by one parent to spy on the other or simply to serve as a bearer of information. While this form of delegating may differ from the dynamics of what Stierlin (1981) refers to, the power inherent in the messenger role may be more than the child can handle. It may, as Sager et al. note, be used consciously or unconsciously to divide the REM couple and conquer the bioparent or to gain favors from all parental figures.

The expelling mode is specifically mentioned by almost all writers as a plausible outcome for adolescents in stepfamilies. Sager et al. refer to this mode as extrusion. The common pattern is that both households are open to the adolescent, but if the REM system itself is threatened by the adolescent, various forms of extrusion may be the outcome of a reciprocal, escalating, negative interaction. It may take the form of subtle disengagement, open hostility, threats of extrusion, planned temporary extrusions, or banishment (pp. 260–61). At times the birth of a mutual child may affect the range of extrusion used; at other times such an event serves as a cohesive centripetal force pulling the REM family together and making extrusion less necessary.

In spite of these dire outcomes in some stepfamilies, it is important to underscore that this family form, which has been predicted to become the norm by 1990 in the United States (Lutz 1983), works well for many, and the authors referred to in this section all seem to strike a hopeful note, reporting that even with the trials and tribulations of clinical populations of REM families, "The potential gratifications make the difficulties worthwhile" (Sager et al. 1983, p. 37). It can be done. Ways for the human service professionals to assist in this process are presented in chapter 8.

Adolescents in Families of Violence

Blum and Runyan (1980) report that of all confirmed cases of physical and sexual abuse, 28 percent involve adolescents between 12 and 17 years of age and that adolescent females are twice as likely to be abused as males, mostly because of the frequency of sexual abuse. Several reports and studies show great variations in child/adolescent reactions to parental abuse, depending on the child's age at onset of abuse, on its severity, and on family dynamics. A review of 25 cases of adolescent abuse in a public welfare department in a midwestern city showed that in about half of the cases the abuse started at the onset of puberty and was related to the stresses of adolescence as well as the problems of middle age of the parents. The intensity and frequency of the abuse appeared to be related to family dynamics such as flexibility, warmth, and use of punishment as a means of control. The other half of the case sample represented continued abuse from preadolescent years or escalation of physical punishment. This group of families showed evidence of psychopathology of adults and children (Libbey and Bybee 1979. See also Bybee 1979; Fisher and Berdie 1978; Garbarino 1980; Lourie 1979; and Timberlake 1979, and for a cross-cultural perspective, see Korbin 1981).

The psychological impairment to abused school-age and adolescent children include intellectual impairment, poor impulse control, defensive functioning, poor reality testing, disturbed thought processes, depressive affect combined with self-destructive behavior, and problems in school adjustment (Green 1978). Linkages between abuse and delinquency have been established by several authors, as reported in Hunner and Walker (1981), and between early sexual exploitation and prostitution (Silbert and Pines 1983).

Several attempts have been made to present a theoretical framework to explain the dynamics of abusive behavior in families (Belsky 1980; Martin and Walters 1982; Serrano et al. 1979). Foremost among these authors are Gelles and Straus (Gelles 1980 and Gelles and Straus 1979), who propose a theoretical model integrating several schools of thought. The topic of adolescents exposed to family violence and sexual abuse will be addressed in subsequent chapters.

Adolescent-Sibling Relations

Much child development and even recent family system and ecology literature implicitly portray parent-child interactions as if parents relate to just one child, or at least one child at the time. Common life experience tells us that parent-child relations are impacted by the number of children in the family and by their gender and spacing. Yet siblings and their role and impact on one another and the total family interaction have been largely ignored. Siblings orbit in the shadows and rarely make it to the limelight. One reason could be that a large part of our professional knowledge builds on clinical observations of families seeking help with *one* child the so-called identified patient (IP).

Other reasons for the low attention to sibling associations suggested in the literature are: general acceptance of the primacy of the parent-child interaction in child development; the influence of psychoanalytic theory, which has tended to focus on sibling rivalry as a factor in the child's psychosexual development to the exclusion of other functions siblings may play for one another; lack of theoretical underpinnings; and the difficult research methodology involved in studying the multiple interactions even in intact two-parent families, not to speak of additional variables introduced by multiple parents and half- and step-siblings (Tsukada 1979; Schvaneveldt and Ihinger 1979). The complexity is overwhelming. Yet there is a strange contradiction in the fact that technology today allows the study of galaxies outside our own, billions of light years away, while we struggle so in studying and understanding family life of the human being on Earth. The family is at least close by, which may be at the heart of the trouble. Everybody is part of at least one nuclear family and most of several more; rare is the person for whom some family variable or other does not evoke some regret, discomfort, or pain that would better be forgotten.

Important groundwork, however, has been laid for development and integration of future clinical and empirical observations on sibling relationships by Schvaneveldt and Ihinger (1979) in their formulation of 22 propositions relating to the sibling subsystem within the total family system — among them — coalition formation, positional shifts, power, rules and expectations, and processes within the subsystem including sex role development among siblings. They also convincingly argue that siblings are both recipients and instigators of much of the family interaction, and the importance of this is not limited to the early years of socialization but continues through the life cycle. None of the propositions specifically addresses the adolescent stage. The authors refer though to the often quoted study by Bowerman and Dobash (1974) of intersibling affect among over 7,000 high school adolescents. Sixty-five percent of them felt close to their siblings, while only a small percent did not feel close at all. Females were more likely to feel closer to siblings than were males. The closeness toward siblings declined somewhat as the adolescent grew older, and siblings in large families felt a little less close than those in two-child families. A finding of an early study by Garigue (1956) that the degree of affection between siblings in adolescence was second only to that felt for the mother is supported by Tsukada (1979), who found that sibling influence increases at adolescence as the credibility of adults begins to be questioned.

In addition to meeting needs for affection, siblings learn from one another in the socialization process. They learn to share tangibles and intangibles, to play by the rules, to settle conflicts, and to promote — or hamper — relations with peers or others outside the nuclear family through introductions or manipulations. With respect to sex role identification, older siblings influence the younger ones of same or opposite sex (Tsukada 1979). The identity formation process is promoted in siblings' comparisons to one another in points of likeness and difference. A fourth function of siblings is to serve in the role as mediator in conflicts between the sibling subsystem and the parental subsystem. Drawing on the analysis by Bank and Kahn (1975), Tsukada gives examples of undermining or strengthening of parent-child relationships as a result of violating or maintaining secrecy in the sibling subsystem. She cites siblings interpreting one another's behaviors to the parents and vice versa and older siblings educating their parents about changes in social customs and their younger siblings about how to negotiate the school and other systems outside the home.

As opposed to earlier days' emphasis on sibling rivalry and other negatives, the trend now seems to be toward greater recognition of siblings as assets. Yet more is not necessarily better as indicated by the finding of over-representation among juvenile delinquents of youth from large families. Rutter and Giller (1984), however, note that the underlying mechanisms of this association remain somewhat obscure. Birth order, spacing effects, and social deprivation appear to be confounding factors. It is not clear if the higher delinquency rate in socially disadvantaged families is actually linked with the family's size as such, with some hardship factor endured by these groups, or perhaps with some predisposing factor such as low verbal intelligence and poor reading skills, which are commonly found among disadvantaged families.

Adolescents in large families appear to have an increased probability of becoming a "parentified" child or surrogate parent. When the parenting tasks surpass the parent's energy and capabilities, authority may be vested in one of the older children to carry out some of the parental functions. Tsukada (1979) notes in her review that while a parentified child may earn respect and satisfaction from this role, the emotional costs may be high in that the responsibilities prevent the parentified child from having his or her own dependency needs met. Depression is commonly reported among parentified children, upon whom the siblings may also displace the anger they harbor against the parents for abdicating their responsibilities or for other reasons.

Similar cautions and concerns are raised by Jeannie S. Kidwell's (1981) study of the effects of sibling spacing, sex, and birth order on perceived parent-adolescent relationships. Secondary analysis of a national sample of over 1,700 male adolescents found that increase in the number of siblings is associated with perception of increased parental punitiveness and decreased parental supportiveness. More positive parent-adolescent relations exist when siblings are spaced very closely (12 months or less) or very widely (4 years or more), and the intermediary spacings of 2 to 3 years are the most negative. This curvilinear relation is contrary to the earlier assumed straight linear relationship between quality of parent-child relations and spacing. Kidwell also found that the middle-born male reports his parents to be more punitive, less reasonable, and less supportive toward him than do either first- or last-born adolescents. The middle-born also expressed a sense of being pushed around in terms of implementation of family rules. However, when spacing was controlled for, birth order differences were no longer statistically significant.

The study results were stronger among male adolescents with male siblings than among those with female siblings. It is not known if similar overall results would be obtained with female-female siblings; an earlier study by Kidwell suggests that spacing relationships do not appear to be of the same importance for females. At any rate, her conclusion of the need for giving attention to the spacing variable in family interaction research is convincing, as is her argument that spacing of 4 years or more seems to create more breathing room for parents as well as children. More psychic and physical energy is available for each child and fewer dependency demands are placed on the parents from several children simultaneously. A more relaxed disciplinary style may result as well as a more positive, emotional parent-child bond (pp. 316–17). Advantageous as wide spacing may be, one wonders, however, how many parents would want to launch an adolescent every fifth year for example. With three children 5 years apart one would have a teenager in the home for 20 years! Some may prefer the other advantageous peak of the curve, spacing of one year or less, even though some obvious natural barriers would prevent making it much less than a year.

Summary

Havighurst's formulation of the eight adolescent developmental tasks sets the stage for the major thrust of this chapter — the adolescent's maturational separation from the family of origin. This process is considered in the light of findings from four large-scale empirical studies on families with adolescents of theoretical propositions with varying degrees of empirical support and of reported clinical observations (Offer et al. 1981; Olson and McCubbin 1983; Lewis et al. 1976 and 1983; and Westley and Epstein 1969).

The delicate balance of separateness and attachment embedded in the family's dual tasks of raising autonomous children and furthering ongoing personality maturation of the parents reaches a peak of intensity during the family life phases of living with and launching adolescents. During these periods even normal, intact families experience the greatest amount of stress and the lowest levels of marital and family satisfaction. The competence by which families cope with these tasks and stresses organizes families along a continuum from optimal families, which meet the adolescent's as well as the parents' maturational needs, to competent but pained families, which raise autonomous adolescents but fail to meet parental needs, to dysfunctional and severely dysfunctional families, which fail to meet the maturational needs of both children and parents.

Stierlin's concept of the parent-adolescent separation as a "loving fight" in healthy families is supplemented by his notion of the binding, delegating, and dispelling modes of separation. Parental and marital needs strongly determine which form prevails. If parenting is the major *raison d'être* of the marital relationship or if the adolescent is needed by one of the parents to meet emotional needs unfulfilled by the spouse, the binding mode is likely to prevail and prevent separation. If the adolescent's needs stand in the way of the parents' own developmental or marital needs, expulsion of the adolescent is the likely mode, providing physical but not psychological separation from the family. In delegating families, separation alternates with being pulled back into the family orbit, the parents vicariously satisfying their own unfulfilled needs, dreams, and aspirations through their adolescents.

The impact of divorce and subsequent single-parenthood is still somewhat murky. The consequences are not necessarily negative, as formerly believed. Some adolescents appear minimally affected by these experiences, and for some they stimulate maturational growth spurts. The outcome is determined by factors such as the quality of the parent-child relationship prior to the divorce, the adolescent's general emotional, mental, and physical health, the degree of parental conflict associated with the divorce and ongoing parental fighting, the postdivorce relationship between adolescent and custodial parent, and ongoing contact with the noncustodial parent.

For adolescents in remarried families, some crucial issues are divided loyalties, discipline, and sexual tensions in the absence of the incest taboo. The first two years of remarriage are experienced as more stressful than later years.

The final section of the chapter ties together the interrelationships between the marital and parent-child subsystems with the often overlooked sibling subsystem. Siblings appear to fulfill several major functions for one another, including meeting needs for affection, influencing socialization and sex-role identification, and serving as mediators of conflicts between the parental and sibling subsystems. The confounding variables of family size, sibling spacing, ordinal position, and sibling gender combinations are discussed as they impact the role of siblings in the adolescent's separation from the family.

This chapter's focus on intrafamily interaction now shifts to the next chapter's attention on the adolescent's developmental tasks outside the family.

Notes

1. The diagram incorporates concepts from Michael Rutter's Simplified Model of Causative Influences (1980, p. 240) and from Havighurst's developmental tasks. It is also influenced by Bronfenbrenner's Ecological Model (1979), even though it does not accurately depict the micro-, meso-, exo-, and macro-systems of that model. Bronfenbrenner's macro-system, for example, refers to cultural inconsistencies and underlying values of the three other systems, so in a sense the macro-system contains the other three and thus should not be presented as being on the same conceptual level. For an accurate chart of Bronfenbrenner's model, see the ecological map developed by Garbarino (1982, pp. 25–26).

2. Family-adolescent interactional variables identified as important in empirical and general adolescent psychology literature are numerous enough to constitute a separate book. Inclusion of concepts and variables for this chapter has been made on a judgment of their usefulness to practice. Several recent adolescent psychology texts contain good basic chapters on adolescent-family relations. Examples are Adams and Gullota (1983), Lambert et al. (1978), and Rice (1981).

3. Several major social work texts incorporate some or all of these shifts: Bloom (1980); Germain and Gitterman (1980); Golan (1981); Hartman and Laird (1983); and Maluccio (1981b).

4. Two typologies discussed in this section do not distinguish between early and late adolescence. The McCarter and McGoldrick (1983) family life cycle typology places the family with adolescents between the stages of the family with young children and launching children and moving on. The typology used by Olson and McCubbin (1983) designates the relevant stage as families with adolescents from 13 to 18. Interestingly enough, reported findings include information about the parents' average ages and age range, but about the 350-adolescent subsample we learn only that the average age was 16, not the age range. Perhaps additional future findings from this recent and major national study on what makes families work will provide comparisons between early and late adolescent groups.

5. Some tendencies of variance among adolescents from different nations and between the sexes are reported in chapter 4.

4 DEVELOPMENTAL TASKS OF ADOLESCENCE: PEERS, IDENTITY ACHIEVEMENT, AND SOME GENDER AND CULTURAL DIFFERENCES

The previous chapter dealt primarily with the adolescent's moving out of the family of origin. This chapter, which completes part I, focuses on maturational processes in relation to peers of both sexes, on the task of preparing for the adult role of work, and on personal identity achievement. Although attention is given throughout this book to variations in development and behavior according to gender, socioeconomic status, and cultural factors, these topics are the foci of the chapter's last two sections.

In studying Havighurst's formulation of eight adolescent developmental tasks, the emancipation from the family has been given the lion's share of space and attention compared with the other tasks discussed in this chapter. This unevenness does not reflect a valuation of family variables as the end-all in adolescent development. Developmental tasks achieved in the peer arena and in community settings — though interrelated with familial processes — are no less important. They are simply different and not the core topic of this book. Knowledge about extrafamilial developmental tasks is included to the extent it is considered helpful for work with adolescents and their families.

Adolescent Peer Relations

Age mates are important throughout childhood; even babies light up and often reach out when they spot other babies as if recognizing that here is somebody like me. Through the parallel play in the sandbox and coopera- tive or competitive play in games and on athletic fields, peers become part- ners in the socialization process throughout childhood. At adolescence positive relations with peers are by many considered indispensable to nor- mal social development. The ability to make mature formal judgments is dependent on the give-and-take among equals, and peer associations pro- vide a safe testing ground for changing conceptions of self through mutual support and shared experimentations (Hill 1981). Yet as a topic peers share the fate of siblings in having been rather neglected by researchers, and in popular thinking, negative connotations of destructive gangs, bizarre youth culture groups, or cults often overshadow the positive impact of peer associations on adolescent development. Of course, the constructive force of the peer group has been utilized, not overlooked, by many educators, recreationists, and therapists.

Peer relations take several forms — from personal friendships to peer group membership. John C. Coleman's study of 700 adolescent boys and girls in England (1974, 1980a and b) found that the middle-adolescent years represent the greatest stress in terms of fear of rejection and insecurity in friendships, especially for girls.[1] Girls tend to seek satisfaction of emotional needs while boys stress action-oriented friendship relations. These gender differences, however, are weak for early and late adolescents.

Peer groups fall into two major categories: cliques and crowds. Cliques are smaller groups consisting of 2 to 9 members, frequently found in schools, recreational facilities, and religious and other organizations. They are closed groups with informal leadership, usually with prosocial activities, and use constructive criticism, manipulation, or rejection as a means of maintaining certain behavior standards of individual members (Lambert et al. 1978; Coleman 1980b). Crowds have been described as an association of cliques. From a study of a little over 300 teenagers between ages 13 and 21 belonging to 44 school cliques in Australia, it was observed that cliques shift from be- ing unisexual in early adolescence to heterosexual in late adolescence (Dun- phy 1963, as quoted by Lambert et al. 1978 and Coleman 1980). In that study, membership in a clique was found to be a prerequisite for crowd membership but not all cliques were associated with crowds, which were larger groups of 15 to 30 members. Crowd members considered one another as "acceptable associates" rather than "real buddies." Activities in crowds centered around parties and dances, while clique members usually engaged in conversation. In late adolescence the crowd tended to disintegrate into loose-knit associations of couples. Other studies have observed that some cliques develop into gangs, generally reflecting a deviant or antisocial subculture.

A concern of many parents is the susceptibility of their adolescent to the demands for conformity required in return for membership in most peer groups. Coleman (1980b) summarizes in his review of empirical findings on this topic that conformity reaches its height in the early adolescent years, diminishing from age 14 or 15. Giving in to peer pressure is associated with status in the group and self-blame; however, studies on conformity could bear replication, and very little is known about how autonomy from peer pressure is achieved.

Many theorists have attempted to explain the increased psychological need for peer group membership in adolescence; most of them focus on the relative importance of influence of parents and peers. The logic of Ausubel's (1954, 1977) theory goes like this: The outcome of maturation is the autonomous adult enjoying primary status in society earned by his or her own efforts at economic independence, emotional independence from parents, and fulfillment of the masculine or feminine sex role. The child, not yet possessing the abilities to fulfill these roles, derives self-esteem and security from the dependence on parents. The preschool child earns this derived status by its very existence; during the school years the status (and subsequent self-esteem) is increasingly derived from the child's actions in school-assigned and other tasks. As biological sexual maturation and growth in intellectual capacities make it increasingly possible for the teenager to earn external primary status by his or her own efforts, a "de-satellization" of the dependency orbit around the parent(s) takes place. In less complex societies it is possible for a teenager to step almost directly into all adult roles, but in modern urban society the peer group serves as an intermediary source of earned status. Thus the de-satellization from parents is concomitant with a developing re-satellization around peers — the former emotional anchorage to parents is replaced by dependence on and support from the peer group. As noted in the previous chapter, the overly dependent child never makes the shift from the parental orbit to that of the peer group; the parentally rejected child was never fully allowed in the orbit in the first place and because of this deprivation is very vulnerable and susceptible to the demands of any peer group that will allow him or her to join the peer orbit.

This line of thinking then implies that peers fill a developmental void that parents are incapable of satisfying. Peer associations become the breeding ground from which the norms, values, and ideologies of the next generation are forged and shaped. Viewing maturation in the peer vs. the parental orbits as independent processes naturally leads to the myth about generation gaps that prevailed during the late 1960s and 1970s. Empirical evidence, excellently summarized by Coleman (1980), shows that rejection of parental values does not automatically follow from the adolescent's shift of allegiance from parents to peers. Peers are more influential in decisions regarding day-to-day behaviors and activities, while parents are more influential with respect to decisions with long-range consequences. In fact, parent and peer views may supplement one another, since friends are often chosen because they harbor the same basic values as the parents do.

When parental interest and nurture are lacking, commitment and susceptibility to the peer group reach the highest levels. Hill (1981) notes, on the basis of his own research and that of others, that choice of peer friendship groups, cliques, and neighborhood friends is strongly influenced by the child-rearing techniques of some parents. Hill concludes that the "most slavishly peer-conforming children clearly appear to have come from the most extremely authoritarian or permissive families" (p. 75).

Three recent studies confirm several of the above conclusions. Greenberg, Siegel, and Leitch (1983) examined the relative effect of perceived quality of adolescent relations with parents and peers in relation to adolescent self-concept. This study of 213 junior and senior high school students (primarily white, middle-class) builds on recent findings that perceived mutuality and attachment of intimate relationships affect mental and physical health and reactions to traumatic life events. The attachment to parents was, as predicted, considerably greater than attachment to peers, and the quality of the parent-adolescent relation was significantly associated with adolescent well-being. Unexpectedly, no difference was found between older and younger adolescents, which gives further credence to other evidence that parents are highly valued throughout the high school years. The findings also confirm other research in that self-concept and ego identity were positively related to warm relations with parents.

Hunter and Youniss (1982) explored changes over time in the control and intimacy functions of parents and peer relations. The 120 study sample adolescents (from fourth, seventh, and tenth grades, and undergraduate college classes and again primarily from Caucasian, middle-class homes) reported greater control exerted by parents than peers across all grades. Intimacy (defined as self-disclosure, empathy, consensus formation, and companionship) was prominent in friendship and surpasses parental levels in mid and late adolescence. However, intimacy in parental relations remained stable as friendship intimacy increased. The combined findings imply that peer influence may be rooted in friendship intimacy and mutual discussions rather than in simple attempts at behavior control. Compliance to parental wishes, on the other hand, may still derive primarily from deference to parental demands, a retained element of the unilateral authority structure of the parent-adolescent relationship. In addition, Hunter and Youniss found sex differences in friendship relations but not in parent-child relations, with females reporting higher intimacy in relation to friends than the males. Male adolescents (unlike females) perceived their fathers to be more nurturant than their mothers. The overall conclusion is that friendship and parent-child relations fulfill fundamentally different developmental needs of adolescents.

The importance of striking some balance between the two sets of interpersonal relations is one conclusion drawn from the study by Larson (1983) of daily life experiences of the contrasting opportunity systems of families and friends. Daily interactions with friends were reported as more conducive to enjoyment than were interactions with families; feedback from friends was positive, while it was more negative from family interactions. However, adolescents spending more time with their friends than with family showed poorer school performance and wider mood variability. In the researchers' opinion, the most fertile context for growth may be found in a combination of the functional constraints of family interactions and the excitement of friends. They conclude that the most fortunate adolescents may be those who find ways to combine both, since during the time spent with family and friends together the teenagers experienced "serious conversation with positive feedback, openness, and positive moods" (p. 748). They had the best of both worlds.

The above discussion shows a move toward better understanding of the interdependence and independence of family and peer groups as arenas for adolescent development. A lopsided attention in the past to parent-adolescent relations may be in the process of correction. Some writers argue that even greater recognition should be given to the importance of adolescent-peer interaction (Seltzer 1982).

The reader may at this point wonder about the consequences in practice of the relative and supplementary nature of parent-peer influences. The Integrated Control-Strain Model of Socialization, developed by Brennan, Huizinga, and Elliott (1978) and Elliott and Huizinga (1984), presents the theoretical framework that most consistently and comprehensively incorporates important empirical findings. It will be discussed in chapter 8.

Adolescent Relations with Peers of the Opposite Sex

Teenagers in the United States have a remarkable fertility rate. Young women below 20 years of age contribute 600,000 live births annually, which accounts for about 17 percent of all births in a year. This birth rate is 15 times higher than the similar Japanese birth rate, double that in the Scandinavian countries, and higher than both the Canadian and Australian rates (Zelnik, Kantner, and Ford 1981). Many of the estimated 1.33 million adolescent pregnancies occurring each year are unwanted, and an increasing number of teenagers opt for legalized abortion, which became an alternative with the 1973 Supreme Court decision. Over 0.5 million such abortions are performed each year, accounting for 36 percent of all U.S. abortions (Schinke and Gilchrist 1984).

Teenagers' proportionate contribution to the overall birth rate rose from 1960 to 1975, when it peaked at 19.3 percent. This rise can in part be explained by changes in the demographic distribution, that is, the sharp proportionate increase of the adolescent population as the baby-boom cohort moved through adolescence. The birth rate for 18- and 19-year-olds has actually dropped markedly, but less so for those between 16 and 17. For teenagers 15 and younger, the birth rate increased up to 1975 with a slow tapering off in subsequent years (Chilman 1980). About one-third of all teenage births are illegitimate, another third of the deliveries take place within the first nine months after marriage, and the remaining one-third of the newborns are conceived after the teenage mother's marriage takes place (McKenry et al. 1979).

As the age of biological and sexual maturation goes down, the median age of first marriage is slowly but steadily climbing, the latest figures being 22 and 24 years for women and men, respectively. So today there is on the average a full decade between the onset of reproductive capacity and the achievement of marital status. However, it may be just as well that not more adolescents rush into marriage, since teenage marriages have a much higher risk of ending in divorce than marriages occurring after the age of 20. In addition, the level of marital satisfaction in adolescent marriages is low; McKenry et al. (1979) list typical problems such as "feeling robbed of adolescence, education, or social position, mistrust of the marital partner, and the projection of blame on one another, and low self-esteem, depression and withdrawal" (p. 25). Yet some teenage marriages survive. Delissovoy's (1973) study of high school marriages (as quoted by Adams and Gullotta 1983) found in a three-year follow-up that 77 percent of the marriages were still intact. These young families showed strength in building strong bonds with in-laws, in seeking emotional support from religious groups, and in true caring for one another.

When the parenting role is added to the multifaceted demands of adolescent developmental tasks and bodily growth, many risks result for the teenage mother and her child. Medical risks to the mother include higher rates of maternal toxemia, death, prolonged deliveries, anemia, postpartum infection, and hemorrhage during pregnancy. However, such confounding factors as poor nutrition and health care may be as accountable for these outcomes as the chronological age of the mother. Phipps-Yonas (1980), incorporating studies that control for such variables, conclude that, given proper health care and nutrition, "there is no evidence of biomedical risk either to the mother or to her offspring associated with pregnancy for the average female over age 14" (p. 405). Unfortunately, few teenagers receive such care.

The babies of teenage mothers are clearly at risk in facing higher rates of premature birth, low birth weight, higher mortality in the first year of life, higher rates of birth defects, and higher risk for physical abuse and neglect than babies born to older women. Several studies indicate that teenage mothers are less emotionally and intellectually involved with their children and show other signs of inadequate mothering. But, as Phipps-Yonas (1980) notes, it is difficult to separate the impact of young age and early childbearing from factors and behavioral patterns that were operating long before the teenager became pregnant. Many empirical studies have probed the complexities of teenage motherhood, but no single profile of the pregnant teenager has as yet emerged.

Most studies explore nonramdon samples of clinic or social agency populations. While much has been learned from studies like Furstenberg's (1976) five-year comparison study of mostly black, pregnant teenagers with a sample of their nonpregnant classmates, generalizability of findings to the general teen population is not feasible. One major national survey by Zelnik, Kantner, and Ford (1981), however, has used a probability sample of 4,392 young women from ages 15 through 19 to study premarital intercourse, use, nonuse, and misuse of contraception, and the extent of pregnancy, abortion, and childbirth. The original sample of young women were interviewed in 1971, a similar random sample (of half its size) in 1976, and a third round of women were surveyed in the late 1970s along with a sample of males aged 17 to 21. Major findings from the 1971 and 1976 surveys include an increase in the percentage of 15- to 19-year-old women who had experienced premarital intercourse from 30 to 41 percent. Although black teenagers showed much higher percentages than whites (64 against 37 percent), the increase for whites was greater than for blacks. On the other hand, whites have more partners and higher frequency of intercourse. Socioeconomic status, family stability, age at menarche, and religiosity played only minor roles as sources of variance. With respect to contraceptive use, 28 percent of whites and 43 percent of blacks never used any form of contraception in 1976. Premaritally pregnant blacks are more likely to carry the pregnancy to term, that is, they have fewer abortions, are less likely to marry, and consequently are more likely to give birth to illegitimate babies. Preliminary findings from the 1979 survey show a further increase in sexual activity among young women (attributable to whites) and increased premarital pregnancy in spite of increased use of contraception. There appears to be a shift from more to less effective methods of contraception. These young women had information — albeit sometimes incorrect — about contraceptive methods, but the shift in their use appeared to be linked with feared side effects, moral qualms, a belief that they were too young or had sex too infrequently to become pregnant, or the fact that they were unprepared because they did not expect to have intercourse. The earlier trend toward fewer marriages among pregnant teenagers continued between 1976 and 1979, paired with a proportionate increase in voluntary abortions. The net effect of sexual activity, marriage, abortion, and contraceptive use is an increase of live illegitimate births in 1979.

These descriptive findings are — as the researchers themselves acknowledge — somewhat disappointing in that no major variables have been identified as building blocks for theories about the chain of events leading up to illegitimate childbirth. There are no simple answers, yet the findings represent a first step toward "separating the wheat from the chaff — a separation of fact from speculation — in regard to behavior that has important personal, familial, and social consequences" (p. 31).

Another road to understanding of teenage sexuality and parenthood is examination of the impact of family and peer relationships. The literature (usually with less empirical support) paints an unclear picture of the effect of the parent-child relationship on adolescent sexual behavior. Walters and Walters (1980), for example, conclude that the quality of that relationship may not be as highly related to sexual behavior as the specific content of parent-adolescent communications about sex. The trouble is that most parents do not discuss sex with their adolescents, though for those who do this discussion "is related to postponement of sexual activity and more responsible use of contraception" (p. 815). Fox (1981) and Fox and Inazu (1982) have found that the more favorable a relationship between a teenage daughter and her mother, the less likely she is to have had sex. They also found that the degree of conflict, the power structure, the general tenor of the marital relationship, and the presence or absence of a husband-father carry over to the daughter's sexual behavior. Parental impact on pregnant teenagers' decision regarding pregnancy resolution was explored in a longitudinal study of 100 pregnant teenagers from a rural area in Michigan (Rosen, Benson, and Stack 1982). Findings from other research that parents rarely exert direct pressure on the daughter and that when they do it is in favor of abortion was confirmed in that only eight teenagers were exposed to direct parental pressure — seven of them in favor of abortion and one in favor of keeping the child. Overall, 66 of the young women opted for abortion and 34 for keeping the child, with 12 of the latter staying single. No influence at all was exerted in 11 percent of the aborters as against 29 percent of those who kept the child. None of these women chose adoption as a solution. Other sources indicate that only about 4 percent of teenage mothers relinquish their children for adoption and substitute care (Schinke and Gilchrist 1984, quoting Chilman 1979).

The influence of peers on adolescent sexual behavior is even more unclear than that of parents, even though peers are the most likely source of information about sexual matters (what is exchanged, however, is often misinformation). The few existing studies reviewed by Schinke and Gilchrist (1984, p. 41) indicate that female teenagers may be influenced as much by role modeling of girlfriends as by direct pressure for sexual activity from boyfriends. Many sexually active adolescents find no enjoyment in it; they go along begrudgingly. Phipps-Yonas (1980), reviewing the sparse studies of male adolescents, suggested that peers play the greatest role in influencing sexual attitudes, activities, and contraceptive use among teenage boys and that weak evidence exists to indicate that males who are highly involved with their families are less sexually active. Even so, parents are rarely used as sources of information or advice.

In general male teenagers have been grossly overlooked by researchers as well as service providers in spite of their obvious participating roles in teenage pregnancies and parenthood. Stereotypes abound of pleasure-seeking irresponsible young bucks getting girls into trouble with only sporadic factual information to correct these off-hand impressions. They are often referred to as the "putative" fathers, a somewhat negative term. A recent study conducted by Zitner and Miller (1980) for the Child Welfare League of America that sought to identify support services utilized by adolescent mothers found that the baby's father played a significant supportive role in the lives of these young mothers. Almost a quarter of them lived with the baby's father at the time of follow-up when the child was 1–1½ years old, and almost half had continued contact with him although not living with him. Many of the young fathers provided financial support and participated in decision making regarding the child. However, only a handful of them had been offered any services or contacts from the agencies the mothers had frequented. Other review articles (by Barret and Robinson 1982; Earls and Siegel 1980; Gershenson 1983; and Parke, Power, and Fisher 1980) underscore the need for empirical investigations of male teenagers' sexuality, participation in and reactions to pregnancy outcome decisions, psychological correlates of fatherhood in respect to self-esteem, developmental state, social correlates and consequences of fatherhood, contraceptive use, and so on. Gershenson (1983) points out in his study of fatherhood in families headed by white adolescent mothers that redefinition is needed since the biological father of the baby is only one of several males serving in the fathering role — males such as the mother's current husbands or boyfriends who are not the child's biological father and the mothers' own fathers or step-fathers. Unbiased empirical knowledge based on direct information from the male teenagers themselves — not secondhand from the mothers or service providers — is sorely needed.

This section on the adolescent's achievement of adult sexual roles is not complete without mentioning the identity formation of the homosexual adolescent, a topic that is even more obscure than the topic of teenage fathers. Malyon's (1981) analysis mentioned three adaptations gay and les-bian adolescents commonly engage in to cope with the dilemma of homosex-uality: "a) repression of same-sex desires; b) a developmental moratorium in which homosexual impulses are suppressed in favor of a heterosexual or asexual orientation; c) homosexual disclosure and the decision to mobilize same-sex desires" (p. 326). The last solution, often referred to as coming-out, frequently involves alienation from the family and confrontation with societal stigma. Even though this process represents an opportunity for emotional and psychological maturation for some, others suffer the unfor-tunate consequences of impoverished socialization (p. 329).

The topic of adolescent sexuality stirs many emotions and evokes illu-sions of sexually active teenagers as suffering from intrapsychic pathology or warped, oedipal strivings or as victims of the social evils of poverty, violence, and racism. In our urge to understand the reasons and conse-quences of the high level of illegitimate live births in the United States, we may be overlooking characteristic subgroup variations among different cul-tures as well as failing to recognize the powerful impact of social expecta-tions from the social-cultural environment as sexual norms are changing (Stewart 1981).

Identity Achievement

In a sense this concept represents the sum total of successful adolescent ma-turation in many areas of living. A large body of research has attempted to validate and expand Erikson's dichotomy of identity diffusion and identity achievement. Bourne (1978a and b) has identified close to 50 such studies, some of which employ self-descriptive Q-sorts, self-report questionnaires, or paper-and-pencil instruments. However, 29 of these studies have utilized the Identity Status Paradigm developed by James E. Marcia (1980) and his coworkers. This paradigm consists of semistructured interviews probing identity formation in two areas: the extent to which the adolescent has experienced crisis with respect to vocational choice and with respect to ideological beliefs. *Crisis* here means active struggle, experimentation with alternative roles, and making relatively lasting commitments in the two areas.[2]

This section will first present concepts and findings from Marcia's work and related empirical investigations judged helpful in assessing and counseling adolescents. Next follows a discussion of one of the two major variables embedded in identity formation as defined by Marcia — vocational or occupational choice. The other major variable, the shaping of ideological beliefs or moral development, is not further elaborated upon here.[3]

First, a few general comments about identity are in order. Identity is one of those basic concepts that everybody knows, that everybody uses with confidence, and that few like to be challenged on. It easily slips away under scrutiny; in Marcia's (1980) words, the study of "identity in adolescence is not a task for the methodologically sensitive" (p. 159). He sees identity as an underlying "self-constructed, dynamic organization of drives, abilities, beliefs, and individual history" (p. 159), that, at a minimum, requires commitments to vocational direction, sexual orientation, and an ideological stance. More important than the separate entities we infer from observable problem-solving responses is the underlying process that fits all the parts into a flexible unity or organization. While the content of identity (relations, beliefs, and so on) changes with age and experience, the underlying structure remains fairly stable over the lifetime. And, at least in the identity achieved individual, the basic organization appears to grow stronger by each life crisis passed through.

What is special about adolescence is that at late adolescence the cognitive, physical, and social capacities for the first time become sufficiently developed to review and synthesize childhood identifications and carve out a self-chosen route into adulthood. Marcia sees good social and physiological reasons for the industry—identity—intimacy progression, but he finds psychological reasons most compelling because vocational commitment is such a powerful component of identity formation. The forerunner of identity, industry is the sense of mastery and confidence in one's skills that brings about a sensitive attitude toward work that is essential to vocational choice. Identity, in turn, brings about the secure sense of self that makes it possible to risk the vulnerability of merging temporarily with another. Paradoxically, says Marcia (p. 160), intimacy is a "strength that can be acquired only through vulnerability; and vulnerability is possible only with the internal assurance of a firm identity" (p. 160). This may be one reason why so many teenage marriages end in divorce — if formed before identity is achieved in both partners the foundation for intimacy is frail and risky. Finally, Marcia points out that identity formation is not just shaped at crucial, crisis points but gradually built by bits and pieces of everyday, sometimes by seemingly trivial decisions (1980, pp. 160–61).

To facilitate the evaluation of where an adolescent stands in the identity process, Marcia has developed four identity status categories. Independent coders, on the basis of the status interview answers, determine the extent to which the interviewee has experienced crisis and has made commitment. Interobserver reliability for these determinations usually is around 80 percent (Marcia 1980). Table 4-1, adapted from Marcia (1980, p. 162), depicts the four statuses.

Table 4-1. Marcia's Identity Statuses

	Crisis Experienced	Commitment Made
Identity Diffusion No ideological or vocational direction; crisis may have been experienced, but without resolution and commitment	(−) or (+)	(−)
Moratorium The person is *in* crisis, struggling with ideological and occupational issues; considers alternatives, but unable to make a choice	(+)	(−) or vague
Foreclosure Little or no evidence of crisis, but committed to values, beliefs, and occupational goals — often chosen by parents or other authority figures	(−)	(+)
Identity Achievement Period of decision making; crisis has been experienced; committed to self-chosen occupational and ideological goals that are actively pursued	(+)	(+)

The list in table 4-1 of four modes of dealing with identity issues in late adolescence is, of course, not all inclusive. However, as Marcia (1980) points out it allows room for greater variations in styles than Erikson's original dichotomy. On the other hand, Marcia's Identity Status Paradigm does not capture all seven strands or domains that Erikson's writings explore as part of identity formation (Bourne 1978a and Grotevant, Thorbecke, and Meyer 1982), namely, the structural, subjective, developmental, dynamic, adaptive, psychosocial reciprocity, and existential perspectives of ego identity. Grotevant, Thorbecke, and Meyer (1982) conclude that while the Identity Status Interview taps some of these seven dimensions more clearly and fully than others, no one dimension is ignored. In any event, Marcia's own work on the Identity Status paradigm and the extensive research it has generated have strengthened Erikson's theory by contributing to its empirical underpinnings. In the process, the paradigm and the interview have been corrected for flaws and expanded in content. For example, Grotevant, Thorbecke, and Meyer (1982) have expanded the interview to include the three interpersonal domains of friendships, dating, and sex roles, which have proven helpful in identification of variations in male and female identity formation, to be discussed later in this chapter.

Bourne proposes future explorations of the relationship between identity achievement and other ego-developmental constructs, such as comparison between ego identity status and ego development as measured by Loevinger's Sentence Completion Test. The review "Personality: Stages, Traits, and the Self" by Loevinger and Knoll (1983), however, does not report any such explorations. Redmore and Loevinger (1979) pursued a related topic in comparing ego development over time with intelligence among adolescents from one private and three public schools. The test-retest correlations show that ego level increases steadily from early to late adolescence, and some but not all of the samples reveal a high correlation between intelligence and ego level.

Along this line, Marcia (1983) himself proposes investigation of 3 variables in early adolescent ego development as predictors of identity development at late adolescence. The 3 hierarchically linked variables are: confidence in parental support; a sense of industry; and a self-reflective approach to one's future. The most basic of these variables is the adolescent's confidence that the parents will not withhold support while the adolescent engages in experiments of autonomy. Without this trust the adolescent will drift toward identity diffusion. With parental support but without a sense of industry, Marcia predicts the outcome to become a characterological moratorium, while trust in parental support combined with a sense of industry but no self-reflection is predicted to lead to foreclosure. If all three variables are present the predicted outcome is transitional moratorium of identity achievement.

Bourne's critical analysis of identity studies rightly points to the limitations stemming from the almost exclusive focus on college students. He suggests that future replication studies should include postcollege and adult populations, college-age youth in other countries, high-school students, and psychiatrically disturbed populations matched with "normal" controls. From a human service perspective it would seem appropriate to emphasize adequate sample representations of ghetto youth and others growing up under conditions of deprivation and discrimination. In addition, Bourne notes that Marcia could have included Erikson's "negative identity" status as a fifth category. By expanding the sample populations as suggested, one would suspect that this fifth category would readily emerge from data of youngsters known to child welfare agencies, youth services, and juvenile court professionals. Adopted adolescents are suspected to encounter special difficulties in the identity formation process; this topic is discussed in chapter 6 in the section on adoption.

Other proposals for direction of future identity formation research include Grotevant's (1983) suggestion of focus on family variables and other specific domains and sequences of the identity formation process in early adolescence as opposed to late adolescence, which has been fairly well explored. And Adams and Montemayor (1983), among other suggestions, propose to search for evidence of observable behavioral differences between the identity statuses.

At any rate, many of the research efforts on identity formation have translated Erikson's purely theoretical concepts into validated constructs of potential utility to work with adolescents and their families. It is this author's observation from classroom and internship teaching that the Identity Status Paradigm provides students with an opportunity to review their own journey into the achievement status and experience and recognize it as a universal, satisfying developmental process. Because this journey for most students has just barely been completed (and in one sense it never is), there is a strong inclination to nudge and steer clients onto the achievement road so that they too can experience the joy of a developmental leap. The danger of imposing one's own values may perhaps be especially present in cases involving young women. The present-day common belief that a woman's identity can be achieved only through commitment to multiple roles, of which motherhood is only one, may be no more universally applicable than the belief of preliberation days that a woman seeking fulfillment in roles outside the home necessarily suffered from unresolved femininity or authority conflicts or, worse yet, was driven by "penis envy." Still it seems as hard today to find an intervention plan that does not include some elements of getting the mother out of the home to develop herself as it was to find any plan in the 1950s that moved a mother's out-of-home commitments beyond the PTA or other volunteer activity. While this picture may be overdrawn — after all, individualizing has always been taken seriously by most counselors — reflections on identity statuses help clarify one's own values and make it clear that outsiders can provide timely challenges, resources, and conditions that promote developmental leaps, but the actual steps toward establishing one's identity can only be taken by the individual himself.

Imposition of the commonly but often implicitly held opinion that everybody ought to arrive at the identity achievement status represents different dangers for clients at various status levels. The diffused and the moratorium client may experience the practitioner's push for change as an additional stress that makes it even more difficult to arrive at a choice and subsequent commitment. Another reaction may be to go along and make premature commitments based on the practitioner's ideas and plans without much questioning; in other words, the outcome is foreclosure, not identity achievement.

With the foreclosed client counselor-imposed values may indeed succeed in stirring up some consideration of alternatives and other crisislike activity, but this may or may not reflect the client's move toward autonomy. It may simply mean that the client is replacing a former authority figure with the practitioner; therefore, the outcome, foreclosure, is unchanged. A safeguard here may be to precede interventive actions by reflections on who is to decide when, where, by whom, and for what purpose "sleeping dog" issues should be stirred up, if at all.

Vocational Commitment and Employment

Considering the importance ascribed to vocational choice and work experience it is somewhat startling that the overwhelming majority of identity status studies are limited to samples of male college students. One exception, reported by Marcia (1980, p. 107) is the Munro and Adams (1977) study comparing college students with high school graduates who went straight on to a job; the latter were more likely to be in the identity achievement status than the college students, who may have responded to the psychosocial moratorium that college provides. Similarly, Finkelstein and Gaier (1983) found in their comparison of 20 economically dependent students with 20 independent nonstudents (bank employees), half of the two samples consisting of 20-year-olds and the other half of 24- to 25-year-olds, that prolonged student status tends to foster emotional dependence and to impact achievement of identity and the sense of self-worth negatively, even though overall self-esteem was not markedly affected. The two researchers acknowledge the need for replication of their small exploratory study and for longitudinal investigation of the developmental impact of the college environment, which in the words they quote from Erikson (1959b, p. 74) is "society's most elaborate device for the artificial postponement of adulthood that could be imagined" (Finkelstein and Gaier 1983, p. 127). They speculate that nontraditional structures of higher education spread over the life cycle may prove beneficial not only for those heretofore deprived of higher education, but also may serve the developmental needs of the traditional student better.

Other empirical investigations, primarily by sociologists and economists, have examined factors associated with career choice and later employment experiences. Lambert et al. (1978), from a review of such studies, list the following factors as having an impact on career choice: desire for security, achievement motivation, need for power and prestige, intellectual ability, parent-child relationship, linkages between vocational fields and personality traits, and sociological influences from peers and the school.

A factor assumed to have a strong impact on occupational values, subsequent employment, and job satisfaction is actual work experience during the teenage years. The current research on the developmental significance of early work experience by Steinberg, Greenberger, and their coworkers (1982) digs into this assumption. They identify two perspectives. The first is the occupational competency model held by several blue-ribbon commissions (Carnegie Commission on Policy Studies in Higher Education 1980; National Commission on Youth 1980; National Panel on High School and Adolescent Education 1976), which holds that early entry into the work place will develop self-reliance, initiative, and autonomy in young people in ways that high school cannot. The growth in personal responsibility is supposed to come about as a result of the demands and opportunities of holding a job — such as punctuality, dependability, and management of one's own money — rather than from the intrinsic nature of the work done. The second view — the occupational cynicism model — holds that the work available to adolescents is by and large menial and dehumanizing and cannot be expected to foster positive work habits and attitudes. On the contrary, the work experience is more likely to contribute to development of extrinsic reward values (work motivated primarily by monetary benefits), rather than intrinsic reward values stemming from the interest that the job holds for the teenager. In this view, high school students who work are in greater danger of developing an extrinsic orientation than their counterparts who do not work.

The number of adolescents for whom these issues are a reality is surprisingly high. Steinberg et al. (1982) report that nearly 80 percent of adolescents will have had a formal work experience by the time they graduate from high school, that about 20 percent of the 14- and 15-year-olds held part-time jobs, and that 43 percent of 16- and 17-year-old males and 37 percent of the females of that age work in the labor force while going to school. The proportion of American teenagers engaged in part-time jobs is greater than at any other time during the last 40 years. What are some of the consequences? In summary, the findings of several studies by Greenberger, Steinberg, and their coworkers are: (1) working contributes to development of personal responsibility (self-management skills, punctuality, and dependability) but not social responsibility (defined as concern for others and tolerance of people of varying social and ethnic backgrounds); (2) working enhances autonomy in girls but not in boys; (3) working leads to less involvement in nonwork activities and relationships with friends and family; (4) working leads in some cases to cynicism and acceptance of unethical work practices; and (5) working leads to an increase of cigarette and marijuana smoking (Greenberger, Steinberg, and Vaux 1981; Ruggiero, Greenberger, and Steinberg, 1982; Steinberg, Greenberger, Vaux, and Ruggiero 1981; and Steinberg, Greenberger, Garduque, Ruggiero, and Vaux 1982). The findings of all these studies cannot be generalized to adolescents in jobs in government-sponsored youth employment programs that have been created to facilitate their development or to urban, disadvantaged, minority youth, but they probably can be generalized to the vast majority of suburban youngsters who have their formal work experiences in "naturally occurring" jobs in the private sector (Steinberg et al. 1981, 1982).

So far vocational choice and work engagement have been viewed mostly from the perspective of what the adolescent brings. The other side of the coin is: What is there to choose from? Several interrelated societal and labor market factors have drastically changed the options. Present-day U.S. industry no longer requires large numbers of marginal workers, who, in the past, frequently were drawn from the adolescent population, but requires instead highly specialized and trained workers. As the percentage of adolescents who graduate from high school has grown to above 80 percent, more and more high school students are looking for part-time jobs, and from an employer's perspective they are not as attractive as full-time workers since they require the same amount of training before they can perform. The end result is that young people between 16 and 24 years of age account for half of the number of unemployed persons, even though they make up only one-fourth of the potential labor force (Robison 1980).

Among the unemployed youth, high school dropouts represent very special problems for themselves and human service professionals. Studies exploring the reasons for dropping out, reported by Douvan and Gold (1966, pp. 503–504), cite difficulties with teachers, difficulties with the school work, or lack of financial resources. The dropouts are characteristically poor students who do not get along with their schoolmates, do not participate in extracurricular activities, and often have very poor relationships with their parents. For these youngsters common barriers to teenage employment such as minimum-wage restrictions, licensing restrictions, and union membership requirements become insurmountable.

Black and other minority youth carry an inordinate share of the unemployment burden; the unemployment rate for non-white teenagers is usually about double that of white youth (17.6 percent against 34.3 percent in June 1984, for example, [Los Angeles Times, 7-7-84]). Unfortunately, it appears that the government-sponsored training programs designed to remedy the inequality have failed to reach the hard-core unemployed black youth (Moss 1982).

The overall youth employment picture finds its counterparts to some extent in other Western industrialized countries. A recent Danish governmental commission, for example, reports that youth between 15 and 24, accounting for 20 percent of the labor force, comprises close to 30 percent of all unemployed; in the Netherlands and Belgium they account for 47 percent, and in Great Britain, 40 percent of all unemployed (Regeringens Ungdomsudvalg, Rapport Nr. 3, 1983, pp. 114–115). Even though these figures may not be totally comparable because of differences in reporting periods, computations of employment statistics, and definition of who is unemployed, they seem to reflect a common structural labor market problem with consequences for educational systems, family policy, and human services.

The Danish report acknowledges that in spite of vigorous and extensive training and job-creating projects, many participating adolescents reenter the unemployment status. As expressed in survey interviews, the participants usually like the projects and find them worthwhile, but some feel they are part of a mere holding action that takes them off the unemployment statistics roster at one end just to return them there at the end of the project. The report describes consequences of youth unemployment as varying from apathy, alienation, and resignation to feelings of worthlessness and powerlessness, with perhaps the most essential problem being a disruption in the psychological identity formation process. It also appears that the economic, social, and psychological consequences increase in severity with the length of time the youth is unemployed (p. 138).

Only faint consolation can be gained from the sharing of misery across countries; the fact remains that youth unemployment is one of the gravest psychosocial problems most Western industrialized societies are confronted with today. It calls for major policy and political innovations that fall outside the scope of this book. The magnitude of the problem is presented here as it is such a powerful environmental reality that must be dealt with in many individual adolescent cases.

Gender Differences in Adolescent Development

There are no ready answers to the simple question of what differences, if any, exist between female and male adolescent development. First of all, information about females is scarce; Offer (1978) states that over the last two decades, there were seven studies of male adolescent psychology for every study of females. This inequity has been somewhat rectified through a proliferation of women studies since then, but this body of research usually addresses the total life span and not specifically adolesence. So far nobody appears to have come up with generally accepted answers to why female development has been overlooked. Some unlikely reasons could be that female adolescents were assumed to be like males with respect to psychosocial development, that they were not sufficiently interesting to be worth studying, or they were considered to be so utterly different from males because of their reproductive capacity that they would require their very own investigations whose time had not come. In any event, the lack of a universal theory of female development and the existing fragmented and sometimes contradictory empirical findings add up to a confusing and unclear picture. Arguments over interpretations of established differences occupy volumes of printed pages and cannot be given the just treatment the topic deserves in this short section. Only a few major points will be made.

The most comprehensive study of adolescent development of both sexes, that by Douvan and Adelson (1966, as summarized by Benedek 1978), involved interviews with 1,045 boys aged 14 through 16 and 2,005 girls between 11 and 18 years of age. The researchers found that boys separate from their parents earlier than girls and fight major battles with their families over independence, while the girls, in contrast, continued dependent relationships with their parents, using parental authority as a source of identity. Douvan and Adelson identified two feminine developmental patterns: unambivalent and ambivalent. The former gain self-esteem from helping others, preference of security over success, little achievement motivation, and daydreaming about marriage and family goals. The ambivalent girls also aspired to become wives and mothers, but they were also concerned about jobs and personal achievement. The four nonfeminine patterns include: achievement-oriented, boyish, neutral, and antifeminine girls who said they did not want to marry and expressed a wish to be boys. The most typical group was the unambivalent feminine girl, while the antifeminine accounted for only 5 percent. One may speculate that a different distribution among these and other categories would emerge in the 1980s were this study from the late 1950s replicated.

Gisela Konopka's (1976b) interview study of close to 1,000 girls 12 through 18 years old in 11 states found that most wanted career, marriage, and family and thought it possible to combine all these goals. The sample, half white and half minority, was evenly divided among adjudicated delinquents, teenagers affiliated with youth organizations, and nonaffiliated and nondelinquent girls. The adjudicated girls twice as often as the others did not think it possible to combine all three goals; they also chose traditional occupations, while the majority of the other girls opted for white-collar, professional, and nontraditional occupations. Practically all accepted a need for being prepared for gainful employment. Seventy-five percent of the girls felt close to adults — most to their mothers, others to teachers or grandparents, and the adjudicated girls to social service personnel.

Burke and Weir's (1978) study of 93 males and 181 female adolescents from three high schools showed that "female adolescents reported significantly greater life stress, and although they received significantly more social support from peers, they also reported significantly poorer emotional and physical well-being than males" (p. 277). As an explanation of these differences, the authors propose (p. 287) that until puberty girls are rewarded for traditionally feminine pursuits as well as for competitive achievements, while societal and familial expectations become diffuse and sometimes contradictory in adolescence. These inconsistent expectations of adolescent females may lead to a sense of uncertainty and lack of control over their lives.

Traditionally, most females have felt confronted with a choice between marriage/parenthood on the one hand and a career on the other, while males have not felt such pressures. Success in career training and subsequent professional work has often been equated with masculinity or lack of femininity; thus many women have come to fear success rather than failure (Watson and Lindgren 1979).

Grotevant and Thorbecke (1982) found that high school juniors and seniors progress equal distances toward the achievement of occupational identity. However, the two sexes (in this study, 41 males and 42 females) progressed along different paths. Occupational commitment for the young men appeared to be related to "an instrumental orientation, challenging tasks, and lack of concern about the negative evaluations of others" (p. 403). For the young women occupational identity was associated with an orientation toward working hard and avoiding competition.

On the five dimensions of the Offer Self-Image Questionnaire (Offer et al. 1981), adolescent boys and girls rate themselves with much greater similarity than disparity. Still, differences are found on two of the dimensions: girls report feeling worse than the boys about self on the self-image scale, but they have more positive feelings about self in regard to social sensitivity and values. Negative feelings expressed by the girls related notably toward their bodies; over 40 percent of normal girls say that they often feel ugly and unattractive. Several research reviewers report no gender difference in overall self-esteem (Offer et al. 1981 and Kaufman and Richardson 1982). However, in certain substantive self-image areas significant differences are found, summarized by Offer et al., to be better body image and higher academic and vocational aspirations in boys and more positive social, moral, and affiliative orientations of young women, who also seem to suffer more pervasive loneliness, sadness, and confusion than boys.

A basic puzzle in understanding these differences is to sort out the extent to which they are gender related and the extent to which they are sex-role related, that is, acquired through socialization. Bienenstock and Epstein (1978) suggest three possible hypotheses that may explain the fact that, despite greater liberality and permissiveness, women continue to "do most of the housework, spend most of the time in the rearing of the children, and make most of the career sacrifices" (p. 88). First, the biological hypothesis holds that the differences merely express the biological design. Second, the cultural hypothesis posits that overt and covert cultural values, stereotypes, models, and education account for differences in sexual behavior. The third position, the one the authors ascribe to, is that a complex interaction between biological and cultural variables account for variations in sex-role behavior. While there is much more evidence supporting the cultural hypothesis than the biological, they agree that much more research is needed to generate information to guide young women experiencing trouble in this area.

With respect to identity formation statuses, males and females have overall been found to be much more alike than different. This holds for the identity achievement and identity diffusion categories and, to a lesser extent, for the moratorium and foreclosure statuses (Marcia 1980 and Waterman 1982). Mixed findings can be ascribed in part to variations among definitions and measurements of the dependent variable, but they may also, as suggested by Marcia and others, reflect the current social confusion offering women greater freedom to explore alternatives.[4] Empirical testing of Erikson's theory reflects that it primarily accounts for identity development in males, with achievement of identity assumed to be a prerequisite for intimacy. For those young women who chose marriage and parenthood (intimacy) over careers, the Eriksonian progression does not unfold in the same way as for men. They have made a choice and a commitment that takes them out of the identity diffusion status, but the choice does not involve a commitment to occupational engagement outside the home, which keeps them out of the identity achievement category as defined. If fulfilling the wife-mother role continues to arouse conflict or ambivalence over not being able to make a career commitment, the women will score in the moratorium status; if the belief is strong enough that women do not have a choice, that biology indeed is destiny, then foreclosure is the outcome.

A good deal of the confusion about conflicting findings regarding foreclosure and moratorium women probably goes back to the fact that some women opt permanently for foreclosure or moratorium. For them it can be said that intimacy becomes identity, albeit uncomfortably so for the moratorium women. For other young women, these two statuses represent only a tentative commitment. They have, consciously or unconsciously, put the identity formation process on the back burner, so to speak, and some day when the last child leaves home (if not sooner) they will resume the process and complete it, making the self-chosen occupational commitment that will put them into the identity achievement status. For them intimacy has preceded identity achievement. The consequence of the tentativeness of choice for some women is that in the foreclosure and moratorium categories, we find a mixture of women — those who are there to stay and those who are making a temporary stopover.

For the adolescent female struggling with these developmental issues, the situation is, of course, quite different from the middle-aged woman who is resuming the developmental path. Because of the rapidity of change in sex-role norms, mothers of today's teenagers may not have the same utility as role models for their daughters as former generations of mothers did. Girls with traditional mothers may often derive validation and identification for a nontraditional identity from friendships with female peers (Morgan and Farber 1982). Instinctively it seems easy to accept the importance of mothers as role models for the female identity formation process. However, two studies by Enright et al. (1980) of seventh and eleventh graders failed to show any influence of mothers' parenting style on the identity achievement of either boys or girls. Fathers, on the contrary, by what the researchers call an "as yet unknown mechanism," clearly influence identity achievement of their sons as well as their daughters.

A ray of hope out of this quagmire of confusion comes from Carol Gilligan (1982), who reminds us that homo sapiens speak with two voices, a male and a female. We have listened for so long to the much louder male voice that it takes special effort to tune in to the female voice, except perhaps when it sings the baby to sleep. From Gilligan's own research on moral development in men and women, she hears through the self-descriptions of those she interviewed the male voice speaking of the role of separation as it defines the self and of great ideas and distinctive activities as the standards of self-assessment and success. She also hears the female voice speaking of ongoing attachments and relationships as definers of identity, of a standard of moral judgment based on nurturance, responsibility, and care, and of personal strength measured by giving to and helping, not hurting, in relations with others. The dilemma of identity and intimacy intrinsic in the adolescent's task of making commitments exposes the self in relation to others and is articulated through the two different moralities of the ethic of care (no one should be hurt) and the ethic of justice (everybody should be treated the same). For both sexes, reaching maturity means merging of the two voices and the two moralities. For the female, the ethic of care converges with the ethic of justice or responsibility when the activity of taking care is separated from the wish for approval by others.

The processes of maturation are different, but the endpoint of maturity the same. Developmental psychology has so heavily emphasized male development that separation (distance) from the mother has become the measure of the child's developmental progress. For the boy child, the mother cannot serve as the sexual role model. He must relinquish the attachment to the mother for the masculine self to emerge. The danger lies in developing the notion that attachment (intimacy) equates loss of self. For the girl child, who does not need to relinquish but to maintain her attachment to the mother in order to develop her female identity, the danger lies in defining self only in connection with others, that is, allowing justification for existence to lie only in the caring for others. One of the great advantages of Gilligan's formulation of the identity-intimacy interconnectedness for adolescent males and females is that it replaces the "battle of the sexes" with constructive, complementary processes leading to maturity and to the capacity to endure the ongoing ambiguity and difficulty of balancing and integrating justice and caring, rights and responsibilities.

Perhaps, as fathers take on more of the psychological caring functions of child rearing and mothers speak more with the masculine voice, the developmental tasks of shaping identity through commitment and intimacy will become less complex for the young. And perhaps one would find, in replicating the study of Enright et al. (1980), that mothers as well as fathers influence identity achievement of their sons and daughters.

Because of the rapid and ongoing changes in sex-typed behaviors and great variations among samples of studies of adolescent males and females, there is an unusually strong need to consider observations and findings reported in this section as preliminary and much in need of further empirical investigations.

Social Class and Cultural Differences in Adolescent Development

The socioeconomic status of the family (usually measured by the father's education and occupation) is almost automatically included in child development and parent-child interaction research. Yet study findings are often contradictory as to actual social class differences, which may be related to the nebulousness of the social class construct, to other methodological difficulties, or to the multidimensional character of human behavior and development. Changes over time may also account for apparent contradictions. Bronfenbrenner (1958), for example, noticed in his review of child-rearing patterns during the period from 1930 to 1955 that the gap between the middle- and working-classes had narrowed as working-class parents have adopted middle-class values and child-rearing practices.

Walters and Stinnett in their 1971 review of research on parent-child relationships carried out during the 1960s conclude that some differences were associated with social class.[5] The findings generally indicated that middle-class parents appear to be more supportive as well as more controlling of their children than lower-class parents. The former are more likely to use reason and appeals to guilt as ways of disciplining their children and less likely to punish them physically than are lower-class parents. A similar review by Walters and Walters (1980) covering the 1970s does not include any discussion of social class. Neither these reviews nor the extensive review by Gecas (1979) of the influence of social class on socialization single out adolescence for special attention.

A few studies have addressed the link between social class and self-esteem, which is a variable central to the counseling of adolescents. In an upwardly mobile society, it is assumed that the higher you climb, the higher the self-esteem. Filsinger and Anderson (1982) list several different studies showing a range from a positive, to a weak, to an inverse, to no association at all between social class and self-esteem in general, and for adolescents no relationship has been established between social class and self-esteem. Building on the findings by Rosenberg and Pearlin (1978) of "virtually no association [between social class and self-esteem] for younger children, a modest association for adolescents, and a moderate association for adults" (p. 53), Filsinger and Anderson tried to pinpoint when and how social status becomes an influential factor during late adolescence. They found support for their hypothesis that self-esteem is not associated with the adolescent's own social status but with that of his or her best friend. This seemingly odd connection becomes plausible when viewed from the perspective of Bandura's (1977a) concept self-efficacy, as Filsinger and Anderson did. Having a best friend of higher social status confirms the confidence of the self-efficacious youth in being able to handle the challenge of higher social status situations, which in turn leads to higher self-esteem. A reversed spiral operates for the inefficacious youth, who avoid challenging situations and seek friendships with those of lower social status. How well this argument holds up under scrutiny remains to be seen, particularly as applied to samples other than white, undergraduate students who were asked to identify the socioeconomic status of their own fathers and the fathers of their best friend during high school. Furthermore, keeping in mind the gender differences discussed in the previous section, the sex variable may well need to be controlled for, which it did not appear to have been in the Filsinger and Anderson study, at least as it is reported.

Adding the major variable of ethnicity to that of self-esteem also reveals seemingly contradictory findings. In the growing literature on black youth, findings often challenge common misconceptions of prevailing self-concepts among black teenagers. Simmons et al. (1978), in comparing 798 black and white adolescents, found that among these children moving from sixth to seventh grade, the blacks appeared to have higher self-esteem than whites. However, girls of both races demonstrated lower self-esteem than the boys, with white girls scoring lowest of all. For black children coming from broken homes, the self-esteem was lower among those attending desegregated schools than those in segregated schools. E.E. Jones (1979), controlling for socioeconomic status, found that black girls from lower status groups described themselves more favorably than black and white girls from middle-class backgrounds. The Jones study also gives some support to the existence of a common black cultural heritage across nationality lines, since U.S. and Jamaican black female adolescents describe themselves in a very similar fashion and both groups differed in similar ways from white U.S. females.

Smith (1982) in her thorough review of the literature on black female adolescents' educational, career, and psychological development, points to the conflicting findings of self-esteem among black youth. Some reports indicate lower self-concepts among blacks than whites, others the same amount or the reversed pattern. According to Smith, black adolescent females have been generally ignored so "painfully little is known about how young black females feel about themselves as emerging adults and women" (p. 285). Based on the limited data, Smith makes the tentative conclusion that "black females have been able to maintain a positive sense of self against what appear to be overwhelming odds" (p. 281). All the researchers referred to here caution about possible limitations associated with measuring instruments and samples, and speak against the general tendency to view blacks as a homogeneous group.

Concrete and clear evidence against such a tendency is found in the Lewis and Looney (1983) study of 18 well-functioning, working-class, low-income black families in Texas with 43 children and teenagers. While the smallness and purposive nature of the sample limit generalizability, the intensive examination and videotaped testing of individuals and family interaction of these families give credence to the study findings. On the Timberlawn Family Competence scale (discussed in chapter 3), the sample families were distributed from optimal to dysfunctional families, but no one was assessed as severely dysfunctional. Such families are usually found in clinical samples and not to be expected in a group of families who volunteered to participate in the study after having been suggested by church, school, or community representatives. What is of importance is the fact that these families, singled out because of their strength, are distributed from point 2 to point 8 on the 10-point Global Health-Pathology scale, with 11 scoring at the healthy end, 4 in the middle, and 3 at the dysfunctional end of the scale. The most competent families' income was on an average $4,000 above the poverty line; the least competent families as a group had incomes more than $4,000 below that line. This confirms the hypothesis that there is a critical threshold of income below which family structure can hardly be maintained; the little available energy is spent in a struggle for physical survival with hardly anything left for meeting the family's psychological needs.

The 33 adolescents who filled out Offer Adolescent Self-Image questionnaires had a distribution similar to the global family ratings. Nine teenagers from the most competent families had a mean score close to or slightly above the mean of 50, and the 16 from the least competent families scored 17 points below the mean, within the pathological range.

In comparison with the healthy middle-class white families studies earlier by the Timberlawn group (reported in *No Single Thread*, Lewis et al. 1976, discussed in chapter 3), the most competent black families turned out to be more like the white families than their working-class neighbors.

Another example speaking against the tendency to assume homogeneity within socioeconomic or ethnic groups is Frazier and DeBlassie's (1982) study comparing self-concepts in Mexican American and non-Mexican American late adolescents. They summarize existing empirical evidence pointing to generally lower self-esteem among Mexican Americans with a few exceptions, but they also note that none of the extant studies controlled for ability level when comparing Mexican Americans and non-Mexican Americans. In their own study of 129 college freshmen who volunteered to participate, no self-concept differences were found between the two groups, who had equal levels of ability. Similar inappropriate comparisons have been noted in research on minority families, where lower-class minority families have been compared to middle-class white families and found wanting (Staples and Mirandé 1980).

Some hopeful signs indicate that the tide is turning — at least with respect to getting more valid data on family and child development variables in minority groups. Staples and Mirande (1980) conclude their review of the 1970s with the observation that the quantity and quality of research on the black and the Chicano family improved over the decade, but research on Asian and Native American families is still very limited. They call for research on minority families as autonomous systems in their own right rather than assessing them according to the standards of white, middle-class American families. They urge the use of qualitative as well as quantitative research designs and the sampling of minority families from different socioeconomic classes.

Evidence of some of these changes is the appearance of many books and professional articles presenting balanced accounts of strengths and weaknesses in minority groups' family living.[6] Not least of these is the first comprehensive text on the psychosocial development of minority children (Powell 1983) from American Indian, black, Pan-Asian, Hispanic groups, and numerous subgroups. Despite these developments, however, knowledge about minority adolescents is still scattered about. Each cultural/ethnic group, as Ogbu (1981) points out, has its own coping skills that must be taught and acquired by its young to adapt and survive in the larger, often hostile environment with limited access to quality education, jobs, and other resources. Yu and Kim's (1983) account of the additional developmental tasks confronting Korean adolescents with immigrant parents probably is shared by other ethnic groups. These adolescents have the double dilemma of not feeling part of the contemporary American society and feeling disconnected from their original ethnic heritage. As elaborated in previous sections of this chapter, all adolescents need to negotiate the delicate shift of dependence from parents, to peers, to self. If the increased dependence and support from peers that facilitate the letting go of the dependency strings to the parents are not forthcoming from the peer group, the temptation grows to remain under the parents' wings or to break away from them altogether. The latter happens, note Yu and Kim, when the youth experiences his cultural elements to be a hindrance and an embarrassment in attempts at assimilation into the majority culture. In their surveys of Korean parents and adolescents, Yu and Kim identified three patterns of identity formation: (1) full Korean identity; (2) mixed Korean-American identity, which strives to retain positive values from the Korean culture while participating as fully as possible in the American mainstream; and (3) full American identity, which includes the very few who resent Asian physical characteristics and tend to "dissociate themselves from fellow Koreans socially and wish to bury or deny Korean cultural values" (p. 155). Interviews with second- and third-generation Korean-Americans indicate additional stresses in identity formation as institutionalized discrimination is experienced. The researchers also note that ethnic awareness movements have been helpful in bringing these American-born Koreans in touch with their "roots" and resolving their identity conflicts.

Finally, how do U.S. adolescents compare with adolescents from other countries? The very few cross-national studies that have been located indicate similarities rather than differences in adolescent behavior and developmental tasks. The Kandel and Lesser (1969, 1972) studies uncovered a few differences in the comparison of 2,327 U.S. and 1,552 Danish adolescents. An authoritarian decision-making pattern is dominant in the United States, while a democratic pattern prevails in Denmark. The researchers suggest that American parents treat their adolescents as children longer than the Danish parents, who appear to exercise greater control in the preadolescent years leading to more self-directed adolescents. The most striking cross-cultural difference was found in the adolescents' feeling of independence. Danish youth experienced a stronger sense of independence from parental influence than their American counterparts; they would more frequently "disregard their parents' wishes about not seeing friends, [say] that their opinions are different from those of their parents, [and] that they are being treated like adults by their parents and get sufficient freedom from their parents" (1969, p. 357). In both countries it was found that independence is enhanced by few parental rules with explanations for the rules and by democratic decision making including the teenager actively in the process. It thus appears that while the prevalence of autocratic vs. democratic parental patterns varies between the two countries, the parent-adolescent relationship patterns and the association between parental behavior and consequences for adolescent socialization is similar.

The Offer Adolescent Self-Image questionnaire has been used to compare normal youth in Australia, Ireland, Israel, and the United States (Offer, Ostrov, and Howard 1981).[7] Teenagers from countries outside the United States are less rebellious and have slightly more positive feelings toward their parents than do teenagers in the United States, who tend to feel somewhat more committed to morals and work-related values. Offer et al.

conclude that "Americans, in short, may be a bit more autonomous and less family-oriented than are adolescents from the other cultures" (p. 108). This contradicts Kandel and Lesser's conclusion that Danish youth showed greater independence than U.S. teenagers. Whether these differences reflect real variations among the studied national groups or whether they are related to sampling, measurement, or timing differences must be determined by further investigative testing. In any event the comparisons made by Offer and his coresearchers imply that turmoil is not the norm of adolescent development in these samples of teenagers from Western cultures.

Summary

This chapter opened with a review of the role played by peers as friends and associates in groups in the transition of dependence on parents, to dependence on peers, to dependence on self. Recent study findings support the interdependence and independence of family and peers as essential but different influences on adolescent development. Associations with peers of the opposite sex have placed U.S. teenagers way above those from other industrialized nations in respect to fertility. The absolute number and rate of illegitimate births have risen, augmenting risk factors such as various medical conditions, death rate, and neglect for the babies of teenage mothers. It is unclear, however, to what extent these risk factors are associated with young age and early childbirth or preexisting behavioral or personality variables. Adolescent fathers have been generally ignored by researchers and service providers alike — one of the few examples of greater attention to the female than the male. In their identity formation process, homosexual adolescents face special hardships in often being rejected by their families or confronted with societal stigma.

The utility of the four categories of Marcia's Identity Status Interview (identity achievement, moratorium, foreclosure, and identity diffusion) is discussed as a tool for assessing adolescent clients and for checking possible counselor-value impositions. Limitations are noted in the heavy reliance on college males in almost all studies of identity formation.

Almost 80 percent of adolescents will have had a work experience by the time they graduate from high school. The mixture of positive and negative consequences of these naturally occurring work experiences is challenging the work-ethic philosophy that work is always good for you. Some negative consequences include less involvement with family and friends and, in some cases, cynicism and acceptance of unethical work practices and increased cigarette and marijuana smoking. Jobs are unavailable to many teenagers who want to work, reflecting the startling statistic that the unemployment rate for non-white youth is consistently double that for whites. The high youth unemployment rate is unfortunately not unique to the United States but is shared by many other industrialized countries.

Differences between male and female adolescent development are not easily ascertained as there is a scarcity of studies on female development. Some evidence indicates that boys have a better body image and higher academic and vocational aspirations than young girls, while the latter have a more positive social, moral, and affiliative orientation but also suffer more pervasive loneliness, sadness, and confusion. The two sexes do indeed speak with two voices — the girls expressing the ethic of morality and caring and the boys the ethic of justice and equity. The growing awareness of the female voice shows some promise for a more mature blending of the masculine-feminine voices in the future.

Contradictory findings challenge the often-reported belief that self-esteem is directly associated with level of socioeconomic status and that black and other minority youth experience lower self-esteem than whites. Minority groups are not homogeneous; competent working-class black families and teenagers are more like middle-class white competent families than blacks on the same socioeconomic level. Mexican-American adolescents do not score lower on self-concept measures than non-Mexican Americans when ability is controlled for.

Comparisons of U.S. adolescents with those from other Western nations reveal greater similarities than differences and indicate that turmoil is not the norm for adolescent development in these countries.

Notes

1. This is not to be confused with the large-scale U.S. study by James S. Coleman, *The Adolescent Society* (1961), which assessed leading crowds in ten different schools and found that membership in the elite crowd is determined, by and large, by athletic ability in boys and social success in girls. Academic success received low rankings in general as a road to popularity and elite-crowd membership. However, in most cases the most popular of all in all the schools studied was the unusual student combining athletic and academic success (as reported in Coleman, John C., 1980).

2. The term *crisis* has been criticized as being too strong since some adolescents test alternatives and make up their minds without actually experiencing the traumatic upset implied in the crisis concept; *exploration* has been proposed as a more accurate term (Matteson 1977).

3. The reader is referred to Martin L. Hoffman's (1980) analysis of "Moral Development in Adolescence" in Adelson's *Handbook of Adolescent Psychology*. Hoffman's review includes Piaget's two-stage and Kohlberg's six-stage schema of moral thought along with other theories and his own proposal for a developmental framework for viewing adolescent morality.

4. The studies by Marcia and his coworkers build on the assumption that the identity formation process is the same for males and females but center around different content areas. Therefore, separate interviews for males and females originally covered different content. This assumption and procedure have been criticized by Matteson (1977) and have later been corrected by the use of one single interview schedule with both sexes (Rogow, Marcia, and Slugoski 1983). Thus, findings of differences between male and female identity status derived from investigations using separate interview schedules probably should be viewed with caution.

5. Similar conclusions are drawn by Rice (1981) in his chapter on the culturally different, which covers studies and governmental reports up to the mid-1970s. One difficulty in dealing with many investigations including the social class variable is that confounding influences from ethnic, gender, and discrimination variables rarely are controlled for.

6. Selected examples of books are: (1) Bass et al., 1982, *The Afro-American Family;* (2) Devore and Schlesinger, 1981, *Ethnic-Sensitive Social Work Practice;* (3) Jenkins, 1981, *The Ethnic Dilemma in Social Services;* (4) McAdoo, 1981, *Black Families;* McAdoo, 1983, in McCubbin and Figley, *Stress and the Family,* Vol. I; (5) McGoldrick et al., 1982, *Ethnicity and Family Therapy.*

7. The OSIQ has not been fully tested on high school students from a variety of socioeconomic and ethnic groups since many schools do not allow testing of students for research purposes. The limited U.S. data available to the Offer research team indicate that there is no significant difference in self-image scores among youth from different social class and racial groups (p. 34–35).

II SERVICES AND INTERPERSONAL INTERVENTIONS ASSISTING TROUBLED ADOLESCENTS AND THEIR FAMILIES

5 EDUCATIONAL AND SUPPORTIVE SERVICES FOR ADOLESCENTS LIVING WITH THEIR FAMILIES

Where do adolescents and their families turn when the school sends that final notice of expulsion, when conflict in the home has reached such un-bearable levels that parents are prompted to request the immediate place-ment of the adolescent, when parents get that feared call from the police saying that they have picked up their child for possession of drugs, or when the hospital emergency room calls to say that their son or daughter was one of five teenagers in a car crash? Where does the youngster turn when he or she just can't make it in school, can't find a job, feels awkward because his or her body is so much smaller or bigger than classmates', feels so down and alone that life is not worth living any longer? While some families manage to cope with the stresses, problems, and crises of the adolescent phase by relying on friends, relatives, and the religious group they belong to, as we saw in the Olson and McCubbin (1983) study, other families desperately need and use support from community services under public and private auspices.

Such services include child welfare, juvenile justice, health and mental health services, schools, vocational counseling agencies, residential and other institutional services, traditional private youth and family service agencies, YWCA and YMCA, Big Sister/Brother organizations, and alternative youth services such as hotline programs, counseling, and residential centers for runaways. Some of these services will be discussed in this and the next chapter as they address problems faced by adolescents and their families, those living in the parental home (this chapter) and those in out-of-home placements (chapter 6). This chapter is introduced by an ecological perspective of the overall service system and the linkages (or lack of them) among its segments. Special attention is given to the parent-adolescent relationship as an important factor and focus for service delivery.

During the 1960s and 1970s growing criticism of the public welfare system in general — and foster family care for children and adolescents in particular — and a shift in the parent/child balance of rights vis-à-vis the state's rights and responsibilities in caring for the young gave rise to reexamination of practice, principles, objectives, and interventions. One result is the conceptualization of "an integrated continuum of care that provides a full range of home-based and residential options and contains an easily activated set of linkages between the various service programs and the other major systems in which the child participates: family, peer group, school, church, and community" (Whittaker 1979, p. 4). This ecological model of care moves away from an illness model to a growth orientation and the engagement of the family as a partner in caring for the young. While the model originally envisioned integration of mental health, health, education, and welfare services, it is primarily in the field of child welfare that it has been translated into reality through the Permanency Planning approach. A range of innovative services under the Permanency Planning umbrella concept is presented in the Child Welfare League's publication *The Challenge of Partnership: Working with Parents of Children in Foster Care*, edited by Maluccio and Sinanoglu (1981). Included are Maluccio's Ecological Practice Framework; The Oregon Permanency Planning Project's "Coming Home From Foster Care" (Lahti and Dvorak); Whittaker's and Finkelstein's models for extensive parent involvement in residential care; use of contracting with parents (Gambrill and Stein); and a task-centered reunification model (Rooney).

Others have proposed related systems of integrated and comprehensive service organizations like, for example, Brown et al.'s (1982) proposed master plan for an integrated family practice service model and Magazino's (1983) illustration of a comprehensive, community-based preventive service agency for families at risk as modeled after the Center for Family Life in Brooklyn, New York (pp. 246–48). None of these models exclusively and specifically addresses the needs of adolescents, but the Permanency Planning principles and procedures appear to be equally applicable to them as to pre-adolescents. In an attempt to incorporate the many threads of innovation, Maluccio and Fein (1983) propose the following integrated definition:

Permanency planning is the systematic process of carrying out, within a brief time-limited period, a set of goal-directed activities designed to help children live in families that offer continuity of relationships with nurturing parents or care-takers and the opportunity to establish lifetime relationships. (p. 197)

The Permanency Planning movement and related innovative programs and philosophies were incorporated in the first major piece of federal legislation concerning child welfare since the Social Security Act in 1935 — the Adoption Assistance and Child Welfare Act of 1980 (Public Law 96-272). This act restructures the role of the federal government in child welfare and mandates that states provide services to biological parents that will prevent separation of children and youth from their families. Where separation is necessary, states are mandated to develop plans and provide support services to enable children to be reunited with their families or, where this is not feasible, to provide services that enable children to be adopted or placed in other permanent homes.[1] The extent to which the spirit of the law is and will be translated into reality depends on the level of funding, inter- and intraagency cooperation, and the ability of the professions involved to engage in the interdisciplinary cooperation essential for successful service delivery.

Interdisciplinary teamwork among human service professionals may be hampered by many communication and cooperation problems. Dunham (1980) lists such difficulties as differences in language ("jargon"), priority given to goals in individual cases, restrictive professional perspectives with respect to theoretical explanations of human behavior and how it may be changed, ignorance about objectives and procedures of other professionals, strong professional group loyalties, and problems in sharing confidential information. Dunham also gives examples of how these barriers may be remedied, and an article by Goldstein, Gabay, and Switzer (1981) presents an excellent example of how problems in interdisciplinary work were overcome in the cooperation between a child welfare agency and a psychiatric hospital in setting up an ongoing system for discharging adolescents to the community.

Educational and Supportive Services

Outside the family, schools are a crucial locus of learning, living, and social development. For some adolescents, high school provides an exhilarating environment unlocking individual talents and social prowess. For others, the learning challenges and relations to peers and teachers become synonymous with boredom, frustration, or defeat. For them preventive and remedial services provided by the schools themselves or by community agencies become essential if school failure is to be prevented from having lifelong effects.

This section will focus on the schools and selected preventive community services, but first a brief word about service terminology. Kadushin (1980) distinguishes between supportive and supplementary services, which are both preventive in nature. He sees supportive services (such as family service agencies, community mental health programs, and child protective services) as the first line of defense in supporting the family's own strength in overcoming the strain in the parent-child relationship system or in enabling parents to carry out their roles as parents in a more acceptable manner (pp. 25-26). In the second line of defense, the parents use the supplementary (concrete and/or financial) services to carry out the parenting function in such a manner that the youngster can remain in the home without harm. Description and evaluation of these services (Jones et al. 1981; Kadushin 1980; and Magura 1981) usually deal with children from birth to maturity and do not specifically focus on adolescents.

With respect to the primary, secondary, and tertiary prevention continuum, it is probably fair to say that public as well as private child welfare agencies have emphasized primary prevention the least. Ameliorative and remedial services (secondary and tertiary prevention) have been favored in funding and staff resources because of the immediacy and urgency of the need for such services. Furthermore, primary prevention programs are difficult to design and to measure for effectiveness. As Gilchrist et al. (1979, pp. 380-81) point out, primary prevention efforts in providing youth with "information-only" or using "scare" tactics have shown to be ineffective. Interpersonal aspects of risk taking, the role of peer pressures, and the social importance of many adolescent problem behaviors require that the youngsters acquire cognitive and behavioral skills that will help them translate information into personal decisions and overt behavior.

In any event, the aim of this chapter is not a comprehensive analysis of these complex policy and practice questions but a limited presentation of how and what services are provided the adolescent age group.

Schools

Rutter (1980, pp. 164-170) makes the case that the belief derived from the studies by James Coleman et al. (1966) and by Christopher Jencks et al. (1972) that schooling constitutes only a marginal influence on adolescent behavior is contradicted by findings from later studies, including his own. Eight variables affecting the quality of the school as a social organization and as an environment for learning have an important impact on adolescent behavior and scholastic achievement. These variables include: a balance of intellectually able and less able children; use of rewards and focus on success; responsiveness to student needs; attractive grounds and decor; student participation in running of the schools; emphasis on academic matters; availability of teachers to students and as behavior models; nature of management of groups in the classroom; and agreement among staff about curriculum and discipline approaches.

Joan Lipsitz (1977) in her review of the fit between what the young adolescent needs and what happens to him or her five days a week in school identifies the following voids in what junior high schools offer.

1. No linkage between what we know the adolescent's tasks to be in terms of separation, individuation, and commitment and what goes on in the junior high school. She mentions particularly an alleged failure to take into account the timing of cognitive growth, that is, it is "as wasteful to present abstract material prematurely as it is to remain oblivious to new mental capacities" for hypothetical thought (p. 123).
2. A failure to acknowledge differential growth spurts. Age segregation and grade organization assume that all youngsters of the same chronological age are at the same point in their mastery of developmental tasks.
3. Poor coordination among schools and other service organizations, such as health care. The schools, Lipsitz says, cannot be held accountable for not educating the young if they suffer from untreated maladies such as asthma, hearing and vision impairment, or disorders of the central nervous system.
4. Examples of elements that work against the education of ethnic minority students are racism, in the form of relatively inexperienced teachers in overcrowded classrooms in inner-city schools, and lack of role models by virtue of the small number of teachers of minority background.

Later empirical investigations have identified school size as an important variable in that schools with more than 600 students enrolled in grades 9–12 tend to become "psychologically unsustainable" in that they discourage participation, create elitism, lead to staff inflexibility, and, "most insidiously, alienate those students who are already academically marginal" (Garbarino 1979 and 1980a).

A landmark development in public education occurred with the 1975 federal enactment of PL 94-142, the Education for All Handicapped Children Act, which is designed to assure free appropriate public education of all handicapped persons between 3 and 21 years of age. This special education

•

(and related counseling or supportive services) is to be offered in "the least restrictive environment." As far as possible, it is to be offered in regular classrooms after assessment and evaluation by a multidisciplinary team leading to an individualized education program (IEP) stated in written form and with assured due process mechanisms as protective safeguards for the child and the parents that the educational plan is developed according to the law. Underlying assumptions of this legislation are (according to Gresham [1983]) that mingling the handicapped children with the nonhandicapped will afford greater acceptance of the handicapped, who are also expected to model their behavior after their nonhandicapped peers. To what extent these laudable objectives have been realized is still somewhat unclear.[2] Far greater attention has been given to preadolescent children with handicaps than to adolescents, partly from a commitment to early intervention principles, partly because teenagers are supposed to have a greater say in determining their own goal, and partly because some professionals are reluctant to work with adolescents because they often fail to cooperate with intervention efforts (Algozzine et al. 1982; Cullinan and Epstein 1979; Cullinan, Epstein, and Lloyd 1983).

Schools have been a natural working field for professional social workers for a long time. The school is an ideal location for carrying out primary, secondary, and remedial interventions to promote learning and socialization of children and youth. Traditionally, school social work has emphasized remedial efforts to help children who for emotional or social reasons had difficulty in learning. This involved direct counseling of the child and the parents, collaboration with teachers and others within the school system on behalf of specific children, and referral to and utilization of community resources. During the 1970s focus moved away from the individual youngster as the problem-bearer to the school system itself as a supportive, indifferent, or detrimental environment for learning and as the target for the school social worker's efforts for change. This appears to be the major shift in the function of social workers in the school setting. Additional elements of the history of the move from visiting teachers to serving as school specialists are presented by Betsy L. Hancock (1982, chapter 1).

While today's school social workers probably would not fully agree upon their functions, six general social work objectives used by Costin (1981) cover all the services actually provided by school social workers. The needs and atmosphere of specific schools call for different blends of these objectives, which here will serve the purpose of organizing some major points from the school social work literature. The overall goal is "to improve the transactions between children and their school-home community environment in order to enhance children's coping capacities and improve school conditions for all pupils'' (p. 41). Costin outlines the following six objectives.

The first objective is to encourage competence and increase problem-solving abilities of individuals. This objective includes all children who are not realizing their potentials for learning in school. They may have formed maladaptive patterns of interaction that make them disruptive in the classroom or on the playground. They may have suffered traumatic events of loss through death or divorce, may have been victims of abuse, may be malnourished or physically ill, may have succumbed to drug or alcohol abuse, may be a pregnant teenager or a parent, may be in trouble with the law, and so on. The task here is direct problem solving or therapeutic work with the adolescent and/or the family. The second objective is to help children and their families obtain resources within the school system and from community agencies. This includes use of existing resources, such as recreational and medical facilities, as well as efforts to develop new, needed services. The third objective is to help make the school environment responsive to the needs of special groups, such as handicapped youngsters. The social workers' role here often involves advocacy for individuals or groups of children, and they sometimes serve as mediators at hearings regarding conflicts between parents of handicapped children and the school administration related to the fairness of the individualized educational plan developed for a child. Other special groups are children in foster care or those returning from residential treatment or other institutional care.

The fourth objective involves facilitation of interaction and communication between individuals and others in their environment, for example, between parents and teachers, with the social worker serving as interpreter of the meaning of requests or behaviors or proposing alternative actions. This function becomes particularly important when the families and teachers represent different ethnic groups. A recent article by McNeely and Badami (1984) gives examples of misunderstanding between blacks and whites as a result of different communication styles, including patterns of communication such as "intermittent versus continuous eye contact, personal versus impersonal interactive modes . . . use of titles and last names versus use of first names, boastfulness versus bashfulness" (p. 22). They underscore the importance of the social worker's knowledge of such communication patterns in efforts to promote harmonious relations between students, teachers, and staff and in improving the school's relations with minority-group parents.

Lessening of interracial misunderstandings is a crucial task for school social workers — one that is not easily achieved and sometimes has unintended consequences. Tyler and Gatz (1977), in comparing development of psychosocial competence through counseling of groups with mixed membership of exemplary and marginal students, found that all changed significantly in the direction of a stronger sense of self-efficacy in comparison with a control group that received no counseling. Marginal students did not gain as much as the exemplary students but did show greater prosocial gains than the control group. All groups had mixtures of black and white students, and although counseling did not focus on racial issues, the marginal black male students indicated that their lives were less impacted by racial prejudice at the end of eight weeks of counseling than they had stated previously. For them the outcome seems to have been that they came "to blame themselves more and the system less for outcomes in the lives of black people, including themselves" (p. 447). The exemplary black male students did not show the same change, and the researchers note that the effect of counseling for the marginal black males could be potentially adverse, which should not be overlooked. Their overall conclusion is that interventions need to become more responsive to socio-cultural factors.

The last two objectives stated by Costin (1981, pp. 42–43) involve influencing interactions between organizations to ease tension and misunderstandings, and influencing social and environmental policy, such as rules regarding corporal punishment and other disciplinary methods, expulsions, and so forth. An example of promoting collaboration and easing tension between organizations is the social worker's role in developing guidelines for reporting cases in which child abuse and neglect are suspected. Fisher and Berdie (1978) note that this latter group of adolescents often get channeled into inappropriate service branches rather than to the protective service system. The reason for this is that abused adolescents, in contrast to younger children, come to public attention because of their disruptive behavior in school, runaway or delinquent behavior that puts them in contact with the juvenile justice system, or because they become mentally ill, turn to drugs, or engage in other behaviors that channel them into the community mental health system. The school social worker is in a central position first of all to spot victims of abuse as early as possible and second to facilitate contact between the adolescent and his or her family and the appropriate service agency.

In some school systems the school social worker single-handedly strives to achieve all these objectives; in others, an interdisciplinary pupil personnel team shares the tasks. Historically, psychologists, social workers, and counselors have served on such teams. Sometimes they are effective, but at other times gaps in service or duplication have been the result of failure of communication and collaboration among these professionals, which have similar and overlapping functions (Berkman and Rosenblum 1982; Buktenica

1970; and Radin and Welsh 1984). Radin and Welsh propose that rather than operate in isolation from one another, the representatives from the three professions should form a unified team to increase the sharing of expertise. By becoming knowledgeable about each professional's training and shared and unique areas of expertise, mutual respect and an atmosphere of trust may develop and form the basis for team collaboration, designating certain activities as common to all three professions and other activities as unique. This would lead to better integrated, more complementary, and more effective services to the students, their families, the staff, and the community.

Another format for interdisciplinary teamwork in schools is exemplified in the "School Consultation Service of the Child and Adolescent Psychiatric Clinic," Bronx Municipal Hospital Center and the Albert Einstein College of Medicine in New York, as reported by Kandler (1979). The consultation team, which has operated for more than ten years in providing services to several schools, consists of specialists with professional training in fields such as education, counseling, social work, psychology, and psychiatry. Typically the team offers psychiatric and psychological evaluations, brief psychotherapy, seminars for guidance personnel, consultations with school staff, classroom meetings with students, group therapy, and direct work with parents, either in groups (PTA seminars, and so on) to teach them about adolescent development, discuss parenting issues or individually to train them as volunteers. Kandler mentions work with culturally and economically deprived parents in the inner city as particularly important in order to teach them to deal with school authorities in such a manner that their children can take best advantage of what the school has to offer. One advantage of operating as a consultation team from the outside is that the school is an ideal setting for rapid delivery of help, and many families and children are willing to meet with mental health professionals on school grounds but would never agree to seek assistance from a clinic or social agency.

Unfortunately, many of these additional services provided by school systems are often the first to be eliminated at times of budget cuts, and an outside consultation team might be a little easier to get rid of than a well-integrated inside pupil personnel team. In any event it seems clear that many high school students need help in coping with barriers to learning — be they located within themselves, in the school, or in their families or communities. The school social worker has an important role to play, and after some apparent weakening and confusion in the role and function of school social work in the 1960s, this branch of social work now seems to be gaining strength. Fisher (1983) cites as evidence for this the increase in the number of positions, general growth of school social work literature, and development of two professional journals in the field, *School Social Work Journal,* published by the Illinois Association of School Social Workers since 1976, and *Social Work in Education,* published by the National Association of Social Workers since 1978.[3]

Medico-Social Services

As stated in chapter 2, adolescence brings with it vulnerability to a number of illnesses. The Select Panel for the Promotion of Child Health (U.S. Department of Health and Human Services, Public Health Service, Vol. I 1981) notes several sources of health-undermining stress — the rapid physical, cognitive, and emotional changes of early adolescence and the shift from elementary to junior or middle school concomitant with entry into the "teen culture." Explorations with smoking, alcohol, and drug use during the adolescent years may have lifelong health consequences. The increase in sexual activity makes adolescents vulnerable to sexually transmitted diseases (gonorrhea, genital herpes, syphilis, and others), which represent a major health problem for the 15- to 24-year-olds who account for 65 percent of the estimated 8–12 million cases of such diseases each year. Pregnancy and delivery complications, abortions, automobile accidents, suicide attempts, and psychosomatic illnesses can be added to the long list of hazards that call for medical care specifically addressing the needs of this age group.

Two major texts in adolescent medicine (Daniel 1977, and Garell 1976) agree that health care for adolescents has been underfinanced and partly ignored and that ideally such a system should contain service at the primary, secondary, and tertiary levels of care. Primary care — the entry into the health care system — includes general medical care (mostly by general practitioners or pediatricians), prevention, and rehabilitation; secondary diagnostic care and specialized tests occur in ambulatory hospital settings; and tertiary care requires inpatient service and treatment. Garell states that the first free clinic for adolescent medical care opened in Boston in 1951; such clinics have grown in number across the United States, especially during the 1960s. They offer primary medical, dental, psychological, and drug abuse care in various combinations. Some care is also available from runaway and crisis centers and juvenile facilities, which because of meager funding often provide emergency care only. Schools would seem to be a logical place for tending to health needs of the young, but their role has been limited primarily to health education with very little direct patient care. In some places, secondary care is offered at hospital-based adolescent clinics where an interdisciplinary team of physician, nurse, social worker, psychologist, youth-worker, and others provide direct, nonemergency health care. The clinic also serves as a referral source and resource for primary care facilities. Tertiary care is sometimes provided in separate adolescent wards at hospitals. The crisis of hospitalization seems to be minimized if adolescent patients are among peers and served by a hospital staff with special knowledge of and training in meeting the needs of this age group. Post-hospitalization services are offered by public health personnel, occupational therapists, or physical therapists, as coordinated by the primary care unit to which the tertiary unit refers the adolescent.

Wright (1981) presents an example of a secondary, hospital-based clinic for adolescents. The clinic's staff, consisting of doctors, nurses, social workers, and psychologists, observed a growing need for services in the area of adolescent pregnancies, but before further expanding the program to meet that need the opinions of the adolescent population were sought through a questionnaire distributed via the schools to half of the county's high school population. The respondents rank-ordered drug and alcohol abuse, problems with parents, grades, venereal disease, and pregnancy in order of seriousness. Male and female respondents differed in many of the rankings, the largest differences being in respect to problems with parents (43 percent for females, 23 percent for males) and venereal disease (28 percent for males, 18 percent for females). This needs assessment resulted in plans to expand the adolescent clinic to include alcohol-related services, and it promoted communication and collaboration among various educational and helping agencies.

Garell concludes his report by listing 11 characteristics of an ideal adolescent health care system, including the need for continuity and comprehensive care by generalists and specialists, easy access, a holistic health perspective, consumer (patient) input and involvement, and elimination of the economic factor as barrier to receipt of care. Such a system makes sense, but unfortunately it remains by and large an unrealized ideal. Many adolescents without means, whether living with their biological families or in foster care, are receiving minimal or no care at all (Swire and Kavaler 1977 and 1978). Federal legislation has attempted to remedy the situation by the EPSDT (early and periodic screening, diagnosis, and treatment) program enacted in 1967 as a part of the Medicaid program and by the Adolescent Health Services, Pregnancy Prevention, and Care Act of 1978, which focuses on services to pregnant adolescents, adolescent parents, and their children. Both programs have had mixed successes with only some states taking advantage of available federal funding (in Fiscal Year 1980 only $7.5 million was appropriated and only 27 new grants awarded according to The Select Panel for the Promotion of Child Health, Vol. II, 1981).

Teenage pregnancy and parenthood require considerable overlap between medical and social services. Howard (1978), in her analysis of child welfare strategy for servicing young-parent families, focuses on (1) prevention of adolescent pregnancy, (2) comprehensive services during pregnancy and immediately postpartum, and (3) comprehensive services for young-parent families. The need to include the father of the child, whether married or unmarried, is also stressed in all categories of interventions.

Care of the child is mentioned last on Howard's list of 29 needed services, which may or may not indicate any prioritizing. Adequate child care facilities are essential and were stressed in Clapp and Raab's (1978) study of 210 unmarried adolescent mothers who kept their babies; 70 percent of the subsample of 30 mothers who were interviewed ranked child care first among hypothetical services of which they were in need. Overall these unmarried mothers fared reasonably well in spite of the minimal degree to which basic necessities such as income and assistance with child care were met. The authors conclude that "[w]ith adequate child care facilities, financial resources, and educational and employment counseling, the adolescent unmarried mother who keeps her child may become the creator of her future rather than the victim of her past" (p. 153).

Many communities provide services in the prenatal period, in connection with delivery, and immediately thereafter. In the national study of services provided during the spring of 1977 to 1.8 million children and their families (Shyne and Schroeder 1978), about 30,000 children of teenage mothers (1.7 percent of the total study sample) and 17,000 pregnant teenagers (about 1 percent) were provided assistance. The most usual services offered the pregnant teenager were health services (in 51 percent of the cases), counseling of the girl (in 46 percent), and counseling of the principal child-caring person (in 38 percent of the cases).

Howard (1978) particularly stresses the need for long-term and full-range comprehensive services to continue through the child's preschool years. It is unrealistic to expect short-term services to have a long-term effect; as she notes, few would recommend attempting to make a 14-year-old immediately self-supporting. Ongoing support services are needed for a large number of young parents to complete their parenting tasks, and preventive services are needed to make all teenagers knowledgeable about what is involved in parenting (p. 224). Such services need to take account of and build upon the fact that a considerable proportion of adolescent mothers generate support systems on their own among relatives, particularly their mothers, as shown in the recent study by de Anda and Beccera (1984) of Hispanic and white adolescent mothers. Illustrations of medico-social services addressing adolescent sexuality, pregnancy, and parenting issues are listed in note 4.

Community Mental Health Care

A recent study entitled *Unclaimed Children* by the Children's Defense Fund (Knitzer 1982b) estimates that only one-third of the nation's 3 million seriously disturbed children and adolescents receive the services they need. The Select Panel for the Promotion of Child Health (1981, Vol. III) quotes an estimate — possibly inflated — that 18 percent of persons in the United States under age 18 suffer emotional and behavioral difficulties and that only 1 percent are served by the mental health sector and less than 10 percent by the general health system.[5]

Of course, the mental health needs of some are at least partially met by other systems, such as the public and private child and family welfare services and the educational and correctional systems. Shyne and Schroeder (1978) studied nearly 2 million children who received public social services and found that 9 percent of the children received mental health services. However, of the 76,000 for whom emotional problems were the main reason for service, 40 percent were recommended for mental health services and only 16 percent received such services. Other supportive services were provided, and 65,000 of them were placed outside their homes in various substitute care facilities and may there have received additional mental health care.

Rutter (1980), who is a distinguished leader in epidemiological studies of psychosocial disorders and psychiatric illnesses, concludes his analysis of continuities and discontinuities across the adolescent years in stating that first among the problems that peak during this period is juvenile delinquency; anorexia nervosa, suicide, and depression approach their peak at late adolescence; drug abuse rises sharply toward the end of adolescence but peaks a little later. During adolescence the sex ratio of emotional disorders shifts from almost unity in childhood to a higher rate for females than males after that time. It is also a period during which those suffering from autism are most likely to develop epileptic seizures (Rutter 1980, pp. 85–86).

The prevalence of mental disorders within minority populations is still unknown in spite of growth in epidemiological and other research within the last decade or two. There is clearly an uneven representation of various cultural and racial minority groups in mental health service settings, which are underutilized by some cultural groups and overutilized by others (Callicut and Lecca 1983). The deleterious effect of institutionalized racism on blacks, Hispanics, and Native Americans is discussed by McNeil and Wright (1983), and the major treatise on psychosocial development of minority group children, edited by Gloria J. Powell (1983), contains seven chapters addressing mental health issues for black, Hispanic, Puerto Rican,

American Indian, Japanese-American, Chinese-American, and Vietnamese children. The picture is mostly grim and full of injustice. Glimmers of hope come from the fact that the groundwork for at least getting at the facts is laid by the efforts behind this monumental book and in the recent allocation of funds in the National Institute of Mental Health for research in the field of ethnic minorities. None of the references given here distinguishes systematically between children and adolescents; these groups are discussed in an intermingled fashion.

An overwhelming shift from institutional care to community-based services characterizes the mental health system, which is so complex that one can easily get lost. That would be particularly true for the adolescents with mental disorders, since their needs are frequently ignored despite efforts by some interdisciplinary professional groups to draw attention to them. Outpatient mental health services are usually provided through free-standing clinics and the Community Mental Health Clinics, established by federal legislation in 1963. The latter were designed to integrate the scattered mental health services, but instead they became just another branch along with the other major branches of psychiatric hospitals, private psychiatric services, and privately operated community shelters for patients discharged from psychiatric hospital care (Segal 1981).

The troika pattern of psychiatrist, psychologist, and psychiatric social worker, established as the prevailing treatment team in child guidance clinics since the early 1920s, still survives in present-day Community Mental Health Centers, where full-time social work positions outnumber those of the two other professions (Lecca 1983, p. 25). This may reflect greater acknowledgement of the role of the social environment in development and treatment of mental disturbances. The intricacies of the mental health service delivery system will not be further dealt with here; readers are referred to thorough accounts by Callicut and Lecca (1983), Compton (1983) and Segal (1981). However, a few adolescent "needles" found in the haystack of mental health literature will be presented as relevant to the current discussion.

A sub-task panel on mental health and infants, children, and adolescents concludes its report to the President's Commission on Mental Health (1978, p. 634) with the following dismal words:

> [The Nation's] mental health delivery system for adolescents is clearly woefully inadequate. There are far fewer appropriate facilities and adequately trained personnel for adolescents than for adults. Clinical training for working with adolescents has been seriously underemphasized. This problem is complicated by the fact that adolescents frequently require a broader range of services than do adults or younger children. Because they are developmentally in an in-between stage — neither emancipated adults nor dependent children — adolescents often require

a wider variety of services if treatment is to be effective. Too often, even when an adolescent has made entry into the mental health system and has been carefully evaluated, recommendations cannot be carried out because an appropriate facility or therapeutic service is not available or is already overloaded. So adolescents are simply "dumped" into adult facilities or otherwise inappropriate services.

The problem is further complicated by a lack of coordination between agencies at Federal, State, and local levels. Communication between welfare agencies, juvenile courts, and school is frequently lacking, with little or no planning for the young person's immediate and longer term needs.

A few positive innovations accounted for in the literature serve to counteract the negative conclusions just stated. Austin et al. (1981), for example, describe one mental health center's successful efforts in offering workshops to eighth-grade students in several high schools in order to expand their knowledge of mental health services, give them an opportunity to meet "real live shrinks," and otherwise demystify psychotherapeutic services. Kellam et al. (1981), in an epidemiological study of why teenagers come for treatment in community psychiatry clinics, conclude that influence by peers seems to be the most powerful factor in teenagers' seeking help. The severity of the behavior problems or level of distress did not seem to play any role. The nature of the presented problems of these 705 adolescents from an urban, black neighborhood ranged from substance abuse, psychiatric distress of various kinds, antisocial behavior, school and family problems, to adolescent developmental problems. The researchers conclude that teenagers are not likely to come for help on their own accord and that clinics need to take into account the positive influence peers have on help-seeking behavior; they also urge replication studies with different adolescent samples.

A Massachusetts adolescent treatment complex, consisting of a day program located in a state hospital, a "community living education aiding teens" (CLEAT) program of residential behavior modification, and a co-op program of clusters of apartments for adolescents who have mastered the basic living skills in the CLEAT program but still need some supervision is described by Walsh and Rosen (1979) as an integrated network of services for severely disturbed adolescents. A more recent illustration of cooperation between public schools and mental health agencies is presented by Freeman, Goldberg, and Sonnega (1983). This Michigan-based program of comprehensive educational and therapeutic services in a day treatment program serves emotionally impaired children and adolescents who formerly were "falling between the cracks" (p. 184). Three types of adolescents are served: the chronically psychotic group; those with fundamental learning problems who have been mismanaged and present secondary characteristics of anxiety, depression, or behavior disorders; and those adolescents with multiple problems, the "hard-core group that bedevils agencies" (p. 185). This last group seems to respond better to the small, self-contained day treatment center with no other children around so that these disturbed adolescents do not have to compete for attention in negative ways than they do to a conventional interdisciplinary service collaboration between schools and mental health systems. These day treatment centers are cofounded and jointly operated by the two systems.

The runaway phenomenon, escalating in the 1960s and 1970s, shows the collective powers of youth to jar legislators and human service providers into recognizing special needs and providing a new service branch. Traditional social service agencies have not served large numbers of runaways for two reasons. The runaways themselves generally do not know of the agencies' existence or they have been disinclined to seek help from "establishment" agencies, and the agencies themselves have often been reluctant to become involved with youngsters who are illegally away from home.

New and often underground services developed as the number of runaways grew during the 1960s; the dangers and victimizations to which many runaways are exposed became recognized, and the "normality" of running away gained acceptance. These services included runaway houses, storefront clinics, hot lines, crisis lines, and detention centers to remove runaways from the law enforcement system dealing with juvenile delinquents.

The passage of the Runaway Youth Act of 1974 legitimized many of these new services, which from then on have been referred to as alternative agencies. This act offers financial and technical assistance to local nonprofit agencies to develop services for runaways, such as housing, counseling, reunification with parents when possible, alternate living arrangements for youths who cannot return home, service networks to facilitate cooperation between runaway house personnel and law enforcement and other official agencies, and referral arrangements facilitating the runaway's access to vocational, medical, educational, and legal services.

Runaway youth centers, usually with colorful names, no doubt have played crucial roles in the lives of thousands of runaway youth and their families. Yet ultimately they apparently have served only a small percentage of youth on the run. For example, in the two large-scale studies reported by Brennan et al. (1978) and discussed in chapter 8, it was found that only 5 percent of the runaways studied turned to the runaway houses for assistance.

Moses (1978) in her analysis of "The Runaway Youth Act: Paradoxes of Reform" points to both positive and negative outcomes of the act (pp. 237–38). On the positive side, an unconventional form of helping — the runaway house — gained status and money. Runaways have been helped, and this movement has provided an example of successful handling of status offenders outside the traditional system. The act is a model of normalization by approaching adolescent problematic behavior as nondeviant. Among the negative outcomes, she mentions the freezing of a spontaneous community response into a "legitimized, federally funded network, leaving little room for flexibility" (p. 238) and the utilization of the runaway-house model appropriate in the 1960s to influence service patterns of the 1970s, although current runaway youth (in the opinion of their advocates) cannot be readily served by the runaway houses as they currently exist. Moses notes that standards "for intervention that reflect the wisdoms of the Runaway Youth Act but permit the inclusion of a broader class of youth [than runaways] need to be set" (p. 238).

Many private organizations have continued experimenting with innovative programs to meet the needs of runaways. Chase et al. (1979), for example, describe a Family Service Association based outreach program that comprehensively addresses the multiple needs of "throwaway" adolescents as an alternative to institutionalization. The program, which offers individual, family, and group counseling associated with summer day camps, socialization skills training, and vocational orientation, is low cost and attained the low recidivism rate of 20 percent of the teenagers served. Another example is the Teaching-Family model program, consisting of 100 group homes across the United States, organized by Boys Town (Maloney 1980). This program builds on the conviction that comprehensive services are needed to address the total situation and not just the isolated behaviors of either parents or the runaway adolescents. The life in the group homes emphasizes family-style living, self-government, structured motivational systems, and teaching of social survival skills.

Among the runaways a sizable group is in need of mental health services. The runaway centers' philosophy has been very strongly against labelling and application of the "medical model," but, as Gordon (1981) notes, "even to counselors steeped in nonconformity" many of the young people coming to runaway houses are "weird" or hopelessly depressed or confused. To meet the needs of those with emotional and mental disorders, strong ties between the runaway programs and the mental health system are urged (Edelbrock 1980). Even with the increase of mental health personnel in runaway centers and a gradual shift toward what was originally visualized as community mental health centers, questions remain about the ability of the centers to deal with seriously disturbed young people. Gordon (1981) suggests that the runaway centers should be considered as part of the community mental health system, as they are in fact "participants in and heirs to the tasks and aspirations of the community mental health center movement" (p. 199).

Other Community Based Public and Private Services

This chapter on educational and supportive services for adolescents living with their biological families would be incomplete without reference to the national network of family counseling agencies that constitute the membership of the Family Service Association of America, established in 1911. The counseling and other supportive services offered to families have much in common with those provided by child guidance clinics, the latter focusing on the child in his or her family and the Family Service agencies focusing on families with children at various ages. Examples of concern for the adolescent age group are the earlier mentioned works by Frances Scherz (1967 and 1971) and the Casebook on Family Treatment involving Adolescents (1967), which is but one illustration of the contributions to family theory and practice from this national association.

Numerous other organizations, such as the Boy and Girl Scouts of America, YMCA, and YWCA offer counseling and recreational services to teenagers. In many communities the Probation Department or other agency associated with juvenile delinquency prevention has operated Youth Service Bureaus, located in communities with high concentrations of adolescents. Two case vignettes illustrate the type of work carried out in Youth Service Bureaus.

Harry is a 15-year-old, black male who could easily pass for 18. He currently lives with his mother, who separated from his stepfather one year ago. At that time the family moved from a northern state to Southern California. Harry enjoys sports and usually spends a good deal of time playing in the park with his friends after school. He also spends considerable time with his girlfriend.

Harry was referred to the YBS by the police after he was caught with a wallet he allegedly had stolen from another boy. Since this was a first offense, he was referred for counseling and no petition was filed in Court.

His mother brought Harry to the office; she wanted him to receive counseling "to straighten him out," but she refused to engage herself in the process. Harry said that "he would do his time" and agreed to come back. He did not return, and only after the worker suggested they meet away from the office did he keep his appointments. The worker saw Harry in individual counseling for six months.

Harry had a major problem in relation to his mother with whom he was very angry and had frequent verbal fights. The marriage between his parents had been a stormy one; whenever it would erupt Harry was shipped off to relatives, and he was once placed in a group home from which he ran away several times. His goal in life at this point was to find a job, buy a car, and leave home.

The social worker centered on teaching Harry communication and problem-solving skills so that he could get along better with his mother, improve his school performance, and participate in an independent living skills program. Since he had supportive relations with his peers, no additional group activities were offered beyond the living skills program. He graduated from high school and moved away from home.

Sixteen-year-old Loretta came to the YSB office with the woman she is staying with after she ran away from home. She claims her parents are overly strict with her and have one set of rules for her and another set of rules for her two older brothers. Loretta has been babysitting for the woman she now stays with, but her parents do not know about her whereabouts. Both the woman and Loretta were concerned about the legal steps the parents might take; the woman is willing to let Loretta stay, provided no legal complications would ensue.

The worker got Loretta's permission to contact the parents without revealing where she is. It was learned that the parents do have different rules for their sons and the daughter. They have no problems with the boys who stay home and take care of their school work, while Loretta stays out until the early morning hours. The parents were willing to come to the office and have some joint counseling sessions with their daughter.

Loretta first agreed and later changed her mind, saying that she is happy where she is. Upon her refusal the parents revoked her driver's license and refused to sign papers that would enable her to attend school in the district in which she was now living. Loretta decided to wait to complete her schooling until she was old enough to be eligible for night school. She came to see the social worker for sporadic appointments; she felt proud of being able to support herself from babysitting for the woman she stayed with and others. Her angry feelings toward her family did not diminish, which was understandable in the light of the punitive actions they had taken against her. The social worker failed in all efforts to reestablish contact between this young woman and her family. As stated in previous and subsequent chapters, such "emotional cut-offs" usually simply mean postponement of dealing with painful issues that meanwhile are likely to impact the young woman's feelings about self and interpersonal relations.

In addition to the educational, health and mental health, and private services presented so far, a crucial agency within the public sector is the protective services, which are by law mandated to intervene in home situations judged dangerous to children and adolescents. When supportive services fail to improve the home situation sufficiently, the decision for out-of-home care is made. This decision-making process has been subject to much study and experimentation, alluded to throughout part II of this book. The latest review of the topic is presented by Stein and Rzepnicki (1984). The final decision regarding out-of-home placement, of course, rests with the judicial system, which also influences the lives of adolescents in other ways, as seen in the brief presentation to follow.

Adolescence and the Law

Children's need for protection and care in order to survive and develop has been used as justification for the almost total control parents have over their minor children. Voices in favor of acknowledgement of children's right to participate in decisions vitally affecting their lives are of recent date, first heard in the early 1960s. Children have been called the last minority to emerge in the human rights movement, and they differ from other minorities in that others have spoken their cause (Margolin 1978).

Though the children's rights movement gained momentum during the 1960s, several manifestos prior to this time have summarized the needs and rights of children and youth. For example, the 1930 White House Conference on Child Health and Protection adopted the Children's Charter, enumerating 19 rights of children. Similarly, the Declaration of the Rights of the Child, unanimously passed by the General Assembly of the United Nations in 1959, recognizes all children's needs for nutrition, housing, education, health and social services, the right to a nationality from birth, and the right of protection against exploitation and neglect. The 1970 White House Conference on Children affirmed these rights and added the right to a wholesome environment free from pollution. Common to all three statements is that they are of a general philosophical nature and not assertions of definitive personal, enforceable rights. At best they are lofty goals for public and private child and family welfare policies throughout the world.

A special Bill of Rights for Foster Children, signed in Congress Hall, Philadelphia, in 1973 expands the 1930 Children's Charter to include special safeguards, resources, and care to meet the needs of foster children. Again the ten articles of the document are desirable aims that are only partially realized (*Social Service Review* 1973).

Finally, as stated earlier in this chapter, the rights of all handicapped children to equal and full access to educational programs were established in the federal Education for all Handicapped Children Act of 1975.

Konopka notes that even though the Bill of Rights of the Constitution of the United States nowhere exempts certain groups from it, many violations of the constitutional rights of children and youth are tolerated (Konopka 1976a, p. 180). However, several U.S. Supreme Court decisions have affirmed children's rights. For example, procedural protections for juveniles were affirmed in *Gault* (87 U.S. 1428, 1967), and *Goss* v. *Lopez* (419 U.S. 565, 1975) holds that a high school student has a due process right to an informal hearing before being suspended for up to ten days (suspensions of longer duration are protected by earlier decisions). However, court decisions do not always affirm the rights of children and youth. A notable withholding of a constitutional right to be heard is found in *Ingraham* vs. *Wright* (430 U.S. 651, 672, 1977), which held that paddling so severe that a doctor kept a student out of school for eleven days does not violate the Eighth Amendment stipulations against "cruel and unusual punishment" and that notice and informal hearings are not necessary before punishment is inflicted.

What are some common arguments against expanding the rights of children and youth? Patricia Wald (1976) in her excellent analysis, "Making Sense Out of the Rights of Youth," mentions three arguments. First is the "immaturity" argument, that children are not capable of making rational judgments. She agrees this may be true of the very young child, but children today mature earlier than previous generations, and even a very young child's interests related to critical decisions in his or her life deserve representation by an independent advocate before a neutral decision maker. A second argument is that expanding children's autonomy will undermine parental authority to the extent of eroding family cohesiveness to the detriment of the child. Wald argues that a strong family unit probably already gives freedom to the child; it is in the borderline high-risk family that children most likely need an affirmation of their basic rights. The final justification advanced in favor of keeping "parental authority over children intact is to protect the child from his own excesses and from exploitation by unconscionable adults" (p. 384). Pat Wald advocates striking a balance between absolute freedom for children of all ages and society's right to set a minimal age for young persons' rights to make extremely serious decisions affecting their lives, such as marriage, drug use, sterilization, and running away to live without any adult supervision.

A general principle of children's rights, advocated by Wald and others, is that children have the same rights as adults "unless there is a significant risk of irreversible damage from exercising such rights or a general consensus backed by empirical data that at a certain age youth do not possess sufficiently developed physical or emotional (mental) skills to allow them to exercise those rights" (p. 389). A similar stance is taken by Franklin E. Zimring (1982) in his analysis of the changing legal world of adolescence. He describes adolescence as a "learner's permit" to demonstrate growing capacity to master adult tasks, and he promotes the idea of a jurisprudence of semi-autonomy for adolescents. He advocates a legal system that recognizes the freedom to make mistakes and insures the adolescents against damage from harmful decisions they have made.

Although parents' rights and responsibilities vary from state to state, certain basic rights and duties are intrinsic to our American culture. Parents have the right to care, custody, and control of their minor children and to their children's earnings. They have the right to administer reasonable disciplinary measures and to make major decisions in regard to health care, extent and type of education, child's marriage, enlistment in the armed forces, adoption, and religious affiliation and to represent the child in legal actions. The corresponding responsibilities include support and protection of the child and provision of food, clothing, shelter, training, education, and medical care. Courts can limit parental rights and responsibilities by giving legal custody to another person or to a social agency. While this deprives the parents of most of the rights elaborated above, they still retain the right to decide about major medical care, marriage, adoption, enlistment, and religious affiliation. A further limitation of parental rights occurs when guardianship of the person is awarded by a court to another person. In this instance the parent retains right to reasonable visitation, determination of religious affiliation and consent to adoption and retains the responsibility for support of the child. Finally, parental rights can be completely terminated by a court. For further detail regarding legal issues related to parent-child relations, abuse, and neglect, see, Caulfield (1978); Fitzgerald (1978); Knitzer (1982a); Ruback (1984); and Wald, P.M. (1976). The reader is referred to Benedek's (1979) discussion of the law as it relates to adolescent females, to Porter (1984) on juvenile law, and to Hoffman's (1976) discussion of consent and confidentiality in adolescent medicine. Finally, the following books cover several aspects of law and adolescence: Brieland and Lemmon (1977); Gottesman (1981); and Rosenheim (1976).

Notes

1. A presentation of the ramifications of PL 96-272 for adolescents and their families goes beyond the scope of this book. For discussions of this federal legislation and its impact on child welfare services, see reviews by Maluccio and Sinanoglu (1981); Maluccio and Fein (1983); McGowan and Meezan (1983); and Waldinger (1982).
2. For a legal analysis of litigation achievements and statutory implementation, see Roberta S. Stick (1984) in Woodey, R.H. et al. *The Law and the Practice of Human Services.*
3. Fisher has compiled more than 2 thousand articles of relevance to school social work into a major bibliography with supplements. Randy A. Fisher, *School Social Work in the Literature: A Bibliography,* and *Update to School Social Work in the Literature: A Bibliography,* Washington, D.C.: National Association of Social Workers, 1977, 1978, 1979, and 1981.
4. Bell, Ca.A.; Casto, G.; and Daniels, D.C. 1983. "Ameliorating the Impact of Teen-Age Pregnancy on Parent and Child." *Child Welfare* 62(2): 167–173.

   Cain, L. 1979. "Social Worker's Role in Teenage Abortions." *Social Work* 24(1): 52–56.

   Cartoff, V.G. 1978. "Postpartum Services for Adolescent Mothers." *Child Welfare* 57(10): 667–674.

   Horowitz, N.H. 1978. "Adolescent Mourning Reaction to Infant And Fetal Loss." *Social Casework* 59(9): 551–559.

McAnarney, E.R., et al. 1978. "Obstetric, Neonatal, and Psychosocial Outcome of Pregnant Adolescents." *Pediatrics* 61(2): 199–205.

Mudd, E.H., et al., 1978. "Adolescent Health Services and Contraceptive Use." *American Journal of Orthopsychiatry* 48(3): 495–504.

Scales, P. 1979. "The Context of Sex Education And The Reduction of Teenage Pregnancy." *Child Welfare* 57(4): 263–273.

Vadies, E., and Hale, D. 1977. "Attitudes Of Adolescent Males Toward Abortion, Contraception, and Sexuality." *Social Work In Health Care* 3(2): 169–174.

5. Gould et al., whose studies the Select Panel refers to, note in a later publication (1981, p. 462) that conservatively the "overall rate of clinical maladjustment in the United States is probably no lower than 11.8%." They base their estimate on prevalence of clinical maladjustment in 25 U.S. studies conducted between 1928 and 1975, and they underscore the difficulty in making estimates because of variations in definitions of psychiatric disorders, the nature of the samples, and variations in who provided the assessment, since parents and teachers are known to select different children as maladjusted. However, the higher the social class of the parent, the higher the agreement between parent and teacher judgments. The Gould report indicates differences according to age, social class, ethnicity, family factors, and geographic region. However, the information is too scarce to be reliable for these variables. The majority of findings showed a higher rate of maladjustment for males than females.

6 OUT-OF-HOME
CARE FOR
ADOLESCENTS

For the families who are not able to utilize the preventive and supportive services presented in the previous chapter to avert placement of the adolescent or to whom such services have not been made available, placement in out-of-home care is another option. Other adolescents have been long-time users of such care facilities. This chapter opens with a review of how many adolescents are in what types of out-of-home care, and it lists pathways to placement in adolescence. Next follows a discussion of three types of facilities: foster family care, community group homes, and residential/institutional care, with emphasis on the first type of care. For almost all of the adolescents in these facilities, efforts are made to maintain contact with the natural family, and a separate section is devoted to the important topic of parental involvement and its consequences. Adolescents who have long been part of the adoption scene and those who enter it during the teen years after severance of the legal parent-child relationship are discussed in the last section of the chapter. The characteristics, philosophies, and policies of these service systems are fully described in many other sources, referred to in this book; the literature has been used selectively as it sheds light on the experiences of adolescents and their families.

Of the close to 1.8 million children served by public agencies in 41 states in the first quarter of 1977, 28 percent (502,000) were in out-of-home care facilities. Table 6-1 provides the distribution of all children in four types of foster care facilities. As expected, the overwhelming majority of these children (79 percent) were in foster family care and the remainder were in some form of institutional group care. Foster family care is the only out-of-home service in which there is an almost even distribution of adolescents and preadolescents; in the three other categories, the adolescents far outnumber the preadolescents.

With respect to ethnic background, the Shyne and Schroeder survey (1978) found that black children were overrepresented in foster family care and underrepresented in group homes and residential settings. Hispanic youngsters were underrepresented in foster family homes and overrepresented in group homes and residential centers. All ethnic groups were uniformly represented in institutions other than residential centers, in which white children were overrepresented.

Articles by Stheno (1982) and Mech (1983) elaborate on the dramatically different placement patterns of minority youth versus white youths in out-of-home care. Based on data gathered on behalf of the Office for Civil Rights in 1980 from 2,400 public agencies about all children for whom the agencies had legal custody, supervisory, or review status, Mech (1983) reports that the national placement rate was 4 per 1,000 children under 19 years of age. Black children had the highest rate of all — 9.5 per 1,000 — followed by the rate for American Indian children — 8.8 per 1,000. The rate for Hispanic children was 3.0, for Asians 2.0, and for white children 3.1 per 1,000.

None of the statistics reported here provides a breakdown according to preadolescent and adolescent ages; therefore it is not known if the same ethnic variation holds up across age groups with respect to out-of-home placements. Hopefully these Civil Rights data will stimulate advocacy groups, planners, and researchers to take a close look at reasons for these highly discrepant placement rates and follow through with policy changes where rates do not reflect conscious choices by the various population groups.

Variations among families placing adolescents in out-of-home care are also found in regard to family composition, maturational history of the adolescent, and the nature of family interrelationships. Malin (1981), for example, identified two distinguishable groups of families — long pathway (LPW) and short pathway (SPW) families — among the 45 requests by middle-class parents for placement of an adolescent in residential treatment care. In long pathway families, early crises and health problems during the first year of the child's life had generated patterns of mutually dissatisfactory and abusive relationships. The school careers of the LPW children were

Table 6–1. Type of Substitute Care by Age of Child During First Quarter of 1977

Type of Facility	Total	Age of Child (N = 502,000)			
		1–10 years	11–14 years	15–17 years	Total
Foster Family Home	395,000 (79%)	205,400 (52%)	114,550 (29%)	75,050 (19%)	(100%)
Group Home	35,000 (7)	5,600 (16)	14,700 (42)	14,670 (42)	(100)
Residential Treatment	29,000 (6)	5,510 (19)	11,600 (40)	11,890 (41)	(100)
Other Child-Caring Institutions[a]	43,000 (8)	7,740 (18)	17,200 (40)	18,060 (42)	(100)
Total	502,000 (100%)	224,250	158,050	119,700	

This table has been derived from Table 5–1 and the table on page 110 of Shyne, A.W., and Schroeder, A.G., *National Study of Social Services to Children and Their Families*, Prepared for National Center for Child Advocacy, U.S. Children's Bureau, Adm. for Children, Youth and Families, Office of Human Development Services, U.S. Dept. of Health, Education, and Welfare, Washington, D.C. 1978.

Because of rounding of percentages in the original tables, the computed numbers of children and youth in placement should be considered estimates only.

[a]These institutions included those serving mentally retarded, delinquent, and neglected children and youth; maternity homes and diagnostic centers were not included in this table.

also problematic in that 90 percent of them were expelled because of behavioral problems during kindergarten and preschool. In the short pathway families the children had few serious problems during the preadolescent years, but the parents were unprepared for the adolescent's reactions during the teen years, combined with stresses of separation, divorce, and remarriage about the time the youngster entered adolescence. Nine of the 25 SPW adolescents in placement were adopted. Further characteristics and backgrounds of adolescents in out-of-home care will be presented in subsequent sections.

Adolescents in Foster Family Care

Foster family care is not generally considered the out-of-home facility of choice for adolescents. The obvious reason for this is that the psychological task of adolescence to achieve emotional independence from parents and other adults is in clear conflict with asking the adolescent to move into a foster family and establish relations with a new set of parents. The rationale for doing so is the expectation that the nurturant and caring environment supposed to be offered by the foster family will promote age-appropriate behavior in spite of the adolescent's impaired relations with his or her own birth parents.

As seen from table 6–1, almost half of the survey sample of close to 400,000 children in substitute care in 41 states were between 11 and 17 years of age. The 11- to 14-year-olds accounted for 29 percent, and the 15- to 17-year-olds for 19 percent of the total foster care population. The frequency with which foster care is used as a resource for adolescents is somewhat surprising. Furthermore, a later survey of teenagers in foster care in Maine (Hornby and Collins 1981) shows that the proportion of teenagers of the total foster care population is growing in that state; it increased from 46 percent of all children in care in 1960 to 56 percent in 1980.

One explanation for the growth of the adolescent foster care population is that many children enter care in their preadolescent years and simply remain in what is supposed to be temporary care for years; almost one-fourth of the Shyne and Schroeder (1978, pp. 118–19) survey population had been in foster care for over six years. Similarly, 27 percent of the Maine teenagers in foster care had been in their current placement for more than five years.

However, as new permanency planning practices become generally accepted and succeed in moving younger children out of the system more rapidly, a drop in the adolescent foster care population should be expected in the coming years. It also seems likely that these "residual" adolescent foster children for whom permanency planning does not work might be the ones suffering from more severe behavior problems or physical/emotional handicaps. Part of the increase in the adolescent foster care population is linked with the growing number of teenagers entering care for the first time. In Maine and New York 22 percent of all children entering care were 13 years old or older. This is considered, in part, to be a result of the juvenile courts' attempts to divert adolescents from the criminal justice system (Hornby and Collins 1981, p. 11).

Teenagers in foster care, regardless of whether they are newcomers to the system or not, commonly experience multiple placements. In the Maine study, 10 percent of those 13 years old or older had ten or more placements and 19 percent had between six and ten placements (Hornby and Collins 1981, p. 13). In a New York study it was likewise found that the 13- to 15-year-old foster children, discharged from foster care, had a recidivism rate way above all other age groups, regardless of other family and child characteristics, namely, 43.6 percent compared with 22.6 percent for the 10- to 12-year-olds (Block 1981, pp. 603, 609).

As established in numerous studies (summarized by Davis 1979, pp. 53–55), the major reason for placement of both younger and older children is parental behavior (neglect, physical and sexual abuse, mental illness, and alcohol and drug addiction); still, many more older children enter care because of their own behavioral problems than do the preadolescents. For example, more than half of the teenagers entering care in Maine are characterized as acting out (runaways, truants, and so forth) and more than a quarter as delinquent. They also experience moderate emotional illness and alcohol and drug abuse more frequently than the younger foster children (Hornby and Collins 1981, p. 12).

Considering the range of deprivations and problems experienced by children in foster care, it seems essential that this service have a dual purpose of providing family life experiences that promote healthy adolescent development and of resolving or ameliorating problems that are personally or socially destructive (CWLA 1975, p. 8).

The changes associated with healthy adolescent development in relation to parents and peers, occupational choice, shaping of a personal value system, and appropriate sexual role behavior culminate in the achievement of that feeling of identity — the sense of knowing where one is going — that comes about through fusion of "constitutional givens, idiosyncratic libidinal needs, favored capacities, significant identifications, effective defenses, successful sublimations, and consistent roles" (Erikson 1975, p. 190).

For most foster children, this bridging what one was as a child with what one is to become that Erikson suggests leads to the desired sense of inner continuity and social sameness means dealing with anger and resentment over past parental rejection and separation and with conflicts of loyalty between the often idealized natural parents and the foster parents. Rarely has the adolescent in placement experienced consistent and appropriate need fulfillment prior to placement and been exposed to parental value systems from which the adolescent can model and develop his own ideology and decision-making capacities. The foster child's "invisible baggage" from the past often includes deep needs to avenge old hurts and vent old angers (Paull 1956, p. 22) or it has led to lack of trust and low expectations of relationships with adults "juxtaposed with a continuing search for a need-fulfilling relationship of the early infant-mother type" (Stein and Derdeyn 1980, p. 91ff). Many adolescents in foster care exhibit problems and needs like these; they obviously represent quite different challenges than those adolescents who have been placed in foster care primarily because of a family crisis and whose preadolescent development has not been marred by multiple separations, rejections, neglect, and abuse.

The demands placed on the foster family by foster adolescents who have been exposed to abuse are many and severe, and the extent to which the foster parents are able to meet the challenge and respond positively to the adolescent's past and accept the importance of even the abusive natural parents to him or her has an impact on the successful outcome of the foster adolescent's development of an adequate sense of identity and feeling of self-worth. In deriving a sense of continuity by linking the past with the future, children in foster care are also at a disadvantage in that "neither his foster parents, his social worker, nor any other responsible adult in his present experience expects to be a continuing part of his life in the future" (MacIntyre 1970, p. 215). Rarely do these professional relationships last beyond the teenager's 18th birthday; yet the impact of foster parents and social workers may be powerful in helping or hindering the adolescent's strivings to cope with past and present events, particularly in the relationship with the natural parents. Two vignettes from Walker's (1971) study of the relation between foster mothers' level of maturity and foster children's behavior vividly demonstrate this point. One type of foster mother has a dogmatic and controlling stance and considers it unimportant to discuss with the child any feelings the child may harbor about the natural parents. One such mother gives the following account of her handling of her foster children (Walker 1971, p. 239):

> Now you take Juanita; she wasn't a bad kid until she got older — you know, a teenager. Didn't she think she had all the answers then! But I let her know who was boss. I cracked her a few times. Then she shut up. If there is one thing I can't stand it's a kid who talks back. Now you take my Tommy; I've had him since he was two. He keeps his mouth shut, does what he's told. You know you can mold

kids if you get them young enough. That's what I like. I got Juanita too late. Now there's hell to pay. But she ain't going to run me. You can bet your bottom dollar on that. If she doesn't shape up she knows she's had it. I'll ask the agency to find her another place. Trouble with our country today is there are too many lippy kids running around. I had a kid sister that I had to watch when my folks went away. She got smart — wouldn't do what I told her to do when the folks were gone. I cracked her one in the mouth — told her to shut her mouth or else. She got the message. We had our troubles then, but now we get along like two peas in a pod. And that's the way it is with Tommy and me. If the agency had ten more like him, I'd take 'em.[1]

Another type of foster mother recognizes the emotional needs underlying the child's behavior, is not threatened by aggression, and understands the importance of the emotional ties with the natural parents. One such mother states (Walker 1971, pp. 240–41):

That night Mary's father called. He had been drinking and he promised her he was going to take her back with him. The next day Mary found out that he took off for Florida. She had to take it out on something or someone. I used to have a favorite tea pot (laughs). Well, while she was screaming how she hated us all she got a hold of it and whammo! But she had to do it, I knew that she had to get the poison out. She went outside and sat by the brook, all sullen. I let her stay out there because I knew she needed time to think things through. After a while I went out and she looked so lonely. I put my arms around her and told her I knew how hurt and disappointed she was and she cried for the first time. I felt so bad for her. She still gets kind of moody once in a while and I know she's thinking about her father and her brothers and sisters. When she's like that I just kind of make myself available and usually she'll tell me about how she feels. . . . She's mad at her dad but cares about him too. She was so happy when I invited him to stay for dinner last week.[1]

In the Walker study 14 children placed with the first kind of foster mother tended to be passive and submissive, which is to be expected since these foster mothers would ask the agency to remove aggressive foster children and since controlling parent behavior tends to reinforce inhibition in children. The children placed with the second type foster mother were able to vent their anger toward their natural parents, to be aggressive in their interpersonal relationships, and they were more invested in family activities and school achievements.

Insight into some of the abuse and hazards that also can be part of the experience of adolescents in foster care is found in the Hornby and Collins study in Maine, in which in-depth interviews were held with 12 of the 500 foster children in the total study sample. Here is what some of them said.

One 16-year-old, raped by her foster father said, "I could never understand why they were foster parents. All the state would have to do is go to the place and they'd know. The atmosphere was just terrible." Another, "I did pretty good until this girl moved in who was on pot. I started smoking and drinking with her. We'd come home late, get in trouble. I tried suicide and they put me in a mental ward." Still a third, "It was like I had an extra nose or something. I'm different. I just didn't like the idea that all of a sudden they could move me around as if I was just a checker on a board." (Hornby and Collins 1981, p. 18)[2]

Associations between the varied foster parent motivations and parenting abilities and the reactions and behaviors of foster children have been confirmed by several other studies, for example, Fanshel (1966), Hampson and Tavormina (1980), Kraus (1971), and Wiehe (1982). Many of these study findings have implications for foster parent selection and training and for the procedures for matching the needs of specific adolescents with parenting abilities of specific foster parents.

Within the last 10–15 years many communities have recognized the need for foster homes especially designed for adolescents, with foster parents who have received training in dealing with teenagers and knowledge about adolescent psychological development. These incentive foster homes usually serve as alternatives to institutional care for youngsters who have had multiple placements in regular foster homes and whose current behaviors preclude them from another placement in a traditional foster home. Incentive homes are also often used for adolescents who return to the community after placement in residential or other institutional care or group homes. The goals for them are usually not reunification with birth families but care until the teenagers reach the age of majority.

To give an impression of the broad range of problems and general instability of family backgrounds of many adolescents in foster care, a few brief case resumes are presented here. The first two are taken from the New York study of adolescents entering emergency foster care (Citizen's Committee 1980, p. 35), and the remainder are from Southern California child welfare agency caseloads.

Billy H. was first referred to the then Bureau of Child Welfare in 1966 by the hospital in which he was born, suffering from a condition which in recent years has come to be diagnosed as "fetal alcohol syndrome." He has spent his entire life in and out of foster care, going home to his mother and returning each time by reason of abuse or neglect. He was admitted this time in February 1979 on court remand on a neglect petition. Shortly thereafter there was a finding of abuse. Billy is now 14 but looks younger than his years and functions much as a seven-year-old. This time the plan is for Billy to remain in care until he can be discharged to his own responsibility.

Charles N. was born in jail where his mother was serving a sentence for prostitution and drug-related charges. He lived in the nursery of the jail for 11 months.

His mother was permitted to visit him twice a day except when she was in solitary confinement — "which was most of the time". When he was 18 months old he went to live with his mother upon her release. In 1976, at the age of 13, Charles was placed because of his mother's psychiatric hospitalization. He returned to his mother after 10 months in care, and remained with her for two years. He came back into care in February 1979 because of conflict with his mother's paramour. He is still in care.

Sue, a 16-year-old Philipino girl had been living with her mother, stepfather, and three younger half siblings since arrival in the United States two years earlier. Shortly after the family settled in the U.S. the stepfather sexually abused Sue who was then placed in a foster home. She showed severe social adjustment problems in school and in the foster home.

Doris, a twelve-year-old black girl was living in a rural foster home. She became increasingly injury prone, was unable to pay attention in school, screamed obscenities at the teacher and was very withdrawn in the foster home. Doris' parents were divorced; the mother suffering from mental illness and the father's whereabouts unknown. As her condition deteriorated it became necessary to transfer her to a twenty-four hour school.

Nancy, a 16-year-old Caucasian girl with cerebral palsy is permanently confined to a wheelchair. She was relinquished for adoption at an early age, but the adoptive parents could not cope with her disability. Nancy was then placed in a foster home where she has made a good adjustment in spite of the just mentioned experiences. She is a very bright, witty young woman who is doing well in the school, where she is the only handicapped person. Her biological mother has recently made inquiries about her, and a reunion with the mother is considered whereas reunification does not seem a realistic alternative.

"Long term" foster care was arranged for three Hispanic adolescent siblings, ages 17, 12 and 11, of whom the older was a girl and the two younger were boys. These children have been in foster care for more than 7 years with many complications related to the frequent appearances and disappearances of the biological parents who were migrant farm workers. They promised reunification several times but with no follow-through. The older girl has reacted strongly to the broken promises and the foster mother needs considerable support from the caseworker to cope with the girls' adolescent maturational problems.

Andrew, a 15-year-old Caucasian boy was placed in incentive foster care because of a very withdrawn, depressed behavior and numerous run-away episodes. His parents were divorced when he was six years old; he lived for a while with his mother and two older siblings. His father remarried and had two younger children in that marriage. The mother became a student and held various jobs for brief periods of time; she was often evicted from the apartments she rented and lived most of the time with her three children in a van, parked close to public toilet facilities. After neglect charges were filed, Andrew, by court order, lived with his father and stepmother for several months; his mother obstructed this placement, and Andrew kept on returning to her. He was doing very poorly in school in spite of good intelligence. Psychiatric examination revealed severe depressive reaction, and placement in a receiving home was recommended until an incentive foster home could be located. The natural mother refused to engage in needed psychiatric care for herself, and the father was unable to take care of Andrew under his new family circumstances. Andrew's two older siblings had become addicted to drugs and they had on several occasions attempted to pressure Andrew to experiment with drugs as well.

Andrew agreed to the foster home placement and to weekly psychiatric counseling. After six months' stay in the foster home his grades in school began improving.

What are the long-term outlooks for adolescents who have spent part or all of their teen years in foster family homes? Empirical studies have not yet provided full answers. Two carefully designed follow-up studies, Fanshel and Shinn's (1978) study of foster children in New York and the Oregon Permanency Planning Project (Lahti et al. 1978) both were limited to children 12 years of age and younger when entering care. At follow-up some of the children were in their teens, but the findings cannot be applied to those who enter care in adolescence. Some major findings from the Fanshel and Shinn study are that between 25 and 33 percent of the 624 foster children who were followed over a five-year period showed signs of emotional impairment and that the children who remained in care did not score lower than the children who returned home with respect to school performance and emotional adjustment. Overall 52 percent of the total group performed below age levels in school, and 11 percent of them were from two to seven years behind. Such an educational deficit naturally carries over to adolescent performance. Zimmerman (1982) in her follow-up interviews with 61 young adults who entered foster care in New Orleans between 1951 and 1969 and had spent at least one year in a foster home without being placed in adoption found that long-term foster care was not in itself injurious to these young adults, of whom only 3 percent entered care at 12 years of age or later. Sixty-nine percent were discharged at age 12 or later. Those who were older at discharge and who had been in care longer fared better in adult social functioning (parenting, self-support, and adherence to the law) than did those who returned home or stayed in care a shorter time. Educational achievement was crucial to adequate adult functioning, but the overall school dropout rate was 56 percent, which Zimmerman calls an indictment of the school system, the families, and the foster care agencies involved (p. 107). These findings are not generalizable to all foster care populations since the sample was not randomly selected but was limited to those who could be located and agreed to be interviewed. The study is also limited in that some measures of necessity relied on recall data.

The finding of educational deficit as a hazard of growing up in foster care gains further support in a later follow-up study of former foster children in New York by Trudy Festinger (1983). Interviews were held with 277 young adults of whom 94 percent entered care before age 12 or younger. They all "aged" out of the system with 34 percent leaving at age 18, about 20 percent at age 21, and the rest in the years in between. In most respects these young people turned out to be more alike than different from their age cohorts in the general population with the exception of educational achievement. Festinger suggests some likely reasons for their scholastic lag to be lowered expectations by foster parents, school and agency personnel of foster children in general; failure to accurately assess the children's potential; and failure to identify and deal with learning deficits and disabilities at an early time. The overwhelming majority (98.2 percent) of this study sample were discharged to their own responsibility; many of them felt ill prepared to establish independent living patterns.

Adolescents in Community Group Residences

Parallel to the development of special incentive foster family homes for adolescents, other alternative residential services have been created in the form of neighborhood group homes, runaway houses accommodating small numbers of adolescents, and temporary shelters combined with educational services and training in homemaking and other independent living skills. In most of these alternative foster care arrangements, the foster parents (or *houseparents* as they are sometimes called) usually play a greater role on the foster care team than has been the case in traditional foster care.

In their survey of group care in various geographical areas of the United States and Canada, Mayer et al. (1978) note that the old distinction between foster care, residential treatment centers, and institutions for dependent and disturbed children no longer holds. They suggest as new working definitions of group care the two categories of *group homes* and *institutions.* The first category consists of homes of different sizes located in residential areas. These include family group homes, owned by an agency, in which foster parents take care of 4 to 6 children; peer group homes, in which child-care staff take care of 5 to 10 children; and group residences with a capacity of serving 10 to 15 children where group interaction is the main form of socialization. The institutions (further discussed in the next section) also cover three different types according to the number of children served and the extent of therapeutic services offered.

Sister Mary Paul Janchill (1983) lists seven types of adolescents who are appropriately placed in group residences: adolescents needing professional

relations with adults rather than with parents because they have had disabling struggles of emancipation with their own parents or foster parents; adolescents returning from institutionalized care; youngsters from homes with
acute intergenerational conflicts stemming from restrictive religious practices or cultural backgrounds; adolescents with psychological impairment
requiring a therapeutic milieu that also affords contact with schools, other
community social systems, and relatives; drug and alcohol abusers or
repeated runaways, who may profit from positive peer pressures and individualized services; youngsters with repeated failures in family foster
homes; and those who are planning for independent living. Sister Janchill
gives a detailed description of one treatment-oriented group residence for 20
adolescent girls with emotional or psychological disturbances.

Other examples of group homes are offered by Gordon (1976); Maloney
et al. (1977); Richter (1977); Rosen et al. (1980); Shostack (1978), Taylor et
al. (1976), and Wilgus and Epstein (1978). Kadushin (1980) also discusses
group homes as one form of foster care (pp. 399–42). Some of the community
group homes are designed to avert predelinquent and delinquent youth from
the formal juvenile justice system. These group homes, often combined with
occupational guidance and training programs, have been sponsored to a
large extent by funding from the Federal Law Enforcement Assistance Administration (LEAA). Other encouraging community-based programs were
sponsored and stimulated by the Juvenile Justice and Delinquency Prevention Act of 1974. Some of these programs have provided evidence of lower
recidivism rates when compared with control groups. However, it is a
general impression that alternative, community-based programs, centers,
and homes for juvenile delinquents have not made sufficient progress in
preventing juvenile crime to stem the tide of the opposing "get-tough"
trend, which demands incarceration for the dual purpose of protecting the
citizenry by removing juvenile offenders from the street and of deterring
future crime. This question will be briefly discussed in the next section.

Adolescents in Institutions

The final type of out-of-home care for adolescents to be addressed in this
chapter is residential or institutional care, which serves a broad range of
youngsters from dependent, neglected children to delinquent or emotionally
disturbed children whose needs cannot be met in a family setting. The upcoming second *National Survey of Residential Group Care Facilities for
Children and Youth* by Donnell M. Pappenfort and Thomas M. Young
(Dore, Young, and Pappenfort 1984) distinguishes among five kinds of

residential care according to the type of children and youth served: child welfare (serving the dependent, neglected or abused), mental health, care of pregnant adolescents, juvenile justice, and substance-abuse facilities. Preliminary findings show that, in comparison with the data from the first national survey in 1966, the number of child welfare facilities in 1981 dropped from 55 to 37 percent of all facilities, while mental health facilities increased substantially from 12 to 25 percent and juvenile justice facilities from 25 to 34 percent. Institutions for pregnant adolescents accounted for 2 percent of residential facilities in both survey years. The 1981 figures include 83 institutions for treatment of drug abusing adolescents; the 1966 survey did not include such institutions as a separate category. In spite of an overall doubling of residential care facilities from 1965 to 1981, the number of beds remained about the same. This reflects a trend away from large institutions to smaller facilities.

Information from the 1981 survey about the children and adolescents occupying these facilities is not yet available. The 1977 data presented in table 6-1, show that adolescents far outnumber preadolescents in residential care (81 percent versus 19 percent) and in other institutional care (82 percent versus 18 percent). The remainder of this section focuses on residential treatment centers, psychiatric hospitals, and correctional institutions.

Residential treatment centers and psychiatric hospital units for adolescents differ in that residential treatment centers are usually under social work administration, direction, and practice and often offer services that meet all the youngster's needs, including educational, recreational, and therapeutic needs. The psychiatric inpatient units, on the other hand, are under medical/psychiatric administration and direction. In these programs schooling is often an incidental part of the program, and a large part of the day may be spent in various therapy activities and group sessions. The adolescents served tend to be more severely disturbed with extreme behavioral symptoms, often representing threats with respect to homicide and suicide (Day 1973; CWLA Standards 1982).

Lordi (1979), in comparing hospital and residential treatment of adolescents, notes that residential centers are indicated when socialization, education, and development of alternative adaptive patterns are called for; these centers are less medical than hospitals but more therapeutic than boarding schools. Hospitalization is indicated when an acute crisis endangers the adolescent or the family, when the adolescent cannot function socially, when no community resources are available, and when other, less restrictive approaches have been tried unsuccessfully. Lordi also distinguished between acute hospitalization to deal with crises and intermediate-length care of 9 to 24 months' duration for those adolescents whose previous remissions have not lasted but who have demonstrated ability to take charge of their lives and can achieve structural change given the intensive treatment program of the hospital. Various kinds of individual and group therapies are offered the adolescent patients and parents are seen concurrently in ongoing therapy, which is expanded to conjoint therapy with the adolescent when that is feasible. Outpatient care is frequently offered after discharge.

All forms of residential care are extremely expensive, and while the need for aftercare is recognized in order to maintain gains obtained during institutionalization, such services are scarce. The national study of residential care by Mayer, Richman, and Balcerzak (1978) confirmed that most group care agencies have some form of aftercare, but it is rarely effective and adequate. The quality of aftercare, they say, depends on the availability of a broad range of facilities, such as school, recreational programs, peer group possibilities, family interaction, community support, and receptivity to the returning youngster. Beyond the availability of services, active and significant work on the part of the discharge worker or team is essential in coordinating and activating all factors in the process. The principles of continuity of care and a spectrum of interconnected services are essential, as spelled out by these researchers and by Maluccio and Sinanoglu (1981) and Whittaker (1979). Unfortunately the economic situation of adolescents in residential care (whether in centers or hospitals) has a strong impact on the timing and appropriateness of discharge. For those who are not entitled to third-party payments or whose parents are not able to pay for continued care, emancipation is not determined by the youngster's ability and readiness for independent living. In many communities public funding stops automatically at age 18; only those who are clearly a danger to self or their surroundings or clearly incapable of self-care remain in psychiatric hospitals or are transferred to board and care facilities about which little is known and written.

Quite a number of follow-up studies have been carried out on residential and hospital treatment of emotional and behavioral problems. Fineberg, Sowards, and Kettlewell (1980) reviewed such studies and concluded that most of those studied showed a success rate of two-thirds to three-fourths at follow-up compared to problems experienced at admission. Their own study (1982) of 105 adolescent patients discharged from a short-term inpatient program showed significant reduction in severity of psychiatric symptoms from admission to discharge as assessed by the patients themselves and their parents. These reductions were maintained at six-week and six-month follow-ups. The major outcome studies of psychiatric hospitalization of adolescents carried out by the Timberlawn research team in Texas (Gossett, Lewis, and Barnhart 1983) also showed that about 65–70 percent of an original group of admitted adolescents showed substantial benefits at five-year follow-up; th benefits were exemplified in markedly improved family and peer relations, "more successful educational and vocational functioning, reduced symptomatic status, and much greater subjective contentment" (p. 83). Almost all of these youngsters had failed in treatment in other inpatient treatment and/or outpatient treatment prior to the hospitalization in question.

For a multifaceted discussion of institutional care for children and adolescents, see *Child Caring: Social Policy and the Institution,* edited by Pappenfort, Kilpatrick, and Roberts (1973). And the following books give numerous case illustrations and treatment considerations regarding adolescents in residential treatment or hospital care: Davids (1974) *Children in Conflict: A Casebook;* French and Berlin (1979) *Depression in Children and Adolescents;* Masterson (1972) *Treatment of the Borderline Adolescent: A Developmental Approach;* Offer, Marohn, and Ostrov (1979) *The Psychological World of the Juvenile Delinquent;* Rinsley (1980) *Treatment of the Severely Disturbed Adolescent;* and Weiner (1982) *Child and Adolescent Psychopathology.* The following case presentation illustrates a common cooperation between foster care and a residential treatment center.

Adolescent Client: Michael Brown, 15-year-old Caucasian male

Family: Father: Mr. Brown, 50 years old
       Mother: Mrs. Brown, 36 years old
       Siblings: None

Agency: Department of Public Welfare, Institutional Unit

Current Situation Requiring Caseworker Interventions

After three years in a residential treatment center, Michael made sufficient progress to be considered for discharge to a foster home and eventually to his mother. His mother has had legal custody since she divorced her husband ten years ago. She is actively participating in discharge planning for her son, but her involvement is limited by a progressive deterioration of her health resulting from multiple sclerosis.

Mrs. Brown first experienced symptoms of her disease when Michael was 7 years old, two years after the divorce. However, her illness was not diagnosed at the time and was felt by numerous doctors to be psychosomatic. She became unable to care for Michael, who was placed in a foster home at age 7; he stayed in this home for little over a year and, unfortunately, he was physically and emotionally abused in this home. He was subsequently returned to his mother, who again took care of him until her illness required hospitalization.

Michael's father, with whom he had sporadic contact, stepped forward and agreed to take care of him. Within one month, the father, who lived by himself in an apartment, requested placement of Michael, who was by then 10 years old. He was sent to a residential treatment center because of depression, his extremely low self-concept, and confusion about the many separations and other issues associated with the traumatic events in his life.

He has responded very positively to the center experience and has gained considerable self-confidence; his mother has kept in close touch with him and a strong dependency relationship appears to exist between the two of them.

The worker has carefully identified a couple of foster parents who in the past have been successful in bridging the transfer from residential care to return to the natural parents. Both the mother and Michael have met with the foster parents, and mutual agreement was reached that Michael should visit the foster home for the next two months and continue to reside at the center. The visits to the foster home were to be stepped up in frequency and length as time went on. The final transfer to the foster home is scheduled to take place at the end of three months.

Both Michael and his mother have expressed strong and justified feelings about Michael's first foster home experience, including anger, fear, and a sense of betrayal by the agency in exposing Michael to abuse and not discovering it sooner. As Michael begins visiting the new foster home, these feelings most likely will be reactivated and the worker's first task might be to deal with the mother and Michael in this respect.

Since Michael has stayed in the center for three years, he probably has developed strong relationships with some of the other children in the center and its staff. While termination can be presumed to be dealt with directly in the center, the dependency worker plans to facilitate a constructive termination by discussing with Michael the meaning to him of moving away from the center, encouraging him to talk about his experiences and friends in the center to his new foster parents, and perhaps even bringing one of his friends with him on a visit to the home and preparing for continuation of some contact with the center after the final move into the foster home has taken place.

The mother is anxious to have Michael return to her as soon as possible, and the worker needs to explore how well the mother will be able to take care of him. Information is needed about the prognosis of her illness, how many hospitalizations are ahead, and how much Michael is going to serve as a nurse for her. In addition the strong dependency relationship between mother and son needs some attention, since it has presented some problems during his stay at the center. Because of her deteriorating health, the mother's dependency needs may naturally become stronger than Michael's emotional health can tolerate. Michael's feelings of responsibility for his mother and possible guilt over not taking care of her need exploration as well.

Another task is facilitation of the best possible school setting for Michael and beginning exploration of his vocational interests and capabilities. He is a boy with very few support systems; the sporadic contacts with the father need to be reviewed from the standpoint of helping to strengthen the father-son relationship. These considerations need to be seen in the light of how long Michael will be able to remain in the new foster home. To what extent his close relationship to his mother will allow him to build meaningful relations to the new foster parents is difficult to assess ahead of time. If these parents and Michael "hit it off" with one another, long-term stay in the foster home may give him the greatest chances for moving forward in his adolescent maturational tasks. Much will also depend on his opportunity for peer relations in this home and the new school. Recreational facilities and ongoing psychotherapy also need to be considered.

While many of the adolescents in residential and psychiatric hospital care have committed delinquent acts, a large number of juvenile delinquents go behind locked doors in quite different types of institutions under the administration of the correctional system. According to common juvenile justice practice, the juvenile court, on the recommendation of the police or the intake worker or on the judge's own accord, can decide that a juvenile should be detained if it is judged unsafe for the adolescent or for society to have him or her at large while awaiting the final disposition of the court. Usually youngsters brought to the court's attention because of parental abuse or neglect are referred to shelters that are not as physically restrictive as the juvenile detention centers, where those who are alleged to have committed crimes are housed. In some communities however, the two groups are intermingled in one institution, and in others juvenile delinquents are locked up in the adult jail. At times, juveniles are referred to community group homes or half-way houses, particularly in case of first- or second-time offenses.

Wald (1976) speaks strongly against the overuse of detention and calls for clearer definitions of who should be detained — such as those who are accused of serious crimes for which they are likely to be sent to a secure institution or those who willfully have failed to appear in court, have threatened witnesses, or tampered with evidence on other recent apprehensions.[3] She also recommends several ways to protect juveniles from delays including limiting detention to 15 days from arrest to adjudication and holding detention hearings within 24 hours after arrest. Finally, she proposes that the detention period be used to activate resources that can facilitate change and offer crisis-interventions to the juvenile and his or her family.

After detention the juvenile may be transferred to different types of institutions. Their relative use is well depicted by figures from Paul Lerman's (1982) analysis of deinstitutionalization trends.

Type of Correctional Institution	Total Number of Admissions, 1974
1. Jails/workhouses	258,818
2. Detention centers	469,462
3. Shelters	21,851
4. Diagnostic/reception centers	17,709
5. Prisons/reformatories	2,266
6. Training schools	58,655
7. Ranches/forestry camps/farms/schools	60,571
8. Group homes/halfway houses	30,745
Total	920,077

The total number of admissions in 1974 constitutes a rate of 1,369 per 100,000 under 18 years. The similar rate for 1923 was 152 (p. 132). Summarizing the trends in all three service branches dealing with youth in trouble, Lerman notes sharp reductions of institutional care of dependent and neglected youth, while mental health and juvenile corrections have experienced sharp rises in institutional care.

The pattern of increased use of institutionalization has also taken place in Great Britain, as reported by Rutter and Giller (1984). They state that increased incarceration may not only be ineffective but may also make matters worse in some instances. From their extensive review of empirical and other literature on institutional placements they conclude that young people's behavior may improve during institutionalization, but the benefits do not seem to last. Most institutions have been built on the "medical model" that assumes that the juvenile after achieving successful changes in the institution will be able to cope with the original environment, which usually does not happen. On the other hand, it is equally misleading to assume that if only the environment is changed, juvenile delinquency will disappear. The latter is contradicted by "substantial evidence of considerable *persistence* of antisocial behaviour over time and across environments" (p. 348). Removal of the delinquent from his home is needed in some cases, either because of severely damaging and irremediable family influences or for the protection of the community. However, the residential interventions cannot be expected to have much impact on recidivism unless the home environment is simultaneously improved, the institutions have the quality of a social structure, and the juvenile forms interpersonal relationships offering firmness, consistency, and kindness that will promote change. Such qualities are more important than a particular theoretical orientation of the institution.

Treatment of juvenile delinquents is perhaps the most troublesome of all issues in today's human service system. Numerous public and private panels and organizations have labored diligently to think up better ways; Zimring (1982), for example, states that a Juvenile Justice Standards Project of the American Bar Association has produced no fewer than 24 volumes of suggested reforms in the juvenile justice system. Progress is incredibly slow, which may be due to the unresolved issue of whether the principle of rehabilitation or the principle of punishment is to determine service content and procedures. Another deterring factor is the sheer magnitude and multitudes of problems to be faced.

Parental Involvement

There is growing empirical evidence that maintaining contact between parents and children in out-of-home placements is positively related to early return home, improvement in parental feelings about the placement, and higher degrees of well-being of the child. One of the few longitudinal studies of adults who spent part of their childhoods in foster care, Weinstein's (1960) study of the "Self-Image of the Foster Child," established that even among those who had been in foster care most of their preadult lives and identified predominantly with their foster parents, the experience of well-being was significantly higher for those who had been regularly visited by their parents than for children who had no such contact.

Taylor and Alpert (1973) in their investigation of post-discharge functioning of youngsters formerly in residential care established that the child's perception of family support after discharge was significantly associated with post-discharge adaptation, as were "other factors that may be interpreted" as continuity of family support before, during, and after discharge — early detection of the problem, contact with professional helping agencies before admission, parental visiting and involvement in treatment during care, and continuity of living arrangements after discharge from care. The crucial importance of parental involvement has been most thoroughly supported by the Fanshel and Shinn (1978) longitudinal study, which established frequency of parental visiting as one of the significant predictors of successful discharge (other factors were the age of the child, his ethnicity, the amount of casework invested, and evaluation of the mother). Parental visiting had other positive effects, such as greater gains in IQ, emotional adjustment, and higher ratings by the classroom teacher.

Somewhat surprisingly, the follow-up study by Zimmerman (1982) referred to earlier in this chapter showed a negative correlation between parental visiting and later social functioning. However, a closer look at this association established that the most frequently visited youngsters were those most likely to be returned home, and in comparison with those who remained in long-term foster care they did significantly less well as adults. For the children remaining in foster care until they reached the age of majority, frequency of parental visiting was associated with more adequate functioning than those who were visited seldom or not at all.

The topic of attachment and bonding between parents and children remains relatively unexplored and not well understood. Jenkins (1981a) elaborates on the concept of filial deprivation as the separation experienced by parents when children leave and as the counterpart to maternal deprivation. She calls filial deprivation a normal phenomenon that parents experience when adolescent children separate emotionally from them. The separation experience, when it happens prematurely or abruptly, has a strong impact on parents. One of the few studies exploring filial deprivation was carried out by Jenkins and Norman (1972), who in answer to the question of how the parent felt on the day the child was placed received the following list of feelings from the mothers: sadness, worry, nervousness, emptyness, anger, bitterness, thankfulness, relief, guilt, shame, numbness, and paralysis. Patterns of clusters of these feelings varied according to the parents' socioeconomic status, ethnic background, and reason for placement. When placement was predominantly caused by the child's behavior problems, parental guilt and relief were characteristic, while anger and bitterness were less so. When reasons for placement were neglect, abuse, or family dysfunction (alcoholism, drugs, and incompetence), anger was the predominant feeling expressed by mothers. The researchers concluded that parental feelings about separation are varied and need to be taken into account in child placement practice.

In her later analysis (1981a), Jenkins, distinguishes between the "tie that binds" and the "tie that bonds," which are sometimes but not always the same. The former may be seen as the biological bond and the latter as the psychological component of the parental tie, that which develops from the caretaking adult who meets the infant's needs. Different models of foster care may emerge if the foster mother can be seen as having the attachment as substitute caretaker while the biological mother retains the bonding to the child. Jenkins refers to studies of divorced familes that found that children do better developmentally when they have access to both parents (discussed in this book's chapter 3), and they liken the foster parents to a noncustodial parent. Jenkins suggests that viewing foster care in this manner may facilitate communication between biological and foster parents concerning the needs of the children.

In any event, for parents as well as children the parent-child relationship is a powerful bond. Even when it is permanently severed, as in adoption, some threads hang on, and the severance has its price.

Adolescents on the Adoption Scene

The Shyne and Schroeder (1978, pp. 126, 131) study of children's services in 41 states found that 40 percent of the 102,000 children legally free for adoption were 11 years of age or older.[4] Adoptive homes were found for 36 percent of the youngsters between 11 and 14 years of age compared to only 13 percent for children 15 to 17 years of age. The older the child the greater the need for subsidies to make adoption possible; 49 percent of the first age group and 41 percent of the second age group required such a subsidy.

Even lower placement rates are reported by Meezan (1980). Only about 2 percent (565) children were 12 years of age or older of the 27,000 nonrelative adoptions that took place in 1975 — the last year for which national adoption statistics are available. This low rate is probably not reflective of the true national figure since statistical information was submitted from only 42 of the states.

Some agencies make special efforts to place older children in adoptive homes, as for example the Spaulding for Children Agency. Of 275 New Jersey placements, 60 percent involved children aged 9 or older and about 25 percent were teenagers (Boyne 1978).

However, despite the inadequacy of the statistical information it seems clear that thousands of adolescents in foster care are legally free for adoption. As the right of every child to a permanent home has gained increased attention and acceptance, the plight of these children has fueled service innovations such as approval of single and/or older adoptive parents and subsidized adoptions (payments to the adoptive family until the adoptee reaches age 18 or 21 in cases of physical and mental handicaps. See Byrne and Belucci 1982; Waldinger 1982). While many teenagers have found permanent adoptive homes via these developments, many still remain in limbo. The general adoption literature does not distinguish between the preadolescent and the teenage child awaiting adoption in foster care, and the waiting may well have different impact and consequences for the two age groups. The words of two teenagers, reported in the public press (Manuel 1981) speak to this point.

Sarah was removed from her home at age 10 with her nine brothers and sisters; for the next five years they moved from one foster home to another. Two or three of them would be in the same foster home, but most of the time they were separated. While in the first home, Sarah did not want it to work, she wanted to go home. In the second home, "the people were nice, but it was like a cute, perfect little family. And it was always them and me. When we'd go camping or have Christmas, it would always be them and me."

Several of her sisters and brothers were adopted; but Sarah as the oldest was overlooked, but she was finally adopted at age 17. She hated herself and felt she could not do anything right. Her new parents convinced her otherwise; she went to college from where she was about to graduate at the time of this newspaper interview. Her plan is to teach children with learning difficulties and eventually marry and raise her own children.

Her sisters and brothers did not do as well as she in respect to school and getting along in the family. Sarah attributes the difference to the fact that one day she was able to accept that her desire to go home to her own parents was unrealistic because she remembered what it was like. Her brothers and sisters were too young to remember that "our parents were always drunk, always beating on each other. They don't remember that my mother was always trying to commit suicide and that I was always stopping her. They don't remember not having food in the house, not having furniture, or heat, or even light bulbs." . . . "They think that our parents were perfectly normal people who really loved us, and that we got yanked out of there for no reason. They think it is not fair, and they have the attitude that the world has ripped them off."

Sarah also noted that her sisters and brothers had shut themselves off from being helped, had isolated themselves. "Foster kids are basically floating around . . . they don't belong to anybody. And for a family to work, you have to want to belong."

A different life story is told by *Iris*, a 18 year old black college freshman. One night when she was 12 her stepfather tried to rape her while her mother was out for the evening. Iris gathered her two younger sisters and her brother and went to a neighbor's house; the next day she applied for foster care. Neither Iris nor her siblings were ever adopted, even though efforts were made to find them adoptive parents. Iris stayed in 10 different foster homes; struggling with her self-blame and hostility. However, she was doing well in school, ranking sixth of 100 in the graduating class, and she won scholarships that enabled her to go to college. At 18 she is very happy to finally be independent, and according to Iris, all her younger siblings "are waiting to turn 18, so they can decide for themselves whether to stay in their foster homes."

These two cases vividly illustrate the complexities planners and deliverers of child welfare services are confronted with. In both these cases the older child of a sibling group was able to take action and some responsibility for caring for younger siblings; they were also bright and, after initial self-doubt, able to reach out and use the support offered them. Sarah and Iris are not typical of adolescents legally free for adoption, many of whom suffer from physical, mental, and emotional handicaps.

Byrne and Bellucci (1982) report that one-third of the 271 children in subsidized adoptive placements are functioning with low intelligence quotients and another one-third are severely emotionally disturbed. From the latter category they present a pathetic case in which the subsidy was limited to medical expenses only.

A 59-year-old widow accepted a very disturbed 8-year-old boy for foster care — a child who had already quickly failed in two foster homes. Her motivation may have been the desire for a companion for a young boy already in her care, for whom she only belatedly applied for board payments. At any rate, her new foster child had, until placement, been very abused. With substantial backing from her community his mother fought against his removal. During foster care this elderly widow worked flexibly with the boy's therapist and provided all community resources as well as warmth and belonging. After a disturbing visit by the boy's psychotic mother, the foster mother wanted the protection of adoption for the boy and herself. Adoption was completed after placement when she was 63, he 12. About four years later he became involved with Juvenile Court for stealing and drugs; still, his adoptive mother persisted. His behavior worsened, and when he was almost 18 the court took over, removing him from the home of the exhausted but far from defeated 69-year old adoptive mother. When residential placement proved unavailable because of his age, the court returned custody to his biological mother (p. 179).[5]

These three perhaps unrepresentative cases raise the question of how much adoption really matters. Aren't past experiences and attachments, capacities of the individual child, ability to reach out and gain a sense of security from support in the foster home, school, and therapy really what matter? It seems that we do not have the answers to these questions yet.

One recent article by Kathleen Proch (1982) makes the point that subsidized adoptions have blurred the distinction between the traditionally temporary foster care service and the permanent adoption system. She notes that some child welfare workers are dismayed and fearful that allowing foster parents to adopt will undermine the adoption system, and others are perplexed that some foster parents reject the offer to adopt a foster child in their care. Thus an underlying assumption held by some practitioners is that the two service forms are distinctly different. Proch wonders, however, if foster parents and foster children perceive the difference. Her study findings from interviews with adoptive foster parents of 56 children and with 29 of these children reveal that 16 percent of these parents could not identify any differences between foster care and adoption and only 8 of the 29 interviewed children could make the distinction. For the children who considered the two services to be the same, a home was a home and a parent a parent. The child's placement history appears to be the critical element. If the child has known no other parents, the psychological bonding takes place, regardless of the legal status of the parents.

The researcher cautions that the study sample may not be representative of adoptive foster parents and children in general, and only 29 of the original study sample of 130 could be interviewed, which makes the findings only preliminary. However, they are in agreement with the conclusions from the Oregon Permanency Planning Project (Lahti et al. 1978) that the child's *perception* of permanence, not the legal status, is the key to how well the child is doing behaviorally and developmentally.

It seems that the importance of gaining adoptive status during the adolescent years is not yet fully understood; neither do we seem to know how to make it possible for potential adoptive parents (foster parents or not) and the adolescent to turn the adoptive process into an optimal growth-producing experience in all cases. Yet many adolescents keep yearning for that person who, in the words of one of the children interviewed in the Proch study, "will put you up in a home where you stay as long as you live" (p. 266). Other adolescents refuse to be adopted, as for example the 13-year-old girl who was fearful that adoption would mean losing her familial tie to her grandmother who had previously taken care of her but was no longer able to do so. Assured that she would be able to visit her grandmother, she agreed to adoption (Colón 1978). Along the same vein, Edwards and Boyd (1975) report that adolescents at times are reluctant about adoption because of fear of having to give up their identity with their biological families. For the foster parents ready to adopt, such rejection can be a crushing experience. However, casework counseling of foster parents and the adolescent may help resolve the identity confusion and insecurity; in some cases the adolescent has preserved his or her identity to the birth parent(s) by simply adding the foster parents' surname to the original name. Joining a family as an adopted teenage son or daughter then becomes very much like joining a family through marriage.[6] Other aspects of identity issues are presented in the next section.

Adoptees' Identity Achievement

Even children who were placed in adoptive homes when they were a few months old experience special difficulties in working through the identity formation process since they, if they know they are adopted, in a sense have two sets of parents to identify with and separate from. The adolescent and adult adoptees' search for "roots," request for opening the sealed adoption records, and attempts to meet the birth parent(s) in person are often seen as reflections of the added identity struggles adoptees are confronted with.

Four types of psychological identity difficulties have been identified by Sorosky, Baran, and Pannor (1975, 1978) in their thorough research on identity conflicts in adoptees. First, they refer to research establishing a direct relationship between age at the time of adoptive placement and severity of emotional problems encountered at adolescence. The adopted child is separated first from the birth mother then, if all goes well, from only one foster mother or other caretaker. While research findings regarding consequences of maternal deprivation may have been given disproportionate attention, adoptees are at a disadvantage in having to cope with changes in parental figures. Sorosky et al. also point to the difficulties the adoptive parents may have in bonding with the child, depending on feelings they have in relation to infertility and entitlement to a child somebody else has borne. Other areas of difficulty are establishment of sexual identity in a family setting where the incest taboo may not be fully operating and difference in use of family romance fantasies (that my real and perfect parents are somewhere else and will some day come and rescue me), which is a healthy game many children engage in when frustrated and angry with their parents. For adoptees the game is a reality, and their fantasies are preoccupied by "highly exalted or lowly debased parents" (1975, p. 20). The latter often predominate as the adolescent struggles with the question: "How could they be good, if they gave me up?"

Anna Freud (1975) considered the argument that children are best served by being returned to their biological parents so as to be spared the additional identity crisis in adolescence false. In her opinion adolescents whose adoptive parents have become psychological parents are confronted with the same developmental task natural children face in separating from them, the adoptee has the additional and intermediary step of separating from the fantasied images of lost biological parents. Fortunately, many adoptees see their adoptive parents as psychological parents. In other cases, the parent-child relationship falls short of what Goldstein, Freud, and Solnit (1973 and 1979) have called psychological parenthood.

Sorosky et al. (1975) point out that adoptees have to cope with the genealogical bewilderment associated with severance from one's racial antecedents. For some adoptees this bewilderment leads to poor self-esteem, identity confusion, and fears of "unknowingly committing incest with blood relatives" (p. 21).

Drawing from empirical studies and their own observations, Sorosky et al. (1975) note that the intensity of curiosity about genealogical background grows at certain points during adolescence. At pubescence the adolescent begins to think of himself or herself as a biological link between past and future generations, while at late adolescence and young adulthood the shaping of one's psychological identity dominates. These tasks build on the past, and when very little or nothing is known about the past the adolescent starts searching. Specific events often trigger genealogical searches; Sorosky et al. (1975) mention occasions such as engagement, attaining adult legal status, requesting a birth certificate, taking civil service exams, taking out life insurance, medical problems, pregnancy, child birth, and death of one or both adoptive parents, at which time the adoptee no longer needs to hold back in searching for information about the birth parents for fear of hurting the feelings of the adoptive parents.[7]

These concerns are common to all adoptees, and the search for birth relatives is part of the identity formation process for many adoptees. Searchers, however, according to Sorosky et al., also include a small group of adoptees who neurotically search for their birth parents. They seem to gain satisfaction from the search process itself and prefer to live with fantasied parents rather than risk disillusionment by actually meeting the birth parents, and they therefore always stop short of reunion. Another distinguishable group are the quasi-searching adolescents, who are merely threatening their adoptive parents much the same way non-adopted adolescents threaten to move out or run away. Accounts similar to those of Sorosky et al. about the influence of adoption on adolescent psychological development and behaviors are found in Goodman and Magno-Nora (1975) and McWhinnie's (1969) analysis of British adoptees.

Identity Formation and Transracial Adoptions

The genealogical bewilderment seems likely to be more intense for adolescents growing up in adoptive homes of different ethnic background from their own. Chestang (1978), in his discussion of delivery of child welfare services to minority group children and their families, describes the movement the view of the black child as unadoptable or hard-to-place, to the up-swing of transracial adoptions in the early 1970s, to the drop in such adoptions as a result of the opposition of black professionals and organizations. The opposition to transracial adoptions is based partly on strained race relations in society in general, partly on fear that a minority child will not be able to develop identification with his or her own ethnic culture, and partly on white families' supposed inability to provide the minority child with the survival skills needed when confronted with hostility and discrimination. Many adoption agencies now follow the policies laid down in the 1978 Federal Indian Child Welfare Act, which are that the option to adopt an American Indian child is first offered to the extended family, next to the tribe, then to other Indian families, and only if these resources are not available, to a non-Indian home.

As many of the transracially adopted children barely have reached adolescence, the empirical evidence regarding their identity formation is still very limited. Preliminary findings seem to indicate that self-esteem of transracially adopted black children (60 children of a mean age of 13.5 years) did not differ from black children placed in black adoptive homes (McRoy, Zurcher, Lauderdale, and Anderson 1982 and 1984). Kim (1978), on the basis of his own research on the adaptation of Korean children placed in white American homes and his anlaysis of other research, concluded that the early adjustment of the large numbers of children from Korea, Vietnam, South America, and other Third World countries many have been accomplished at the expense of developing their unique ethnic identity. It remains to be seen to what extent the many well-meaning efforts to transplant children from one culture and nation to another and across ethnic lines within the United States will turn out to be a deficit rather than a plus. Barbara Joe (1978) in her defense of intercountry adoptions argues that such adoptions should be retained as one resource for children living under extremely depriving conditions, but other alternative programs such as population control and economic and other aid seem more appropriate for taking care of the world's needy children. In any event, apart from the considerable moral issues involved, the psychological soundness of transracial and transethnic adoptions have not stood the test until a considerable number of these adoptees have reached young adulthood with positive ethnic identity paired with pride in their citizenry.

The Sealed Record Controversy and Other Aspects of Genetic Searches

Adoption laws are designed to protect the best interest of the child and to transfer irrevocably the rights and responsibilities of the biological parent(s) to the adoptive parent(s).[8] Confidentiality of agency records and court proceedings and the sealing of court records and the original birth certificate have been strictly maintained on the assumption that the child's well-being and the development of the adoptive parent-child relationship are best served by no contact with or intervention of the biological parents after adoption placement. Additionally, the biological parents have been free to live their lives without intrusion by the relinquished child, the adoptive family, or anybody else (Jones, M.L. 1979).

Since the late 1960s, however, a growing number of adolescent and adult adoptees have returned to the agencies and courts that arranged their adoption to learn about their biological parents. Some request information only; others want to meet their birth parents. It is estimated that only a small minority of adoptees feel a need to locate their birth parents (Triseliotis 1973 and Jones, M.L. 1979).

In some states the adoptee at age of maturity has a legal right to see his or her original birth certificate but not to search the adoption record itself. The quest for opening of the sealed record has turned into a controversy among lawyers, social workers, adoptees and natural and adoptive parents. Some claim that the adoptees have a constitutional right to know who their birth parents are. Others maintain that the rights of the biological parents to privacy and of the adoptive parents require that the seal of records should remain unbroken, while a third voice speaks for some modification and compromise between the rights of parents and adult adoptees (Anderson 1977).

Empirical studies are beginning to provide data on which adoptees initiate genetic searches, why they do it, and how they feel about what they learn. An example is the exploratory study by Simpson et al. (1981) of 41 genetic searches conducted in Minnesota as a result of that state's 1977 Open Birth Record Law. The data were gained from record analysis and interviews with a random sample of 10 of the 41 persons who requested information about their origins. Two-thirds of the 41 persons were women, and the group ranged in age from 21 to 68, with over half of the searches conducted for the 21- to 35-year-olds. The majority requested access to the original birth certificate as well as more genetic information and person-to-person contact with the birth parents.

Four major types of motivation for a genetic search were identified: desire for more genetic information about their parents, in-depth information about their roots, natural curiosity, and information to pass on to their children. Most of the 41 persons had attempted to get the desired information before the 1977 law was passed.

This group of adoptees had positive experiences in their adoptive families, and the majority of them informed the adoptive parents about their request for a genetic search. The public agency conducting the searches was successful in meeting the requests in most cases as far as birth certificates and genetic information were concerned, but the agency workers were able to arrange personal contacts with the birth parents in only one-third of the cases.

A later report of a private Virginian agency's attempts to facilitate reunions of adult adoptees with their birth parents (Depp 1982) builds on observations from such cases. Nine adoptees were women and three men. Ten of the adoptees returned questionnaires about their experiences; six of seven adoptive parents and three birth parents also responded. The findings of this very small investigation support findings of other studies that "adoptive parents are capable of coming to appreciate the adoptee's need for a reunion," and reunions enhance the relationship between the adoptee and the adoptive parents, regardless of whether positive or negative relationships existed before the reunion. Two of the birth parents in the Depp study felt that the reunion was a positive experience for themselves as well as for their daughters; the third birth parent felt that the experience was negative for both. Meeting the birth mother was considered a positive experience by six adoptees, confusing by six, and negative by one; however, eight of the ten adoptees reported that, overall, the reunions had helped them to establish a better sense of identity.

Many of the variables identified in the above and other research as associated with search for biological parents have been systematically studied by Sobol and Cardiff (1983), who compared nonsearching adoptees with those who had requested information or reunion. Previous studies were limited to samples of adoptees who actually had taken such steps, and their descriptive characteristics could not be taken as search variables without establishing their presence in nonsearching adoptees. As hypothesized, data from the 120 sample adoptees' responses to questionnaires and their self-concept and social readjustment measures established increased searching to be related to "a traumatic adoption revelation, knowledge of circumstances of birth and adoption, strained adoptive family relationships, poor self-concept, the experiencing of stressful life events and a belief that having been adopted made one feel different and incomplete" (p. 477). Replies to the open-ended questions about reasons for the degree of searching activity revealed that seachers were motivated by wanting more information about their roots and wanting to increase their sense of identity and fulfillment. Almost one-fourth wanted to establish a relationship with the birth parent. The nonsearchers gave as a reason for not searching the fear of hurting either adoptive or birth parents, and one-fifth stated that given their satisfaction and identity with their adoptive parents they saw no reason for seeking further information. Interestingly, the older the child was at adoptive placement and the more knowledge they had about the circumstances surrounding their birth, the more likely they were to search. The researchers speculate that having some information may have served as a starting point in contacting the bureaucracies and dealing with resistance to searching.

Similar findings are reported by Aumend and Barrett (1984), who also compared searchers and nonsearchers. The nonsearchers reported knowing less than searchers about their biological parents, and they expressed less concern over the reasons for the adoptive placement. The nonsearchers also had more positive self-concepts than the searchers, which supports the findings of the Sobol and Cardiff study. Aumend and Barrett, however, underscore that despite these differences among the two groups of adoptees, overall these adult adoptees did not have low self-concepts, as the majority scored above the sixtieth percentile on the Tennessee Self-Concept

Scale and scored positively on the Attitudes Toward Parents Scale. Their findings regarding self-concept are in accord with the study by Norvell and Guy (1977), who compared self-concept in adopted and nonadopted adolescents.[9]

In spite of the greater sophistication of research methodology in these comparative studies as opposed to convenience samples of all searchers, Sobol and Cardiff (1983) appropriately caution against interpreting the findings as indicative of actual developmental experiences. Because of a tendency to draw recollections from the past that are in accord with the present, the searching activity as such may not in fact have been prompted by the relations with adoptive parents, fantasies about biological parents, and so forth. What can be concluded, say Sobol and Cardiff, is that "searchers, on looking back over their developmental history, are left with a *current* feeling of discomfort about the past" (p. 483). Whether such a feeling is antecedent or consequent to searching remains for future research to explore.

Sobol and Cardiff conclude that professionals need to deal with requests for information about biological roots not as an expression of a neurotic need but as a legitimate attempt to seek the opportunity to enhance the feeling of completeness, which does not need to threaten the relationship of the adoptee with his or her adopted family.

This chapter concludes with a word about the disrupted adoptions — those that failed and resulted in the adolescent's removal from the adoptive home. A surprisingly high number of adoptions work out well, even for older children (Kadushin 1980), but for those for whom the placement failed, the experience can be devastating. Many of these children are sooner or later referred to residential treatment centers. A recent special issue of *Residential Group Care & Treatment* (Powers 1983) presents gripping accounts of adoption failures and describes how devastating consequences may be averted. The issue closes with a very sensible proposal for establishment of special adoption cottages in centers where these children, who according to Powers are anywhere from 4 or 5 years old to middle and late adolescence, can be helped to deal with the past family history and prepare for another try. Such special-focus units are suggested not only to contribute to more optimal preparation of specific older and troubled children for adoption but also to be a center for accumulation of knowledge about adoption for special-needs children and adolescents.

Notes

1. Reprinted with permission from *Smith College Studies in Social Work* 41 (3). Copyright 1971.

2. Reprinted with permission from *Children and Youth Services Review* 3. Hornby, H., and Collins, M.I., "Teenagers in Foster Care: The Forgotten Majority." Copyright 1981, Pergamon Press, Ltd.

3. For further information on detention see Sarri (1974) *Under Lock and Key: Juveniles in Jails and Detention* and Young and Pappenfort (1977) *Secure Detention of Juveniles and Alternatives to Its Use.*

4. Adoptive homes were found for 54 percent of white children, 37 percent of blacks, and 49 percent of Hispanics. The highest rate of home finding was for 1,000 Asian-Pacific children, of whom 83 percent were placed in adoptive homes; the lowest, 27 percent, was for the 2,000 American Indian/Alaskan children (Shyne and Schroeder 1978, pp. 131–32).

5. Reprinted from CHILD WELFARE, Vol. LXI, 1982, Number 3, p. 179. Copyright © 1982 by the Child Welfare League of America. All rights reserved.

6. Another way of facilitating adoption for teenagers is the process of "open" adoptions, in which actual contact with the biological family is encouraged (Borgman 1982).

7. In assessing the motivation or dynamics of search for biological parents it is difficult to sort out what stems from the cut-off from these parents and what may be associated with influences of the adoptive home. A rare longitudinal study of adopted adolescents in Sweden by Bohman and Sigvardsson (1981) found that at age 11 a cohort of 624 children relinquished for adoption at infancy and subsequently placed in adoptive or foster homes or reclaimed by their biological mothers, were suffering considerably more maladjustment and disturbances than their classmates. At age 15 the adopted adolescents had largely overcome their handicaps. Regardless of genetic background these adolescents were no more at risk than the general population if living in adoptive homes of good standards that were capable of raising a non-biological child. The children raised by their mothers, however, continued at age 15 to be at considerable risk for maladjustment and school failure as were the children who, because of the mother's or the agency's indecision, were placed in foster homes. It may be that the initial identity struggle at puberty was counteracted by the stability of the adoptive homes, while similar support was not available to those in foster homes or residing with their mothers. It would be interesting to see if the identity formation taking place in late adolescence and early adulthood is achieved in different manners by the three groups. It is not known if this longitudinal study is planned to continue.

8. The Child Welfare League's 1978 Adoption Standards also contain guidelines for services to be provided to adopted adults and for disclosure of identifying information about the birth parents.

9. Norvell and Guy hypothesized a more negative self-concept among the adoptees than among nonadopted adolescents, but no support for the hypothesis was found in the mean self-concept scores of 38 adopted and 38 nonadopted adolescents. The researchers refer to earlier study findings that "adoption is a negligible factor if good object relations between the adopted child and his parents are maintained and if the parents are relatively secure" (pp. 445–46). They did find an inverse relationship between self-concept scores and age at the time of adoption (mean scores for children placed before one year of age: 148.2; between 1 and 3 years of age: 140.1; and placed at 4 and older: 133.0). This finding is speculated to be a result not so much of the adoption status itself, but of the "shifting and temporary family relations" experienced by children placed for adoption when older. The focus of future studies on this topic should, according to these researchers, be on parent-child interaction as it relates to adjustment in adoption cases.

7 INTERPERSONAL INTERVENTIONS

Within the context of the services described in chapters 5 and 6, the human service professional translates the overall service objectives into realities for adolescent clients and their families through direct and indirect interventions. The latter include policy analysis, program planning, development, evaluation, administration, supervision, and case management. Important as these are for the quality of the end product, they are not the topic of this book. The focus of this chapter is on direct, interpersonal helping activities with adolescents and their families. Several counseling and therapeutic modalities are at the human service professional's disposal. This chapter presents some pros and cons in the choice of one modality over another depending on what the adolescent client wants and needs, what parental preferences are, what the agency is sanctioned and charged to do, and what the human service professional's education and training render him or her competent to deliver.

This chapter covers the following topics: a theoretical stance, the empirical foundations for interventions with adolescents, and assessment considerations for the adolescent client as an individual and as part of a family. The chapter discusses interventions at three systemic levels: family treatment (including consideration of the sibling subsystem), group counseling, and individual treatment. As one theme of this book is the adolescent's relation to the family, greater attention is given to family treatment than to the two other modalities.

Family versus an Individualistic Perspective

Adolescent-family interaction can be viewed from many angles. One is an adolescent-centered approach, seeing the family as the context of the adolescent's striving for autonomy. This approach usually identifies unidirectional parent or family factors that impede or promote adolescent maturation. Another perspective is family-unit centered. This approach sees the family itself as a social organism connected with larger social and cultural systems influencing its structure, boundaries, values, and interactions, and thus adolescent development as well. Reiss, Oliveri, and Curd (1983) call the former, primarily psychological stance the "up-from-adolescence" approach, in which the family is seen through the window of adolescence; the latter, primarily sociological perspective is the "down-from-society" approach, where behavior is understood to be part of the patterns of social forces. They urge that in order to gain fuller understanding of how social relations influence individual development, and vice versa, both perspectives need to be integrated.

Most human service professionals dealing with family-related problems would readily agree with this, since one-sided attention to either the individual or the family is unlikely to provide the practitioner with a valid picture of the situation. The need for a dual perspective is reflected in recent increased acceptance of ecological and system theories, which depict the family as an interlocking, interdependent set of forces impacting the family internally and linking it with external social and cultural conditions. One important outcome of this development is a move away from the almost exclusive focus of former days on the mother-child relationship to the inclusion of the father and siblings as equally essential factors in the family interaction.

A conscious attempt is made throughout this book, particularly in this chapter, to convey when an individualistic stance is taken and when a family-oriented system perspective is used, the latter being the prevailing orientation. The word *attempt* is used advisedly since it is very easy to slip from seeing a person as a part of a family to seeing him as an individual because the individualistic stance for so long has been so deeply ingrained into our thinking. Some hope for eventual mastery of both perspectives can be derived from the information graciously shared by one of the great family theoreticians, Murray Bowen. Bowen states that it took him more than ten years to develop the ability to shift with ease between individual and family system orientations and finally to maintain the two side-by-side without getting lost in either (in Carter and McGoldrick 1980, p. XV).

This distinction is not intended to engender compulsive or academic exercises of disentangling mixed-up theoretical threads. The reason for the distinction is the pragmatic one that taking an individualistic versus a family system stance makes a tremendous difference in how practitioners approach specific cases. If the adolescent's troublesome behavior is seen as rooted inside the person, then interventions should address the individual. It may be that something failed to develop or something has gone awry, perhaps because of the quality of the psychological potentials the person started out with and perhaps because the nurture offered by the environment was insufficient or ill-matched to the person's needs. The practitioner with this perspective may well tend to the inner workings of the adolescent by individual therapy, utilizing insight-oriented techniques in the context of a supportive or even corrective emotional experience through the therapeutic relationship. Simultaneously the practitioner may work with family and environment to bring about an atmosphere more conducive to the adolescent's growth and well-being. If, on the other hand, the adolescent's behavior is seen as not simply rooted in family interactions but as an intrinsic part of that interaction, then that becomes the locus for the practitioner's interventions. If one accepts the view of Jay Haley (1973) that the success of the individual's growth and development is determined by how one participates in one's natural group and its development, then any attempt to deal only with the behavior of the individual identified as having problems will turn out to be counterproductive. Haley mentions two ways by which "adjusted behavior" can be brought about without growth. If a young person reaches the developmental time for moving out of the family but the family is incapable of moving into the stage of releasing the adolescent, he or she will manifest behavioral symptoms. These symptoms may be alleviated through medication. Or the adolescent may be seen in long-term individual therapy helping the person gain better understanding of past experiences and self rather than the present life situation. In both instances growth is blocked and delayed since it can only be brought about through situational change, that is, by bringing about the family group's ability to let go. Therefore, the family situation is what must be dealt with. Looked at from this perspective, family therapy is obviously not just another mode of therapeutic intervention. It is the only way.

Even though this author's leaning is toward a family-system perspective, the aim of this book is to stand on the Bowenian platform with room for individualistic and family system orientations side-by-side.

One further comment about the author's theoretical biases. Whether one holds the above dual perspective or an individual or a family orientation, one can easily commit the error of forgetting that theories are constructed to achieve some sense of order in a seemingly chaotic field of unconnected relations. Theories, principles, and concepts do not really exist; they are products of our minds, mental tools that help us do our work. If taken as final and unalterable truth and if used to give the authoritative explanation of the behaviors of individual clients and families and how our efforts helped bring about change, then violence may be done to our clients' integrity. That becomes a danger if our theories or practice wisdom do not leave room for crucial individual or environmental factors that contribute to the behavior we are trying to help our clients change. The only way to guard against this danger is to constantly keep in mind and deal with the problem as the client or the family sees it.

Empirical Foundations

Four reviews specifically address the helpfulness of therapeutic interventions with adolescents and their families; thcy are briefly presented here. Pool and Frazier (1973) conclude in their review of early family therapy studies from 1969 to 1973 that it is difficult to assess the success of the application of conjoint family therapy, multifamily therapy, crisis intervention with families, and experimental methods with families because very few objective criteria were applied and there was hardly any use of psychometric measurement of personality or attitude changes. Breunlin and Breunlin (1979) combined their general literature review of family therapy approaches to adolescent disturbances with a summarization of the studies involving adolescents, that were included in Gurman and Kniskern's (1978) comprehensive analysis of 200 studies on outcomes of marital and family therapy. Of the 217 adolescents receiving family therapy reported in 9 of the 200 studies, 75 percent showed improvement, which was an improvement rate slightly higher than for clients of all ages. Deterioration was reported for 3 percent of the adolescents. Breunlin and Breunlin note the increase in empirical evidence but also call for additional research on specific variables of family therapy that are linked with positive changes in adolescent disturbances. Olson, Russell, and Sprenkle (1980) in their general review of marital and family therapy during the 1970s likewise draw on the Gurman and Kniskern review, and they organize other outcome studies around specific topics, such as juvenile offenses and family therapy addressing adolescent psychopathology.

The most comprehensive review has been carried out by Michael G. Tramontana (1980), who reviewed studies on individual, group, and family therapy with adolescents between 12 and 18 published between 1967 and 1977. Of 33 studies included for review, only five were judged to be exemplary in methodological scope.[1] A computed median rate of positive outcome of 75 percent of treated adolescents (based on 20 studies that allowed such computation) against a rate of 39 percent for untreated adolescents points to superiority of psychotherapeutic interventions. Tramontana underscores the special difficulties associated with measuring outcome in adolescent cases, namely, the fact that treatment of adolescents is often combined with other types of interventions and joint interventions with parents, so that it is difficult to isolate which intervention contributed how much to outcome. The impact of the maturation factor is, of course, particularly strong at a period of development with profound changes, such as adolescence. He also wisely proposes changing the tacit assumption that unless long-lasting changes occur, they are not of much value. Less stringent standards could be considered. In Tramontana's opinion research on psychotherapeutic outcome with adolescents is about 15 years behind outcome research for adults, and it also falls below the number of studies with children. He tentatively concludes that therapy with adolescents appears to simply be an "amalgam of principles, approaches, and techniques borrowed from work with adults and children rather than being derived from systematic investigations of the special treatment needs of adolescent patients" (p. 448).

Hall (1984) reviews studies of three treatment approaches to solve parent-adolescent conflict. Two of these approaches — intervention with either the adolescent or the parents only — have hardly been evaluated. Evaluation of the third and much-used approach — treatment with both parents and adolescents — shows mixed results in that parents appear to gain more than their adolescents. And "[t]raining in communication and problem-solving skills has been at least minimally supported and appears preferable to traditional family therapy" (p. 491). However, Hall underscores that while many studies describe interesting treatment approaches, most evaluations suffer from methodological shortcomings.

With regard to families involved with protective and preventive services, a research review by Jones, Magura, and Shyne (1981) confirms that many families make considerable gains within a few months of service while other families require services extended for years to cope with their child-care responsibilities. As far as the content of services is concerned, these authors found that counseling alone or concrete services alone are not as helpful as a combination of the two. Likewise, direct services to several family members (children as well as parents) were found more helpful than services to either parents or children alone. Apparently, outreach efforts are needed to enable families to use the services. Examples of such efforts are providing transportation, escort services, advocacy efforts with other institutions on behalf of the families, case management, and resource utilization, since no one agency is likely to be able to provide all needed services.

Other elements of effective practice with these families, according to Jones et al., are: team approaches, so that a family can get to know more than one staff member; the use of groups to overcome isolation; creation of self-help groups; use of volunteers; quality of the worker-client relationship and worker competence in teaching parenting skills; and understanding of developmental tasks and how developmental achievements are enhanced in children.

Assessment

The Ecological Diagram of Adolescent Behavior in figure 3–1 may serve as a map or guide for the assessment process. What information is actually gathered, assessed, and used in individual cases depends on a multitude of factors. Among them are the agency's function, resources, and legal mandate; the reasons for the adolescent's contact with the social worker; the wishes and wants of the adolescent and the family; and the social worker's orientation, capabilities, and training.

A child protection worker about to present findings to the family court of a home situation in which sexual abuse of an adolescent has allegedly taken place may have a different assessment task at hand than the in-take social worker in a walk-in community clinic for teenagers in a vocational guidance center. A school social worker receiving teacher complaints about an adolescent's increasingly disruptive and aggressive behavior has another assessment task, as does the community mental health social worker struggling to determine if the bizarre, incoherent behavior of the adolescent in front of him is an expression of normal adolescent mood swings or of an emotional disturbance with possibly high suicide risk, requiring immediate psychiatric attention.

In such situations the professional helper assesses where the teenager is in the adolescent phase compared with chronological age and determines whether it is one or more of the developmental tasks that is causing trouble, how severe and pervasive the presented problem is, and whether the problem is experienced by and painful to the teenager alone or has spilled over to relations with family members, peers, teachers, and so on. What are the environmental circumstances in the parental home, independent living quarters, or out-of-home care facility? Do the interpersonal relations and environmental circumstances hinder or help the adolescent's development? What are his or her own intellectual, emotional, and relationship capacities? What is the state of physical health? Is the teenager an early or late pubescent maturer? What is the degree of motivation to change that brought or sent the teenager to us? Does he or she have any life goals? These and many other questions pass through the mind of the human service professional in the effort to get acquainted with the young person seeking assistance. What ties all these considerations together in the practitioner's mind is the three-pronged framework of motivation-capacity-opportunity of the problem-solving practice model so well explained by Helen Perlman (1957 and 1970). Different practice situations call for expansion and elaboration of any one of the three cornerstones, but in this author's long experience with practice and teaching, all three have to be considered and taken into account. The triangle of the problem-solving model captures the essence of human behavior. It seems good for all seasons and places.

As the adolescent moves from early to late adolescence, we observe a shift from using behavior to cope with conflict toward a greater ability to verbalize emotions and conflict. We observe growth in impulse control and sublimatory capacity, in capacity for self-observation and reality perception, a lessening of preoccupation with body image and changes, and a shift toward adaptive versus protective use of defenses. Oldham, Looney, and Blotcky (1980), in their article on clinical assessment of symptoms in adolescents, further elaborate on the interplay between these individual-level characteristics and family- and sociocultural-level factors; they also compare two adolescents to illustrate normative behavior of early and late adolescence.

Even though clinical observations and common sense confirm the importance of factors associated with the human body, these factors and their constitutional/genetic base are often almost overlooked or at least not taken sufficiently into account. It is difficult, if not impossible, to determine how much the adolescent's behavior is influenced by unalterable constitutional factors and how much by the secondary alterable behavioral response patterns the adolescent may have gradually developed in order to cope with his or her own or the environment's reactions to a handicap or other unalterable biological conditions. The unalterable bodily/somatic factors must be realistically accepted in the joint goal-setting for client change, and much can be done in assessment, prevention, and intervention to alter responses of parents, siblings, teachers, and others to constitutional and temperamental variables.

A practical tool to help the adolescent as well as the social worker better understand the interrelationships between life events and current behavior is the Life History Grid for Adolescents, described by Anderson and Brown

(1980). Another helpful assessment device is an instrument specifying components of readiness for independent living after discharge from transitional treatment centers. This instrument, developed by Ehrlich (1980), covers 9 specific skills for independent living, 11 aspects of appropriate personal and social functioning capacities, and 4 aspects of participation in community life.

A third concrete outline for assessment of psychosocial difficulties in children (newborn to 18 years of age) is presented by Hess and Howard (1981) as an ecological model — drawing on family theory, crisis theory, systems theory, and social psychology. The text by Cullinan, Epstein, and Lloyd (1983) contains a chapter on assessment of educationally related behavior areas and assessment procedures; the focus here is on school and learning behavior of children and adolescents with behavior disorders. For some purposes, particularly measurement of change over the intervention period, the Offer Self-Image Questionnaire (OSIQ), referred to several times in this book, is a very helpful tool.

For adolescents suffering from mental/emotional disturbances, the recently revised "Diagnostic and Statistical Manual of Mental Disorders (DSM-III)" published by the American Psychiatric Association (1980) is an essential diagnostic tool. This latest formulation of the DSM system incorporates assessment on five different axes, of which the first three deal with the person's psychological/behavioral functioning, the long-term personality, and the physical condition. The fourth axis rates the severity of psychosocial stressors, and the final axis rates the highest level of adaptive functioning within the last year. Williams's (1981) article gives a good overview of this multiaxial system.

The Texas-based Timberlawn research group has developed several scales of equal utility for practice and research. One of them is the Gossett-Timberlawn Adolescent Psychopathology Scale (published in full in appendix A of Gossett, Lewis, and Barnhart 1983), which provides detailed ratings in the following areas: autonomy, diagnostic severity, subjective discomfort, environmental effect, school performance, breadth and depth interests, intimacy of relationships, and maturity of object relationships; that is, the direction and nature of the person's most meaningful relationship ties, insight, and motivation. This assessment packet also includes a "liking" scale to be filled out by the person making the assessment and an Onset of Symptomatology scale. The third major scale developed by the Timberlawn group is a family evaluation scale, to be briefly reviewed in the next section.

The Beavers-Timberlawn Family Evaluation Scale (published in full in Lewis et al. 1976; Lewis and Looney 1983; and in Gossett, Lewis, and Barnhart 1983) requires ratings based on observed family interaction data on six separate scales measuring family structure, mythology, goal-directedness, autonomy, family affect, and the global health-pathology scale. This evaluation system was used in the studies reported in chapter 3, which classified families in four major categories: optimal, competent but pained, dysfunctional, and severely dysfunctional families. Many other family assessment instruments have been developed in recent years; the author is experimenting with the use of several of these scales in a number of settings but is not as yet ready to recommend any one of the scales over the others. The reason for singling out the Beavers-Timberlawn Family Evaluation Scale is that it is the only scale growing out of clinical work with adolescents and their families. Selected references of research-based scales and assessment outlines from the clinical literature on work with families are listed at the end of this chapter.

Interventive Modalities

An almost bewildering number of interventive approaches have been tried in work with adolescents and their families, and given the meager empirical foundations, it is a difficult task to select among them. Sugar (1979) in a humorous vein states that he at times is tempted to use all the 300 different techniques reported in the literature "singly or together — or even to invent another three hundred approaches!" (p. 509). A number of books with a psychiatric orientation, including one edited by Sugar (1975), give examples of several modalities within a number of theoretical frameworks. Among them are Achenbach (1982) *Developmental Psychopathology*; Ellis and Bernard (1983) *Rational-Emotive Approaches to Problems of Childhood*; Esman (1983) *The Psychiatric Treatment of Adolescents*; Feinstein (1980) *Adolescence: Perspectives on Psychotherapy*; Meeks (1980) *The Fragile Alliance*; Novello (1979) *The Short Course in Adolescent Psychiatry*; Rinsley (1980) *Treatment of the Severely Disturbed Adolescent*; and the guidebook for a broader based therapeutic practice by Stein and Davis (1982). The latter book is a collection of summaries of published articles or books addressing specific adolescent behavior problems, and each section is introduced by the authors' overview of the state of the art in dealing with the particular problem in question. Jones and Pritchard (1980) have edited a British book entitled *Social Work with Adolescents*. The following sections will deal with the three major modalities: family treatment, group counseling, and individual counseling of adolescents and their families.

Family Treatment and Therapy

In the infancy of family therapy the prevailing attitude was that this modality was never the one of choice for adolescents because their psychological task is to extricate themselves from the family in terms of emotional and other dependencies. However, it soon became clear that this separation process does not take place until both the adolescent and the parents are ready to let go. Therefore, a crucial dimension for differential assessment is to determine how far the adolescent has progressed in the various developmental tasks and how the immediate and larger environment helps or hinders his or her progress.

To recapitulate some ideas presented earlier in this book by Stierlin, Scherz, and Rhodes, some crucial ideas in the adolescent's process of physical and psychological separation from the nuclear family are as follows. If the family has low tolerance for experimentation and change (that is, if family cohesion is tied with low adaptability and rigidity), the adolescent's striving for autonomy becomes a threat to the survival of the family as a system, and the dysfunctional expelling or binding modes of separation become likely. If the marital relationship cannot survive under the pressures of an increasingly autonomous adolescent, the expelling mode is the likely outcome, providing physical but not psychological separation from the family. If the marital relationship is primarily centered on parenting and cannot survive without the children as intrinsic parts of the cohesive family system, the binding mode is likely, allowing neither physical nor emotional separation from the family. Still another pattern is a mixture of the binding and expelling parent-adolescent interaction patterns, the delegating mode, in which the adolescent goes and comes.

Ideas about families' varying capacities for coping with stress over the family life cycle (as elaborated in chapter 3, based on the Timberlawn family functioning categories and the Olson and McCubbin Circumplex Model) are well utilized in the transgenerational and life cycle stress approach to family treatment presented in Carter and McGoldrick (1980). The interplay between the two major types of stress — the Developmental Interaction (DI) and the Multigenerational Transmission (MT) effects — is crucial to the outcome of the adolescent's separation from the family. The DI effects assert that each family member's development is shaped by, and in turn shapes, the other family members' development. As the family moves forward in time, this developmental interaction stress (on the horizontal axis) flows from predictable and unpredictable events. The MT effects are linked with the multigenerational history of the family unit, which concerns the vertical flow in the family system of patterns of relating and functioning that are transmitted from one generation to the next, primarily through the mechanism of "emotional triangling" as formulated by Bowen (1976). The flow, say Carter and McGoldrick, includes family attitudes, taboos, expectations, myths, and loaded issues with which everybody grows up. They call it the hand we are dealt — a given that it is up to each person to do something with and about. The central idea is that there are emotional and other tasks to be fulfilled by the family system as it moves through the life cycle stages that require changes in the status of family members, and the transition from one stage to the next involves a complex emotional process. These ideas are fully elaborated by Carter and McGoldrick and by Terkelsen in Carter and McGoldrick (1980); they also draw attention to the basic — and often overlooked — fact that the family is the only system that can be joined only by birth, adoption, or marriage and that can be quit only by death. The divorce process results in ex-membership, not discontinuance.

In regard to family therapy within this perspective, the question is whether the family is experiencing difficulties within a life cycle stage, in which case the task is one of helping the family rebalance itself within the present systemic organization, or whether the family has derailed itself from the life cycle, in which case the family needs help getting back on the track by what Lynn Hoffman (1980) calls a quantum leap. The two types of changes are referred to as first order and second order changes, and it follows that the nature of the therapist's task and interventions will vary according to the type of change needed and required. N.J. Ackerman (1980) spells out the therapist's involvement with the cross-generational changes taking place in families with adolescents, an assignment that may challenge even the most seasoned therapist. But, as he says, if the therapist can weather the storm, as with the families themselves, the rewards may be substantial.

Of the many models of family therapy, the structural and strategic approaches are of special relevance to work with adolescents. These two models, which overlap to a large extent, both require the therapist to be quite active and problem and change oriented. A major thrust of the strategic model's application with adolescents is to "put the parents in charge" as elaborated by Cloé Madanes (1981) and Jay Haley, who in his latest book *Leaving Home: The Therapy for Disturbed Young People* (1980) offers many suggestions for the therapist's efforts to enlist families in active problem solving. Many of the case examples, however, indicate caseloads of adolescents with quite severe emotional disturbances. The structural model, developed originally by Minuchin (1979, 1981 and Minuchin and Fishman 1981), in work with black and Puerto Rican families of low socioeconomic status. This model — later expanded to families from all walks of life —

centers on change of the family's structural interaction patterns, as individual malfunctioning is seen as a consequence of a dysfunctional family
structure and subsystems. By restructuring the family unit, individual
behavior can be changed. The therapist promotes such restructuring by
joining the system and by use of confrontal and many other techniques.
Aponte, who has continued the model's application to poor families, also
gives full accounts of the history and dynamics of this approach (Aponte
1976, Aponte and Van Deusen 1981). A third problem-oriented family
model is the one developed by Nathan Epstein and his coworkers.

The dominance and impact of adolescent stage problems on family life
are also reflected in the fact that 8 out of the 12 cases selected for inclusion
in Peggy Papp's (1977) book on family therapy deal with adolescent problems. The full-length case studies contributed by a range of therapists, including social workers, illuminate the many different approaches and
techniques that may be employed to help families cope.

A model emerging from task-centered social work practice is the Task-
Centered Family Treatment approach by William J. Reid (1981, and in
press), which is characterized by planned short-term, structured interventions consisting of conjoint interviews with two or more family members to
help resolve difficulties or problems in interpersonal relations or by confronting the family as a whole. The family's problem-solving work is
organized around tasks family members agree to carry out with the practitioner's help either within the sessions (session tasks), in the home between
sessions (home tasks), or in the family's environment (environmental tasks,
which may be carried out by family members or the practitioner). Each
problem is always understood in the light of such contextual factors as patterns of family interactions, functioning of individuals, environmental factors, and so on. These factors may serve as resources for or obstacles to
problem resolution. The TCFT model, which is in early stages of testing
with families of various compositions and problems, makes use of some of
the assessment and interventive techniques developed in the structural,
strategic, and problem-centered system therapy introduced in previous sections. Theoretically the model builds on problem dynamics (Reid 1978 and
1981), general system theory, and communication theory.

Other illustrations of application of family therapy to social work practice are found in the latest edition of Florence Hollis's book on psychosocial
therapy (Hollis and Woods 1981), which includes a case example involving a
family with adolescent children. Several such cases are also found in the
book by McGoldrick, Pearce, and Giordano (1982), *Ethnicity and Family
Therapy*. The popularity of family therapeutic approaches for work with
adolescents is additionally reflected in *International Book of Family Therapy*,

edited by Florence W. Kaslow (1982), which presents chapters from Argentina, Australia, Belgium, Canada, England, Israel, Italy, Norway, South Africa, and the United States.

Guidelines for deciding when family therapy is indicated as the major intervention modality chosen over group or individual counseling for adolescents or parents are beginning to appear in the professional literature. Meeks (1980) suggests the following four indicators for the use of family therapy: (1) Crisis situations. Family interviews may be helpful in revealing whether the adolescent's crisis behavior (runaway, suicide attempt, illegitimate pregnancy) represents an ill-advised attempt to emancipate from a family system plagued by chronic problems or if the behavior reflects a temporary developmental conflict. (2) Situations in which the adolescent's difficulties are tied with problems in separating from the parents. Such families, says Meeks, come on their own accord when the youngster tries to extricate himself from the family bonds or when the school or other institutions or agencies note the adolescent's immaturity. He also points to the situation where the adolescent is being used to satisfy parental needs or to play the role of mediator, confidant, or spouse surrogate. The therapist's general tendency to side with the adolescent in these situations needs to be checked, since the parent will only become more clinging in his or her efforts to hold on to the adolescent if the parents feel the therapist is on the adolescent's side. (3) Families who consistently externalize problems are also candidates for a family therapy approach, even though it is very difficult to change the destructive relationship patterns. (4) Meeks mentions the need for family therapy in cases where the adolescent is required to carry a scapegoating role in order to maintain a neurotic family homeostasis. In these cases, the family therapy often needs to be supplemented with individual therapy for the youngster, who may have difficulties in letting go of the scapegoating role that so far has at least assured a place in the family structure.

Another list of indicators and of contraindicators of family therapy in adolescent cases is presented by Offer and VanderStoep (1975) and by Stierlin et al. (1977). Hall (1984) suggests separate treatment of adolescents and parents is indicated when anger is a significant problem, while treatment together is preferred when anger has been reduced through separate treatment or when conflict initially is low. All the guidelines presented in this section for choice of intervention modality build more on clinical experience than on systematic empirical observations.

To complete the list of books on family therapy and adolescence, I mention *Adolescent Crisis. Family Counseling Approaches* by Leveton (1984); *Family Therapy Techniques for Problem Behaviors of Children and Teenagers* by Schaefer, Briesmeister, and Fitton (1984) and *Practicing Family*

Therapy in Diverse Settings by Berger, Jurkovic, and Associates (1984), which includes chapters on settings serving adolescents. So far family therapy has been discussed primarily as a tool for promoting change. An additional important function to be served by family therapy is prevention of developmental and other family problems.

Prevention in Family Practice

Claude Guldner's (1983) growth-promoting family therapy model represents a prevention approach to family practice. This model builds on the underlying assumption that families have a natural inclination to develop their potentials and strive to reach optimal functioning levels. Growth-promoting family therapy may be offered as a continuation of crisis- or problem-solving therapy, not for the purpose of reaching deeper levels, which is another and common reason for extension of therapy, but with the aim of helping the family develop its strengths and potentials. The model may also be offered as a preventive service, preparatory to life cycle passages; the reason here may be some concern or apprehension in the family over its capacity to cope with upcoming life cycle tasks, even though no specific problems are identified and no crisis present. Finally, growth-promoting family therapy is offered in one- or two-session formats to well-families in much the same style as medical or dental check-ups. If, in the latter case, the family becomes aware of a need for expanding its repertoire in respect to attitudes, behaviors, or communication processes, a few additional sessions may be scheduled to carry out the specific task. Usually a follow-up session is then scheduled three or six months later to assure that the changes have been integrated to the benefit of the family.

The family system is seen as having at least three life stage cycles operating at the same time: the cycles of the individuals, the marital couple, and the family as a whole. Additional system levels include the extended families and community networks. The therapist may enter the family system at one or more of these levels. Guldner sees the patterns of family structure in the context of eight issue areas identified from his own experience and other family theorists: boundary, power, affective, communication, and negotiation issues; contextual issues of time, space, and energy within the individual and the family; task performance issues; and self-esteem. These issues are approached through the eight modalities of experiential, strategic, structural, interactional dynamic, behavioral, problem-solving, and educational modalities. Techniques used include reframing, sculpting, constructed imagery, video feedback, home tasks, and growth-promoting actions among family members in the sessions.

Two case examples given by Guldner involve families with adolescents. One of them, the Dell family, consist of the father Harry (46), mother Bertha (46), Tom (16), Greg (14), and Nell (12). The parents were concerned about their parenting roles and they felt a growing need for reaffirming the marital relationship, which had been given somewhat short shift compared with energies devoted to parenting and their careers. The Dell family contracted for four family enhancement therapy sessions — a four-week family enrichment workshop with parallel adolescent and parent groups, a marriage enrichment weekend for the couple, and one joint session including Mrs. D's parents. In the therapy and workshop sessions, the family learned new problem-solving models related to adolescent developmental issues, parent-child conflict resolutions, behavioral techniques of establishing goals and rewarding their attainment, insight into self and others in the family context (including how the grandparents and the parents' workplaces affected family functioning), new ways of dealing with anger and of dyadic communication, creation of clear boundaries of the marital subsystem, and enhancement of Bertha's competence as a parent in relation to daughter Nell. Frequent conflicts between Nell and Bertha's mother in which Bertha was bypassed reflected old, unresolved conflicts between Bertha and her mother. By the strategy of shifting Bertha out of the role of go-between into actively seeking her mother's support in dealing with Nell and discussion of their differences in parenting styles, Nell was relieved from being the locus of the acting-out of her mother's and grandmother's unfinished conflicts. Guldner illustrates how various techniques were used to bring about these changes. For example, Harry was given the home task of finding time for some activities by himself three times a week without feeling guilty about it. Harry had seen his desire to have more time for himself as self-centered, a view shared by his wife. The therapist reframed Harry's desire as normal for his developmental stage at mid-life and helped Harry to see that in meeting his own personal needs and maintaining a strong bond to the family Harry would provide a good model for his adolescent children in their growing need for separateness and individuation from the family.

Guldner is very clear about the need for extensive training for growth-promoting family therapy. Beginners, in his experience, do not work well as primary prevention service providers since most therapy training starts with a focus on pathology. In contrast, the growth-promoting model requires a focus on family competence and strength, and it may be easier to work from that perspective after problem-oriented therapy has been mastered. In addition, Guldner and others in *Prevention in Family Services* recognize the difficulties in convincing communities of the benefits of a primary prevention approach.

This section of family therapy concludes with a discussion of the role played by siblings in adolescent family work and the ways in which siblings may become involved.

Interventions and the Sibling Subsystem

The general tendency to fail to take into account the sibling subsystem, as mentioned in chapter 3, has meant that siblings traditionally have been overlooked as resources and/or targets for intervention (Rhodes 1977). Murray Bowen's three-generational family system approach is to be given a large part of the credit for a slow change in this respect; it is difficult to totally ignore the siblings when they have to go into the genogram, that is, the "intergenerational map of three or more generations of a family" (Hartman and Laird 1983, p. 215).

In healthy families siblings often support one another in the move out of the parental nest. In families with the extreme forms of binding and expelling, siblings are often cast into the rigid roles of "well" or "bad/sick" children, creating very complex family interactions. As the parents are preoccupied with the behaviors of the bad child, the well child may sneak out of the family unnoticed and achieve higher levels of autonomous functioning, often with a sense of guilt over having escaped at the bad sibling's expense (Rhodes 1977). Other patterns of separation of well siblings and their interplay with a sick sibling are spelled out by Bank and Kahn (1975), as reported in Tsukada 1979). One pattern is that of flight and avoidance as described above — the well adolescent is sustained by persons outside the family or other well siblings in the avoidance of becoming entangled in the sick child-parental triangle. Another strategy is a coalition between the well child and the parents against the sick sibling. In the role of the "white sheep" the child derives satisfaction from the alliance with the parents to the detriment of the sick sibling. A third possibility is an alliance between the well and the sick siblings against the parents; this may provide the well child an opportunity to rework prior unresolved conflicts with the parents and allow the sick to make a move toward disengagement from the parents. A fourth pattern, described by Bank and Kahn (1975) is the well child taking on the role of go-between, which has much in common with the parental child role. The well child feels loyalty toward the sick sibling as well as to the parents and can perform an important role as mediator in helping the parents to let go and in encouraging the sibling to move on.

The relationship among siblings in incestuous, abusing families has been subject to study, particularly in order to find out why some children are singled out for abuse and the siblings are not. Herrenkohl and Herrenkohl (1979) compared abused children with their nonabused siblings and found that the abused children were more likely to remind their parents in negative ways about themselves, they were considered "different" from birth, and they exhibited more behavioral problems than the siblings. Mary deYoung (1981) in her analysis of the siblings of incest victims notes that siblings often realize that incest is taking place and sometimes, consciously or unconsciously, actually collude to set the sibling up as the victim. In other instances siblings may be envious of the extra attentions bestowed on the incest victim. Feelings of guilt and anger may lead to psychological disturbances in siblings years later. DeYoung states that many siblings of incest victims grow up to live normal, healthy lives, but others are deeply affected by the experience. A consequence of these observations is a strong recommendation to focus on the entire family when intervening.

Tsukada (1979) points to Murray Bowen's concepts of "differentiation of self" and "triangulation" as appropriate theoretical frameworks for understanding the interrelationship between sibling interaction and parental alliance. Variations in self-differentiation among family members — as postulated by Bowen (1976) — are reflected in the four types of well siblings. The least differentiated of all is the sick sibling, while the well sibling in coalition with parents against the sick is only slightly more differentiated, since he or she does not perceive the scapegoating process or feel any loyalty toward the sibling. The go-between and avoidant siblings have differentiated themselves sufficiently from the parents to at least be able to identify the nature of the parental projections; however, the go-between may become too involved in the family and inadvertently entrench an unhealthy power distribution within the family. The avoidant sibling runs the danger of distancing and disengaging from the family to the point of denial of any need for emotional ties with the family. Within all of these patterns a range of interactions may be found, from the productive to the dysfunctional. As Tsukada points out, many combinations are possible between different types of well siblings and different kinds of familial triangles.

The following case vignette illustrates the role of an older sister in helping her younger sister's release from a binding relation to the mother.

Agency Setting: General Hospital's Social Service Department. Thirteen-year-old Rita was referred by her teacher for a complete neurological examination because of emotional, perceptual, and learning difficulties, particularly in math.

Rita lives with her mother, an 18-year-old sister, and her maternal grandmother in a public housing project. An older sister, Chris, left home to attend college, to which she had earned a scholarship. Rita's father committed suicide when Mrs. J. was five months pregnant with Rita. The family has survived on Social Security payments. All women in this three-generational family suffer from asthma. Mrs. J. has always been extremely close to her mother, from whom she has never been separated except for a three-week period shortly after she was married. Mrs. J. has held secretarial jobs on and off and is currently enrolled in a job training program to upgrade her skills.

Rita is a very shy, stuttering youngster who stayed in close proximity to her mother when talking with the social worker at the Social Service clinic. Rita has been more affected by the asthmatic condition than her older sisters. Mrs. J. is very ambivalent about the demands that Rita, who was an unwanted child, has placed on her. At the same time, Mrs. J. is extremely overprotective toward Rita. When the school suggested that Rita be transferred to a moderate learning disability class in a different school, Mrs. J. vehemently refused to give her permission for fear that Rita would get lost in the process of making a bus transfer to or from the new school.

The worker, sensitive to Mrs. J's extreme need to hang on to her youngest child, offered individual counseling to Mrs. J. for a four-month period. Simultaneously, the worker engaged in environmental work on behalf of Rita in working with school personnel to make a transfer possible and in obtaining an examination at a specialized Speech and Hearing Clinic. The worker also supported Mrs. J's application to the housing authorities for a better apartment.

Against the mother's wishes, the oldest daughter, Chris, on a visit home from college insisted on talking with the social worker in support of Rita's transfer to the appropriate school. The mother finally reluctantly gave her permission for the transfer after the worker had assured her that services would be continued until a successful transfer had taken place.

Rita, with support from the worker and the big sister, made the transfer without getting lost; after three months in the new school, Rita had made some new friends (she did not have any in the previous school), and she made progress academically.

Mrs. J. had several severe asthma attacks immediately after the transfer, but she was able slowly to engage herself more actively in the vocational training and she secured a new position.

The J. family's contact with the clinic lasted almost one year. It is an example of how preventive and supportive services consisting of a blend of individual counseling, securing collaboration with a sister who made it out of the system (and perhaps feels guilty about it), and utilizing other community service providers can lessen extreme dependency bonds between a parent and an adolescent.

Some of the propositions formulated by Schvaneveldt and Ihinger (1979) on the basis of empirical and theoretical findings are paraphrased below as they may serve as suggestive guides for practitioner consideration of sibling involvement in specific cases. It needs to be kept in mind, however, that these propositions generally lack sufficient empirical support to be used as predictive rules.

General Proposition (p. 461)

1. The higher the number of siblings in a family, that is, the stronger the sibling subsystem, the less parents influence the children.
2. Sex role identification is facilitated by opposite-sex siblings, and the impact is greatest from elder to younger siblings (p. 462).
3. Sibling affect emerging from sibling interaction is influenced by age, sex, spacing of siblings, and degree of parental cohesiveness (p. 463).

Propositions Relating to Parental Coalitions and Sibling Subsystems (pp. 458, 463)

4. When parental coalitions are so strong that no child is allowed to ever form a winning coalition with one parent against the other, strong coalitions are to be expected among the children.
5. When a parent is clearly dominant, a coalition between the weaker parent and a child is likely to form, which may in turn lead to formation of sibling coalitions against the favored child.
6. Parents nearly equal in power but without a strong parental coalition are likely to have children who engage in intense and bitter sibling rivalry to take advantage of the shifting coalition opportunities offered by the parents.

Propositions on Sibling Solidarity (pp. 459–60)

7. Sibling solidarity is increased by (a) interaction that is mutually regulated to maximize rewards and reduce cost and by (b) the degree to which siblings serve as a bridge for one another to the adult world.
8. Sibling pioneering activities viewed positively by the parents serve to generate harmony in the family; if viewed negatively, conflict between the pioneering child and the parents will be generated.
9. Sibling departures provide clues to the emotional well-being of siblings in the family to the extent siblings provide mediating services between parents and other siblings.

Rules of Fairness

10. Conflict interaction in the sibling subsystem is lowered when parents apply justice norms with consistency and congruence to arbitrary situations (p. 462).

Parental Sibling Function

11. Designation of parental power to a sibling is accepted by siblings who will grant power to that sibling.
12. A sibling holding resources considered desirable holds power and authority over siblings.
13. A sibling exercising coercive powers of intimidation creates alienation in the sibling system.

Group Counseling and Interventions

Much of the general group therapy and group treatment literature has been developed from practice with adolescent groups. Because the peer group takes on special significance in the adolescent's socialization into the non-parental world, perhaps there is no age group for whom a group approach is more natural or appropriate than adolescents. The conditions in the group interaction that are assumed to promote positive changes in the group members have been examined by Yalom (1975), who asked adult group therapy participants to organize Q-sort cards of group items into categories of helpfulness. From the answers Yalom extracted 11 curative factors, including altruism, group cohesiveness, universality ("same boat" experience), interpersonal learning (input and output), imparting information guidance, catharsis, identification, family reenactment, self-understanding, instillation of hope, and existential experiences. Corder, Whiteside, and Haizlip (1981) replicated this procedure with 16 adolescents, ranging from 13 to 17 years of age, from four therapy groups. The adolescents' choices were strikingly similar to the adults' judgments of helpfulness in the group. Highest rankings were given to catharsis, interpersonal learning, existential factors, group cohesiveness, and universality. Least helpful as judged by both adults and adolescents were guidance from and modeling of other group members. The two groups differed in importance ascribed to insight category items, such as "Discovering and accepting previously unknown and unacceptable parts of myself." Adults ranked this item as number one, but it was ranked very low by adolescents, which these researchers attribute both to adolescents' general defensiveness against recognizing conflicts within themselves and to the therapists' nonconfrontal therapeutic efforts. On the other hand the adolescents gave high rankings to opportunities for cathartic expression of feelings, which would require group therapists to maintain a delicate balance between techniques promoting expressions of feelings and not getting too close to the resistance toward insight. In another article Corder and Whiteside (with Koehne and Hortman as co-authors, 1981) present techniques for handling loss and addition of members in adolescent psychotherapy groups.

In analyzing the powerfulness of the group, Weisberg (1979) notes that the group approach focuses on "the processes by which decisions are made rather than on judgments as to the adequacy or inadequacy of the participants' behaviors" (p. 183). He states that the group generally has fewer restraints on behavior than the family and provides an education, "a crash course," in socialization and interpersonal skills. Group therapy, like family therapy, is carried out within various theoretical frameworks and for dif-

ferent purposes, such as maturation of group members, furthering socialization, problem solving, task achievement, or to provide a corrective emotional growth experience or healing. Whittaker and Small (1977) compare
assumptions, goals, techniques, role of therapist, role of client, strengths,
and limitations of three approaches: the psychodynamic approach, aiming
at "personality and behavior change through free interaction in a carefully
structured social environment" (p. 5) for children 4 years old through adolescence; the behavioral approach, aiming at behavior change by application of principles of social learning for behavior disordered children; and
the guided group interaction approach, using group interaction to shape
behavior primarily of older delinquent adolescents who participate in daily
group sessions that are highly structured. In terms of empirical validation,
only the behavioral approach has produced a strong base of many studies
showing effectiveness in behavior change.

In any event group approaches are used in multiple settings. Hancock
(1982) describes the many uses of groups by the school social worker in the
form of developmental groups, group-centered counseling, problem-solving
groups, task-centered groups, and support groups for children who have
recently experienced loss or conflicts such as adolescence or newly divorced
parents. Over half of the chapters in the book edited by Berkovitz entitled
*Adolescents Grow in Groups: Experiences in Adolescent Group Psycho-
therapy* (1972) address preventive services in clinics, offices, and community
groups. The remainder deals with hospital and residential settings serving
adolescents.

Strategies for group work with adolescents from a task-centered perspective are discussed by Garvin, and Rooney offers an example of such group
work in the public schools (Reid and Epstein 1977). Larsen and Mitchell
(1980) present guidelines for task-centered, strength-oriented group work
with delinquents in order to diminish self-defeating behaviors. Closely
related to task-centered group treatment is social skills training and life
skills counseling, which are both gaining in popularity. The former approach in a 1982 special issue of *Child & Youth Services* Journal (LeCroy)
reviews the use of social skills training with adolescents and its application
to court-adjudicated youths and to emotionally disturbed adolescents in a
day treatment program. The life skills counseling approach is fully reported
by Schinke and Gilchrist (1984); this approach, addressing all aspects of
everyday life, may be carried out individually or in groups, and it has growing empirical evidence to support its effectiveness.

One of the most carefully designed, experimental studies of the use of
groups in rehabilitation of prosocial and antisocial boys is reported by Feldman, Caplinger, and Wodarski (1983). This successful experiment delineated

the group process with the leader of the group as the group's moderator, which in turn alters the group members' behavior. While group composition was a powerful factor, it was shown to change with the changing profiles of peer behaviors. The researchers conclude that "the most rapid and potent therapeutic changes among groupmates took place in integrated groups [prosocial mixed with antisocial boys] that were treated by experienced leaders" (p. 278).

Other examples of application of group processes are found in MacLennan and Felsenfeld's (1968) *Group Counseling and Psychotherapy with Adolescents*; in Kerslake's chapter on group work with adolescents in Great Britain (Jones and Pritchard 1980); Goldberg and Goldberg's (1982) article on group work with former cultists; Lieberman's (1982) use of mixed-age groups; in Raubolt's (1983) discussion of group composition and leadership style in brief, problem-focused group psychotherapy with adolescents; and several examples are found in Northen's (1982) book, *Clinical Social Work*.

The psychosocial needs of the adolescents in question, the agency setting and function, and the availability of appropriate groups influence the practitioner's decision about which of the group approaches to select. Berkovitz and Sugar (1975) discuss indicators and contraindicators for group therapy within outpatient settings, with adolescents in hospitals and residential settings, and with adolescents with specific problems such as obesity, mental retardation, illegitimate pregnancy, drug-abuse, and in foster homes and welfare programs. Their summation of general themes and indicators includes: recommendations to "provide a miniature real life situation for study and change of behavior"; develop new ways of dealing with situations and skills in human relations; provide new models of identification; help adolescents feel less isolated; provide protection from adults while undergoing change; and "uncover relationship problems not evident in individual therapy" (p. 22). They find group therapy generally contraindicated for adolescents who are too deviant from the rest of a specific group, for some adolescents categorized as "narcissistic," and for those with deficient control. For them "group therapy may be inadvisable due to potential excess group contagion or stimulation leading to disorganization" (p. 23).

Individual Counseling

The third major intervention modality encountered in work with adolescents is individual counseling, which may be offered concurrently with family and group therapy or independently of these. Again the modality choice depends on the adolescent's needs and wants, the presented problem, and his or her "developmental age" in relation to self, the biological family, and to peers. The process of individual counseling with emotionally disturbed adolescents in a community setting is presented in *Effective Counseling of Adolescents* by Rabichow and Sklansky (1980), who operate within a psychodynamic personality perspective. Exclusive focus on counseling of adolescent girls is provided in Doris Lamb's (1978) sensitive and thoughtful book. Several practice experiences and studies support the values of short-term and task-centered approaches to individual counseling of adolescents (Bass and Hofstad in Reid and Epstein 1977 and Norman 1980). Other evidence points to the advantages of concurrent utilization of individual, family, and group approaches (Chase 1979 and Kellam et al. 1981). The latter reference also emphasizes the powers inherent in peer counseling, which may be offered in a one-to-one context or in a group.

A study comparing the relative effectiveness of family therapy versus individual therapy was carried out by Wellisch, Vincent, and Ro-Trock (1976) in an inpatient psychiatric institute. Twenty-eight adolescents (between 13 and 22 years of age) were selected from the intake population if they met the criterion of having an intact family. The patients were randomly assigned to either a family therapy group or individual therapy. Both programs were short term — eight sessions in duration. In comparison with therapist activities in the family therapy sessions, therapists in individual sessions tended to be less directive and verbal. Self-report measures as well as observational measures of family problem solving and community readjustment measures at three-month follow-up were used. Of the adolescents in individual therapy who returned to the families who had received no treatment, 43 percent were readmitted to the inpatient setting within three months, whereas no one was readmitted from the family therapy group. The patients from the latter group also returned to work or school in fewer days than those who had been seen in individual therapy. Findings regarding changes in nonverbal and verbal positive and negative behaviors are difficult to interpret.

This section on interventive modalities with adolescents closes with an additional reference to the Stein and Davis (1982) collection of article digests describing individual, group, and family techniques applied to a broad range of emotional, physical, interpersonal, antisocial, sexual and substance abuse problems and suicidal behaviors.

Notes

1. As the methodologically sound studies in five different areas may have special interest, full references to them are given below (they are not included in the bibliography of this book).

1. Jesness, C.F. 1975. "Comparative Effectiveness of Behavior Modification and Transactional Analysis Programs for Delinquents." *Journal of Consulting and Clinical Psychology* 43: 758–779.
2. Massimo, J. and Shore, M. 1963. "The Effectiveness of a Comprehensive Vocationally Oriented Psychotherapeutic Program for Adolescent Delinquent Boys." *American Journal of Orthopsychiatry* 33: 634–642.
   Shore, M. and Massimo, J. 1966. "Comprehensive Vocationally Oriented Psychotherapy for Adolescent Delinquent Boys: A Follow-up Study." *American Journal of Orthopsychiatry* 36: 609–615.
   Shore, M. and Massimo, J. 1969. "Five Years Later: A Follow-up Study of Comprehensive Vocationally Oriented Psychotherapy." *American Journal of Orthopsychiatry* 39: 769–773.
   Shore, M. and Massimo, J. 1973. "After Ten Years: A Follow-up Study of Comprehensive Vocationally Oriented Psychotherapy." *American Journal of Orthopsychiatry* 43: 128–132.
3. Persons, R. 1966. "Psychological and Behavioral Change in Delinquents Following Psychotherapy." *Journal of Clinical Psychology* 22: 337–340.
   Persons, R. 1967. "Relationship between Psychotherapy with Institutional Delinquent Boys and Subsequent Community Adjustment." *Journal of Consulting Psychology* 31: 137–141.
4. Redfering, D.L. 1972. "Group Counseling with Institutionalized Delinquent Females." *American Corrective Therapy Journal* 26: 160–163.
   Redfering, D.L. 1973. "Durability of Effects of Group Counseling with Institutionalized Delinquent Females." *Journal of Abnormal Psychology* 82: 85–86.
5. Ro-Trock, G.K., Wellisch, D., and Schoolar, J. 1977. "A Family Therapy Outcome Study in an Inpatient Setting." *American Journal of Orthopsychiatry* 47: 514–522.

Selected References on Family Assessment

Ackerman, N.W., and Behrens, M.L. 1974. "Family Diagnosis and Clinical Process." In Caplan, G. (ed.) *Child and Adolescent Psychiatry, Sociocultural and Community Psychiatry. American Handbook of Psychiatry.* Second edition. Vol. 2. New York: Basic Books.

Bolton, F.G. 1983. *When Bonding Fails. Clinical Assessment of High-Risk Families.* Beverly Hills, Calif.: Sage. (This book deals with assessment of adolescent parenthood in chapter 9.)

Compher, J.V. 1982. "Parent-School-Child Systems: Triadic Assessment and Intervention." *Social Casework* 63(7): 415–423.

Esptein, N.B.; Baldwin, L.M.; and Bishop, D.S. 1983. "The McMaster Family Assessment Device." *Journal of Marital and Family Therapy* 9(2): 171–180.

Epstein, N.B., and Bishop, D.S. 1981. "Problem-Centered Systems Therapy of the Family." In Gurman, A.S., and Kniskern, D.P. (eds.) *Handbook of Family Therapy.* New York: Brunner/Mazel.

Geismar, L.L. 1980. *Family and Community Functioning. A Manual of Measurement for Social-Work Practice and Policy.* Second, revised and expanded edition. Metuchen, N.J.: The Scarecrow Press, Inc.

Hartman, A., and Laird, J. 1983. *Family-Centered Social Work Practice.* New York: The Free Press. (Outline for family assessment, pp. 345-353.)

Hepworth, D.H., and Larsen, J.A. 1982. *Direct Social Work Practice. Theory and Skills.* Homewood, Ill.: The Dorsey Press, chap. 11.

Homan, A.M. 1983. *Family Assessment. Tools for Understanding and Intervention.* Beverly Hills, Calif.: Sage.

Hudson, W.W. 1982. *The Clinical Measurement Package. A Field Manual.* Homewood, Ill.: The Dorsey Press.

Moos, R.H., and Fuhr, R. 1982. "The Clinical Use of Social-Ecological Concepts: The Case of an Adolescent Girl." *American Journal of Orthopsychiatry* 52(1): 111-122.

Olson, D.H., et al. 1982. *Family Inventories. Inventories Used in a National Survey of Families Across the Family Life Cycle.* St. Paul, Minn.: Family Social Science, University of Minnesota.

Tomlinson, R., and Peters, P. 1981. "An Alternative to Placing Children: Intensive and Extensive Therapy with 'Disengaged' Families." *Child Welfare* 55(2): 95-103. (Contains a framework for assessing the disengaged family.)

8 INTERVENTIONS WITH SPECIFIC GROUPS OF ADOLESCENTS

This final chapter presents examples of interventive considerations and services regarding three selected groups of adolescents: those who come from divorced and remarried families, those in foster care and adoptive homes, and runaways.

Divorce and Stepfamily Counseling

Divorce counseling has grown out of the need for effective interventions that help divorcing parents go through the process of breaking up the family in ways that protect the developmental growth of the children and adolescents involved. As discussed in chapter 3, the impact and consequences of divorce are varied and are not yet fully known and understood. The goal of divorce counseling — as far as the children are concerned — is to deflect the bitterness or hatred in the marital relationship away from the children, to create a truce area or "demilitarized zone" around them, as the Group for Advancement of Psychiatry (1981, p. 117) calls it. The divorcing parents are aided in developing enough common interest in the welfare of the children to allow for co-parenting. This is accomplished through increasing self-esteem and diminishing feelings of failure, guilt, and blame so that a more balanced view of the ex-spouse may develop. The children's pain and trauma are recognized, and they are helped to accept the divorce as real. Even though it is recognized that only a beginning step can be taken in coping with the trauma at the time of divorce, the committee suggests that courts recommend divorce counseling in all cases involving children and that more research be carried out to establish the relative benefits of individual and family therapy or group workshops, the most beneficial length, spacing, and numbers of sessions, and the long-term consequences of divorce for children of different ages.

Goldmeier (1980) describes a framework for intervention in divorcing families that emphasizes development of coping tasks appropriate for the three stages of divorce. The first stage is the divorce process, which includes the decision to divorce and the restructuring of roles and relationships. The second phase is family dismemberment. This period between divorce and remarriage involves coping mechanisms aimed at "maintaining family and personal integrity in the face of the loss of an important member" (p. 40). Family reconstitution, or phase three, includes restructuring of the roles and relationships including the new spouse. Goldmeier suggests that guilt, fear, and loneliness are the most prominent impediments to problem solving as the family members pass through the phases of the divorce-to-family-reconstruction continuum. Interventions to assist the involved persons need to be flexible in terms of timing and types; some need to address relationship building, while others focus more on developing practical skills and clarification of person-situation configurations.

Other writers point to the usefulness of Minuchin's structural family therapy framework for understanding and assisting the family at the crisis of divorce transition (Kaplan 1977; Ahrons, 1980). According to Ahrons, the spousal relationship not only determines how the divorced family redefines itself but also sets the emotional climate for the redefinition and the boundaries of the new co-parental relationship. In order to reduce contamination of parental roles by spousal conflicts, a clarification of the boundaries of the two subsystems is needed. The behavioral rules growing out of this clarification process about how each parent will relate to the child in the future are crucial to the child. And the actual relationships that develop between the child and each of the parents have significant influence on the effect of the divorce on the child's development. Ahrons, in her research on a random sample of divorced parents drawn from court records, found great variation in how well divorcing parents manage to separate the spousal and parenting roles. There was a major difference between those parents who were able to "discuss, plan, and negotiate child-rearing with each other directly and those who were not. Parents who were not able to interact with each other were similarly unable to separate parental from spousal subsystems" (p. 439). When they would get together to discuss child-related issues, they would end up discussing the marital relationship and divorce-related inequities. Major tasks for divorce counselors are helping the divorcing spouses disengage from their spousal roles and develop new rules for the ongoing parent-child relationships and for the co-parenting roles. In this process of helping the family redefine itself as a binuclear family, living separately in two households, the counselor or therapist needs to help the family members to consider the divorced family as a continuing but different family system. Ways by which this can be done, over and beyond counseling sessions, are providing the divorcing parents options for access to other divorced co-parents to serve as role models and providing support in groups of divorcing families or through workshops and lectures. For the children, co-parenting affords continuation of attachment bonds to both parents, and with clear separation of the spousal and parental subsystems, children are much less likely to be drawn into the spousal conflicts. Ahrons (1983) elaborates on the role changes and the redefinition of family boundaries and rules as the family moves through five transition stages: individual cognition, family metacognition (family system begins to change in response to recognizing that a problem exists), separation, family reorganization, and family redefinition, which frequently includes remarriage and incorporation of a stepparent into the postdivorce family. Ahrons (1983) provides a case illustration of how one family coped with the stresses of each of these phases. Kaplan (1977) provides other examples of reorganization of family structure, while Abelsohn (1983) gives a detailed account of the impact on three adolescent girls of the restoration of parental functioning in one postdivorce family.

One type of divorce counseling, referred to as custody mediation, seeks to arrive at a custodial decision based on which parent can meet the emotional, cognitive, physical, and social needs of the child more effectively and fully. In some cases the choice of joint custody is used as a viable alternative when both parents are capable of sharing the ongoing parenting. While joint custody appears to work well in some postdivorce families, empirical support for this alternative as an optimum approach for all children is still very modest (Derdeyn and Scott 1984; Vanderkooi and Pearson 1983; Watson 1981).

Treatment considerations and techniques for helping postdivorce families blend and become stepfamilies are offered in four fairly recent books — Carter and McGoldrick 1980; Sager et al. 1983; Visher and Visher 1979; and Wald 1981. All make important contributions to this fast-growing specialization of counseling and therapy, and all contain numerous case examples of which many include adolescents. The principles for interventions, the phases of the counseling process, techniques, and modalities discussed are too numerous and complex to summarize. A few points specifically addressing the needs of adolescents in stepfamily counseling have been selected for inclusion here.

McGoldrick and Carter (1980) give several rules for treatment of which the following are relevant for adolescents. The relationship between a child/adolescent and a stepparent takes time to develop. The shift to active stepparenting may take several years, and in "the case of older adolescents, it may not be appropriate to expect the shift to occur to any great degree at all" (p. 293). Feelings of loss may be especially great in children for whom the remarriage ends a long and close single-parent/child relationship, so the shift to a new system may take a long time. If a child is presenting a problem, it is important to involve all parents and stepparents in treatment as soon as possible to resolve the child's difficulties. Stepparents may need help in "backing off" and putting the natural parent in charge in the case of "child-focused uproar," becoming reinvolved when the uproar dies down. Finally, McGoldrick and Carter alert therapists to difficulties related to the brought-together families' being at different life cycle stages and to look for "hidden agendas" in sudden requests for changes in custody, visitation, and financial arrangements (p. 293).

Both Visher and Visher (1979) and Sager et al. (1983) recommend groups for stepchildren. For adolescents the tasks appropriate for groups are mourning the loss of the nuclear family, which may take longer than for younger children as they have a longer nuclear family history, integration into the remarried family, overcoming feelings of isolation, and testing their sense of reality. Visher and Visher suggest restricting groups agewise because of rapid developmental changes to ages 10–13, 14–16, and 17–19 years.

Sager et al. have found use of an adaptation of MacGregor's (1964) multiple impact family therapy very helpful. This approach, originally developed in the mid-1950s to provide brief and intensive family treatment to families with adolescents who had a long distance to travel, calls for assignment of a therapist to each family member or at least each subsystem of the family. At large sessions including all family members and therapists, the professional person assigned to the units would speak for that unit and model adaptive behavior. The families treated by Sager et al. did not have long distances to travel, but the model was found useful in helping with difficulties some subunits in remarried families had in communicating and working toward common goals. This approach has been especially effective in dealing with emergencies, but is not continued for long because of its expense. Furthermore, Sager et al. recommend the use of multifamily therapy as the treatment of choice for remarried families with adolescents, who gain support from one another and welcome opportunities to talk about their ambivalent feelings toward their noncustodial parent of the REM adults, among other topics. Usually the multifamily therapy group has a maximum of four families and two co-therapists. Twenty or more members may form the multifamily therapy group, which works in 90-minute sessions (Sager et al. 1983, pp. 110, 262–63).

Adolescents in Out-of-Home Care

Interventive Services Provided for Adolescents in Foster Care

The activities described in this section are limited to those of the front-line child welfare worker who has responsibility for the ongoing direct contact with the adolescent in care and his or her natural and foster parents and for coordination of services from other professional or lay persons.

One point that should be emphasized is the importance of the involvement of the adolescent in the decision about out-of-home placement in the first place, about type of foster care and the duration of care. It is highly unlikely that an adolescent who has not even been consulted about placement decisions will be able to relate to the foster parents and others in a cooperative fashion. The adolescent may also be capable of suggesting alternative solutions overlooked by the parent(s) and the worker.

During the preplacement period as well as after placement has taken place, the child welfare worker is the key figure in coordinating needed supportive and adjunctive services, in facilitating and maintaining the adolescent's contact with the natural parent(s), in helping the adolescent adapt to the foster home, and in facilitating contacts between foster parents and natural parents. Because of the caseworker's central role in the adolescent's life, regularity and stability of direct contacts between worker and adolescent are particularly important. In the Shyne and Schroeder (1978) national study, actual contacts between the child and the public child welfare worker were reported in only two-thirds of the cases. And in these cases, contacts decreased as the length of stay in care increased. The average number of contacts was one a month.

A similarly discouraging picture emerges from Zimmerman's interviews with young adults formerly in foster care. Only 3 of the 61 interviewed mentioned understanding the worker to have responsibilities beyond monitoring what went on in the foster home and the child's development, for example, the responsibility to help the natural family toward rehabilitation. Even those who were emancipated from foster care did not recall discussing with their caseworkers topics such as sexual issues, job finding, education, or finding a place to live after leaving foster care. Even allowing for faulty memories of these youngsters and for the possibility that the workers supported the foster parents in carrying these roles, Zimmerman seems justified in concluding that the placement agency needs to make its position and function clear to the child through foster parents, social workers, natural parents, and the social worker's responsibility for interaction and communication among all parties involved, not the least of whom is the foster child him or herself. The former foster children who recalled helpful social workers mentioned that they responded to their needs and helped them when they asked for something — be it getting a tutor or finding something out about their natural families. All those who did not feel helped sufficiently said that the workers did not talk to them or did not hear what they had to say and subsequently did not meet their needs (Zimmerman 1982, pp. 115–16).

This picture is not complete, however, without considering how many children and adolescents one worker can truly listen to in one day. As the caseloads keep increasing in size, the herculean task of meeting the emotional, social, and other needs of the children in care becomes more than even the most dedicated and most highly educated expert can possibly fulfil. New administrative and management systems are called for in placement agencies; otherwise we are simply adding another human injustice — worker burn-out — to that of not meeting the *in loco parentis* responsibilities for the children in care. Such innovations are being experimented with, but child welfare policy and administrative issues go beyond the scope of the current analysis.

The decision about the extent of the social worker's direct work with the child may be guided by the conclusion drawn by Timberlake (1979) from her study of abused and nonabused children in foster care. For the nonabused children, who seemed to have a pretty good understanding of the reasons for placement, the social worker's intervention can focus primarily on significant persons in the child's life rather than working directly with the child. For the abused foster children, the needs are different in that these children experience greater confusion about placement, are more severely depressed, and have lower levels of school performance and stronger overt aggressive behavior patterns. Here direct work with the child, as well as work on behalf of the child, is called for. For the direct treatment, Timberlake (pp. 288–89) mentions goals such as working through loss and grief, decreasing self-defeating actions, building social relationships, and enhancing self-image. Even though Timberlake studied preadolescents in foster care, the need for differential services most likely applies to adolescents as well.

Mouzakitis (1984) proposes that treatment be applied differentially to the two distinguishable groups of nonchronically and chronically abused adolescents. For the latter group, the author proposes long-term insight-oriented therapy, possibly combined with group therapy for the adolescent who may need to be placed out of home, preferably in a treatment-oriented group home rather than a foster family home as foster care by and large has not been successful. For the nonchronically abused, short-term crisis approaches appear to be effective, but equal attention must be given to the parents and the total family; Mouzakatis observes that exclusive focus on the youngster can be counterproductive. While short-term foster home placement may be needed in some cases, it should be avoided so as not to alienate the adolescent from the family. Ziefert (1981) proposes that group foster homes can be a helpful alternative to an individual foster family placement. In her observations, younger adolescents appear to do better in a nuclear foster family setting where he or she is the youngest or the only child. Older adolescents seem to do better in group settings. However, individual cases need to take into account "the youth's own wishes for independence, self-sufficiency, and more intimate peer relationships, evolving relationships within the family, planned length of residence, and the need for and ability to tolerate provision of nurturance and warmth" (Ziefert 1981, p. 168). In all these cases the overriding concern is protection of the adolescent from further abuse, and the decision to return a youngster to the biological family must weigh the risks. Server and Janzen (1982) suggest that risk is present when the mother does not believe reports of sexual abuse, the father denies such abuse, the nonabusing parent is incapable of protecting the child, or the parents lack motivation to change the family system. Extreme vulnerability is present when the abuser's psychopathology prevents comprehension of the detrimental effects of the abuse or when the mother is so tied to the abuser that she is unable to relate positively to the daughter.

Boatman and Borkan (1981), as a result of treating 40 incest families, discuss the pros and cons of individual, group, and family therapy. *Individual therapy* is used primarily with the younger child as the sole treatment modality and sometimes in conjunction with family therapy to give the therapist an opportunity to check the child's perception. Some children are also uncomfortable about discussing the sexual experience in the presence of others. However, others and particularly adolescents are embarrassed about discussing the sexual experience with the therapist alone and prefer the group approach. A disadvantage of individual therapy is that it tends to perpetuate the sense of secrecy associated with incest. *Group therapy* offers great potential for peer support to abused adolescents; the sharing of experiences of incest and its aftermath of medical and court examinations can help the youngsters overcome their feelings of being "damaged goods." Boatman and Borkan share the observation that a male therapist in a group of adolescent girls elicits seductive behavior on the part of many girls; the use of opposite-sex therapists offers the group an alternate model for male-female relationships. However, group therapy is limited in altering long-standing psychopathological behaviors in some of the girls and in affecting the home situation directly. *Family therapy* may be helpful in bringing about change in the family system, particularly if the family is not too disorganized. These authors have found that teenagers who are not able to participate verbally in family therapy sessions use what goes on in these sessions to go deeper into personal issues in the individual therapy sessions. Family therapy is often used to help relocate parenting responsibilities to the parents, as the sexually abused daughter often has taken over aspects of the wife/mother roles. Changing such patterns, of course, requires both the mother's willingness and capacity to take on these roles and a strengthening of the marital relationship. Hoorwitz (1983) discusses the progressive steps involved in moving from excessive closeness between father and daughter (who holds a hierarchical position as powerful as the mother) as eliminating the closeness between father and daughter, developing an alliance between mother and daughter, and resumption of the parents' authority in the family by providing protection to the child and encouraging an improved marital relationship. Hoorwitz charts variations in these steps depending on whether the husband holds a dominant or a dependent position vis-à-vis the wife (Hoorwitz 1983, p. 523).

Other proposals of interventions with abusive families are given by Barth, Blythe, Schinke, and Schilling (1983), who successfully have offered small-group, short-term training in self-control and child management skills to maltreating parents. Susan J. Wells (1981) suggests helping families increase their verbal accessibility skills as preparatory to family therapy, utilizing crafts, games, role-play, and other action-oriented techniques. Gradually as the family's verbal skills improve other techniques may be used. Family therapy, however, is contraindicated in families close to breakup, families with a member so self-centered that he or she cannot participate in joint interviews, or in families where the parents are incapable of acting as parents and who are better served without the children being present. Several other interventive strategies are proposed in Kathleen C. Faller's book, *Social Work with Abused and Neglected Children. A Manual of Interdisciplinary Practice.*

To return to the social worker's tasks with adolescents in foster care, several authors (Euster et al. 1984; Joseph 1971; Lee 1977; MacIntyre 1970) stress the importance of offering group experiences to adolescents for the purpose of dealing with their feelings of uneasiness in living with strangers, the reasons for placement, the foster parents' view of their natural parents, and the burden of depression. Group experiences help clarify psychosexual roles and normalcy and help in the task of identity formation. For adolescents who have spent years in foster care, this latter task may also be facilitated by the worker's pulling together a dossier of life events from the adolescent's past and about his or her birth family.

Zimmerman's (1982) study revealed that sibling deprivation was especially strongly felt by foster children; siblings were the persons these youngsters wished they had seen more of while in placement regardless of the length of time they were in foster care. Zimmerman urges that the professionals involved make every effort to maintain sibling relations during placement as siblings represent a great resource for providing family continuity and support. Timberlake and Hamlin (1982) suggest that placement of a child in out-of-home care represents a crisis for the family, and while time may not allow for meeting with the sibling group at the point of placement, special efforts should be made to meet with the group on earliest follow-up. In meeting with the group, the worker can help the siblings recognize and express their fears and anxieties about one of them having had to be placed. Often siblings feel that they are at fault and perhaps could have prevented the placement. The purpose of the meeting also includes working on immediate problems at hand, encouraging a realistic view of the situation, and developing plans for visiting and communication with the placed sibling (Timberlake and Hamlin 1982, p. 550).

The social worker's cooperation with the foster parents involves administrative, educational, and supportive functions. Kline and Overstreet (1972) spell out the details of the content of the worker's collaboration with the foster parents from preplacement to the child's adjustment in the foster home, including relations to the natural parents and eventual discharge. One area that often has caused friction between foster parents and social workers is the foster child's moral development. To one social worker's question of why foster parents are so "hung-up" on values, a foster mother (Felker 1978) states that foster parents are supposed to *parent* the youngster, which includes attention to the shaping of values of the adolescent. Furthermore, the foster parents live with the adolescent, and it is not as easy to be tolerant of a child sitting across your table three times a day as it is to be tolerant once a month in the social worker's office. This foster parent suggests workshops in value clarification and moral development theory and provision of opportunities for foster parents to get together and share their feelings about value-loaded areas of behavior as some of the ways in which collaboration can be improved.

Colca and Colca (1978) offer four vital roles in which the worker can support foster parents of delinquent youth.

> (1) Being a sounding board for both the youth and the foster parent, (2) assisting the youth and the foster parent in resolving difficult situations, (3) helping to clarify to the foster parent the dynamics of the treatment process they are living through with the youth, (4) and advising the foster parents and child of available resources. (p. 36)

Such resources include adjunctive services from health and recreational agencies, schools, educational and vocational testing, counseling, and job training. These services are equally important resources in discharge and postdischarge services for adolescents in foster care, in general. A particularly vulnerable group is the 13-to-15-year-olds who have the highest recidivism rate (Block 1981).

Festinger (1983), as a result of her follow-up study of young adults in New York who moved from foster care to independent living, suggests that planning for discharge should start many years before it actually takes place. She proposes that this planning ought to include, educational and career counseling; vocational training and employment; training in independent living skills (budgeting, locating housing, training in shopping and cooking, and so on); sex education and family planning; information about kin and other ties; and information about community facilities and groups that provide companionship and linkage to the adult world. In many communities services like these are almost nonexistent. Furthermore, Festinger proposes review of policies and practices governing discharge to ascertain that young women receive the same preparation as young men; to assess reasonableness of maximum limits on earnings that can be retained by foster adolescents to allow them to save up for postdischarge living; and review of discharge grants. (Festinger mentions that New York State allows up to $500 for purchase of furniture and rent if need is established.)

Finally, a crucial aspect of the foster care worker's overall tasks is collaboration with the Foster Care Review Board, family court or juvenile court, and other segments of the legal system responsible for decision making and ultimately responsible for supervision of permanency planning in all cases of children and adolescents in out-of-home placements.

Special Services to Meet the Needs of Adoptive Families with Adolescents

As more and more older children are placed in adoptive homes, many of them with emotional or physical handicaps, additional supportive services from placement agencies are called for. The need for actively involving the adolescent in the search for an adoptive home, and for pre- and postplacement services to adoptive parents as well as the adolescent are crucial tasks for the adoption worker. In many of these cases, work with the foster parents also becomes essential to facilitate the move from a foster home to the adoptive parents. A growing literature deals with the placement process of older children. Ward (1979 and 1981), for example, spells out the nature of the working relationship between the caseworker and the adoptive parents and describes the bonding process between parents and child. Other examples of articles are by Chestang and Heymann (1976); Gill (1978); Meezan and Shireman (1982), and Katz (1977).

Postplacement services are considered particularly important in facilitating the integration of adolescents into adoptive families. Meezan (1980) mentions such pioneering postplacement services as "(1) case work services, (2) the use of volunteer families who have already adopted special needs children, (3) strong linkages to community resources in order to help the family provide for the individual needs of their special child, (4) social events, and (5) parent groups" (p. 36).

Families who adopted infants or younger children may need assistance in responding to their adopted child's need for sexual learning (Shapiro and Seeber 1983) as the children approach adolescence, and Pannor and Nerlove (1977) describe one agency's group program for adoptive parents and their adolescents to discuss the adolescents' feelings about being adopted, their interest in finding out about their biological parents, and to help the adoptive parents differentiate the problems associated with being adopted and those attributable to normal adolescent development. These short-term group experiences were helpful to the parents and the adolescents as both sides felt relief over being able to talk about matters that formerly could not be brought up.

Dynamics and Treatment of Runaway Youth

Running away from home before reaching legal age is not a new phenomenon in the United States (Gordon 1979 and Libertoff 1980). Since Colonial times children and adolescents have run away to escape poverty and unhealthy family or work conditions, to seek adventure or simply to assert independence. A rise in runaway behavior has been observed during periods of social, cultural, and economic changes and sometimes during war situations. The unrest associated with the Vietnamese War is often linked to the noticeable increase of runaways during the 1960s. The fact that many of these runaways came from middle-class homes is by some viewed as the reason for the arousal of sufficient public concern to pass the 1974 Runaway

Youth Act, which for the first time makes federal funding available for the care of runaway youth.

A great deal of confusion exists on the reasons for runaway behavior. Just as psychological theorists argue over the validity of the "storm and stress" theory of adolescent development in general, the "normality" of runaway behavior is debated. Multiple theories have been advanced to explain the behavior; some focus on psychological features of the child or of the parents, some on the parent-child interaction. Other theories seek explanations in environmental and societal conditions. Yet few of these theories have been validated and thus they have limited value as guides for practitioner interventions.

Three federally funded studies form the best sources of information: The National Statistical Survey on Runaway Youth, conducted by the Opinion Research Corporation in 1976, and two studies by Brennan, Huizinga, and Elliott at the Behavioral Research and Evaluation Corporation, Boulder, Colorado. Their book *The Social Psychology of Runaways* (1978) gives a full account of the studies. The first, the HEW-Colorado Study of Runaways, utilized two samples, a probability sample of 2,000 households and a smaller sample of runaways obtained from a number of institutions. The youths and their parents of both samples were interviewed. The second study reported by Brennan et al. for The Office of Youth Development National Study, involved interviews with a national sample of 7,000 youths from ten U.S. cities; 800 of these reported to have been engaged in runaway behavior. This section draws on these and later, smaller studies and clinical reports.

Defining and Describing Runaway Behavior

The term "runaway" has been defined in many different and often vague ways, which makes comparison among studies hazardous. Most definitions specify the age of the youth and an absence from home without parental permission; however, they vary in the specified length of time gone from a few hours to several days. Brennan et al. (1978) define a typical runaway as a young person between 10 and 17 years of age, inclusive, who has been absent from home at least overnight without permission. Other terms such as *throwaway* and *pushout* are used to designate children whose parents have asked them to leave, have abandoned them, or have subjected them to such abuse and neglect that leaving becomes almost a necessity (Nye and Edelbrock 1980).

Abandonment is usually associated with younger children. Yet abandoned adolescents are not rare among clients of runaway centers. Fourteen-year-old Joe, for example, arrived in Los Angeles with his family from the midwest. He was handed a dollar and asked to buy a quart of milk. When he came out of the store his family had left. And 15-year-old Molly, living with her mother and stepfather, came home from school one day to find their apartment stripped and empty with no word for her (Vils 1982). The stunned despair and pain generated by such events seem almost too much to be borne by anyone. Equally gripping are the anguish, hurt, guilt, and futile searches that many parents live through, sometimes for years, before they learn if their child is dead or alive. The emotional turmoil experienced by those directly involved is another reason why facts and verified explanations of this behavior have been hard to come by.

Estimates of the incidence of adolescent runaway behavior vary depending on the definition used and on the source from which information is drawn, for example, police records, self-report records of youth survey samples, the Federal Bureau of Investigation's Uniform Crime Reports, clinic and school records, or records from runaway centers. Adams and Munro (1979) quote one national estimate of approximately 700,000 runaways in 1973. Nye and Edelbrock (1980), utilizing the Opinion Research Corporation (ORC) 1976 National Statistical Survey, present the estimate that 733,000 youths between 10 and 17 years of age ran away or were missing for at least 24 hours during 1975. Single-parent households reported higher incidence of runaway behavior than four-person families which in most instances were two-parent, two-child households. The highest rate of runaways was from households with eight or more persons. Rates for white and black families were almost the same, while Hispanic households were above the national rate. This higher rate may be explained by the cultural difference that Hispanic children are relatively free to live with a relative for a while (Nye and Edelbrock 1980).

The 1976 national survey showed an almost even gender distribution — 53 percent males and 47 percent females. Adams and Munro (1979) note that runaway behavior generally would be assumed to be characteristic of males, but in one New York study over half (8,000 out of 14,171) of the runaways under 18 years of age reported to the police were girls. A number of other studies confirm that female runaways are not uncommon, but the interpersonal dynamics of runaways may be different for boys and girls. Young et al. (1983), for example, summarize that females are more likely to leave home because of restrictive family relations, while male adolescents appear to run because of rejecting or detached family relations.

Empirical Findings on Runaway Behavior Prior to the Brennan, Huizinga and Elliott Studies

The research literature review conducted by the three researchers — excellently reported in chapter 2 of Brennan et al. 1978 — identified three major themes. First, runaways are seen as sick individuals suffering from various psychopathological conditions and characterized by impulsivity, superego deficiencies, depression, low self-esteem, and loneliness. Studies unraveling these findings are primarily based on work with runaways in treatment centers or medical settings and have been carried out by researchers like Jenkins, Levanthal, and Robey to mention a few.

The second theme in runaway research is the sociopathic and criminal tendencies of runaway youths found to be truant, drug abusing, and engaged in theft, assaultive behavior, sexual promiscuity, and so on. There is a strong overlap between the first two themes, which are in stark contrast with the third theme — the view of runaway behavior as a healthy act (examples are studies by Blood and D'Angelo (1974), D'Angelo (1974), English (1973), Goldmeier and Dean (1973), Homer (1973), and Walker (1975)). In this perspective, running away is seen as a positive coping strategy. to protect psychological growth and mental health threatened by intolerable, cruel, and hopeless living and family conditions. Specific factors within this perspective associated with runaway behavior are escape from scapegoating or differential treatment by parents of siblings and expulsions by parents or from the school environment. Other reasons for healthy runaway are rebellion against middle-class values, search of adventure, or part of the normal process of emancipation from parents.

The multitude of explanations offered by the 150 reviewed studies were categorized by Brennan et al. into three major explanations.

1. The psychological, personal explanation, locating the "cause" in the adolescent who is singled out for treatment intervention, focusing on his or her psychological dynamics.
2. The social structural/environmental explanation, building on the assumption that anyone living under compelling conditions of parental abuse and rejection and physical violence could be expected to escape.
3. The social-psychological explanation, which considers the two previous ones as oversimplifications, assumes that "runaway behavior results from an interaction between certain kinds of social conditions and the individual personality of the child." (p. 43)

The majority of studies have utilized the pathological or environmental perspectives, and only a handful have used a social-psychological orientation. The three researchers consider the latter perspective the only one holding promise for a coherent explanatory theory of runaway behavior. They formulated this social-psychological theory as a foundation for the two Colorado studies. As this theory has much to offer as a guide to interventions with runaways and their families it is presented below in some detail.

The Integrated Control-Strain Socialization Model. As implied in the name, this model builds on two sociological-psychological theories — control and strain theory.

Control theory (Reiss 1951; Hirschi 1969; Nettler 1974, as reported by Brennan, Huizinga, and Elliott 1978), holds that two types of bonds — internal and external controls — emerge from early socialization in the home. Internal control bonds, defined as *commitment*, involve feelings of belonging, self-esteem, and commitment to the values of the family or other groupings. External control bonds, defined as *integration*, involve actual participation in group interaction, filling specific social roles, and being a viable part of the group. The two types of bonds, commitment and integration, in combination form the individual's tie to the social order, be it the family group, the peer group, or other groups. The stronger the bond, the stronger the individual's investment and satisfaction, and the more the individual has at stake in maintaining the tie and consequently in adhering to the group's values and norms. In simpler terms, the internal commitment bond can be described as the inside-the-person "feeling" part of one's social ties, while the external integration bond is the actual behavioral experience of being part of a social organism.

Only under certain conditions do the two bonds develop from the socialization process in the home. The bonds vary in strength from strong to weak, depending on the promoting or hampering quality of the socialization. The capacity for bonding, developed in the home, usually operates in similar fashion outside the home, provided similar conditions prevail in the outside groupings. In case of weak family bonding, it is possible (but not likely) that a positive school or peer group may promote development of the capacity for commitment and integration.

In case of strong family bonding a number of stresses and strains may erode the bonding. And, according to strain theory (Durkheim 1951; Merton 1957; Cloward and Ohlin 1960; Elliott and Voss 1974; as reported by Brennan, Huizinga, and Elliott 1978), as the individual experiences in real or imagined ways that his or her needs and social goals can no longer be achieved, the two forms of bonds or social controls begin to weaken. The attenuation of bonds is accompanied by lessening of the adherence to the group's values, and the individual becomes alienated from that social context. The sources of strain may be drastic changes in family composition or interpersonal family crises connected with death, divorce, relocation, illness, and so on or, in the case of an adolescent, his or her failure in school or apprehension by the police.

The youth with severely attenuated bonds to the family and subsequent feelings of alienation is very vulnerable to peer influence. Given prior strong bonds to conforming peers, support from them may carry the youth through the period of strain with the family and the former strong family bonds may eventually be restored. If the youth had prior weak bonds to peers, the alienated youth may be powerfully drawn toward nonconforming peers. However, it seems reasonable to expect nonconforming peers to have potentially much stronger controls over youth who have never experienced strong family bonds and commitments than over the youth with attenuated family bonding.

Combining the strength of family and school bonds with deviant or conforming peer associations produces four delinquent runaway types and four nondelinquent runaway categories. This typology, derived from Integrated Control-Strain Theory, was largely validated by the findings of the Brennan et al. studies in that the sample runaways clearly fell into five discrepant categories:

Short-Term Runners:
1. Crisis escapists (including 39 percent of the sample; 65 percent returned home on their own from friends)
2. Casual hedonists (17 percent, seeking good times; return home on their own in one or two weeks)
3. Crisis escapists — unhappy runaways (differ from crisis escapists in intention of action, usually planned. Majority were younger age ranges)

Long-term Runners:
4. Pursued and curtailed escapists (34 percent of sample, planned and permanent split, leave home because of bad home situation, do not return voluntarily; from older age group, includes many girls)
5. Deliberate, independent (5 percent of the runaways; planned departure with intended permanent break; come from older age brackets primarily from Anglo background; youth experiences happy episodes)

With respect to the actual runaway experience, Brennan et al. (1978) found that parents did not expect the youngster to run away in the majority of cases. The most common precipitating factor was long-term family problems, with personal problems stated as the second most frequent reason, while problems with school, friends, or the police usually did not precipitate runaway behavior. Two-thirds of the runaways had no plan to run, took along nothing but the clothes they wore and a little extra money, and left without a destination. Half of them returned home within three days after having traveled less than 10 miles. Only 5 percent used runaway houses, and that the same percentage suffered violent or sexual victimization. The majority of the runners had no contact with police. Among those who did, the non-Anglo, lower-class, older, and female runaways were arrested more often than their counterparts.

In comparing their runaway and non-runaway sample families, Brennan et al. found several highly significant differences among the two groups in regard to family characteristics and parent-child relationship variables. The runaways experienced far less parental nurturance, interest, acceptance, satisfaction, and positive labeling. On the contrary, they experienced high levels of expressed rejection, parental dissatisfaction, and negative labeling. The runaways also showed significantly higher scores than the non-runaways on disciplinary actions such as deprivation of privileges, affective punishment (making the child feel rejected, unworthy, or bad), social isolation as discipline, and a greater amount of physical abuse (pp. 168–69). The researchers conclude that the composite pattern of parental behavior in these families suggests that the parents have physically or emotionally discounted or expelled the youngster. This pattern is clearly in accord with Helm Stierlin's (1973, 1981) expelling mode of parenting (presented in chapter 3 and further discussed below as part of interventive considerations).

However, variations in family experiences found in different subgroupings of runaways based on sex, age, social class, and ethnic differences lead Brennan et al. to caution that family conditions alone do not account for why particular adolescents run away; many other impinging components must be taken into account as well.

A similar need to differentiate between family relations of subcategories is underscored by Gullotta (1979). He sees family relations of the youth leaving without parental permission as suffering from temporary communication weaknesses, while the parental abandonment of the throwaway is seen to be so severe and emotionally tearing that the bond between parent and child is broken, not on the initiative of the child but of the parent.

In Foster's (1962) study comparing 100 runaway delinquents with 75 non-runaway delinquents and their families, the runaways were found to come from homes with a much higher incidence of parent-child separations, with the most frequent separation being from the father before the age of 5 years with no subsequent return. A significantly higher incidence of step- and adoptive parenthood was also found in the runaway sample.

A more recent follow-up study by Olson, Liebow, Mannino, and Shore (1980) compares the social functioning of 14 former runaways, who received services from a runaway center 12 years earlier, with that of their 12 siblings. Data were drawn from 44 intensive interviews with the former runaways, their parents, and their siblings. None of the runaways went beyond high school, with 8 of the 14 dropping out before graduation. All of the 12 siblings received their high school diplomas on time, 6 graduated from college, and 2 completed graduate school. Only 6 of the former runaways were employed, whereas all of the siblings were. More than half of the runaways had mental health problems, while only one of the siblings did. In regard

to family relations, the runaways not only felt that their parents had un-
justly inflicted heavier household burdens on them than on their siblings,
but they also felt that they were less deserving. The parents viewed the runaways as always having been difficult, while the siblings were seen as more
easy-going and reasonable. The parent-adolescent relations appeared unchanged over the 12-year period; the researchers comment that the rancor
may have faded somewhat, but former hostilities and bitterness might even
become more crystallized.

While generalizations cannot be made from this study sample — which
the researchers call a series of 14 case studies rather than an empirical study
sample — the strong differences found among children growing up in the
same families led to the conclusion that running away cannot be explained
just in terms of social structure or social forces; personality and psychological variables in the context of family dynamics apparently play a role as
well.

As far as the runaway's school experience is concerned, the Brennan et
al. studies revealed that runaways in comparison with non-runaways receive
significantly higher levels of negative labeling by teachers and perceive
themselves as blocked from access to desirable social roles and occupational
opportunities. For runaways the rates of beatings by teachers, expulsion,
and truancy are twice that of the non-runaways. Runaways also have higher
levels of attack by schoolmates. Family conflicts and school failures are frequently mentioned as antecedents of runaway behavior in professional literature in general. However, some consider school failure to be of prime
importance in that the school failure starts the spiral of parental displea-
sure, disappointment, nagging, and eventual rejection. Others maintain
that it is the family conflict that makes it impossible for the youngster to
cope with the school situation. The Brennan studies anticipated higher parental pressure for educational success among runaways, but the findings
indicate that these parents were markedly uninterested in their children's
academic performance. This may imply that for the majority of runaways
school failure may have had little influence on family relations.

Closely linked to school experiences is the runaway's peer relations. Runaways differed from the non-runaways in that they spent more time with
their peers and less with their parents. They associated more with delinquent
peers, and were under greater peer pressure to engage in delinquent acts
than were their non-runaway counterparts (Brennan et al. 1978, p. 229).

A major and clear conclusion drawn by Brennan et al. is that runaway
behavior is primarily generated by family context influences. Evidence for
this conclusion are: dominance of family variables in a multivariate analysis
predicting runaway behavior; extremely high statistical significance of dif

ferences from non-runaways in regard to family interaction variables; and, even though some runaways did not experience family problems, the great majority of runaways in all subcategories of the taxonomic system experience severe and critical stresses in the family.

A final comment on the findings. The taxonomies of runaways contained a reasonable explanation of why the youngster would run away in 80 percent of the cases, while for 20 percent of the runaways no clear reason could be identified. These unexplained cases were distributed across the subgroupings of the taxonomic system. The researchers speculate that, since the present social-psychological framework does not and was not planned to include all important personality variables, it is possible that unidentified intrapsychic factors in these cases may account for the runaway behavior.

Interventions with Runaways and Their Families

Literature on runaway youth is replete with strongly voiced opinions about the utility of individual counseling for the adolescent, family therapy, group counseling, and other specific interventive strategies. However, little systematic research reveals the actual effectiveness of any particular strategy, even though some small-scale clinical studies give important insights into the dynamics of certain therapeutic approaches.

Homer (1973), for example, in a frequently quoted study, concludes that "an effective help must determine whether a child is running from conflicts aroused by parental values or to a subculture that sanctions forbidden behaviors" (p. 473). Of the 20 runaway girls in her sample, 7 girls were classified as "running from" and 13 as "running to." For 6 of the 7 "running-from" girls, who all had intrapersonal conflicts as well as family problems, a family-communication-oriented approach of family therapy proved to be of significant help. For 9 of the "running-to" girls, therapy was virtually useless, resulting in no change of behavior and frequent running away. Helping to set limits and pointing to consequences of the acting-out behavior appeared to be of some help to the remaining 4 of the "running-to" group. Homer asks what alternative types of intervention might have been helpful for the 9 girls who were not helped and who appeared unable to develop internal controls. External control of their behavior was required, and unfortunately, this could be obtained only through commitment to the Department of Youth Services.

Bass (1977) reports on helping seven out of ten runaway girls at a juvenile detention center and their families through utilization of a time-limited, task-centered casework approach, involving the girls as well as their parents.

His article presents the practical steps leading to joint interventions with the parent(s) and the girl at the center, the making of reciprocal written agreements about behavioral changes, and tasks to achieve behavioral changes. Follow-up home visits are made to assure that agreements are adhered to and to offer further counseling in the home or at the office.

On the basis of their overall findings, Brennan et al. (p. 311) recommend four objectives for intervention strategies that could be brought to bear on any runaway situation.

1. Strengthen weak or attenuated social integration bonds (especially in the family and school)
2. Strengthen weak or attenuated personal commitment bonds (especially to the family, school, work, and community at large)
3. Reduce attenuating strain conditions (especially in the family and school), and
4. Minimize exposure to delinquent peer association and structure channeling (if possible) of the youth into more positive peer affiliations.

The authors give many constructive and helpful suggestions about how these general objectives may be obtained through specific direct interventions with the runaway and/or the family and indirect interventions with schools, courts, and other community agencies (pp. 311–61).

Two helpful guides to direct intervention are offered by Stierlin (1973) and Orten and Soll (1980). Stierlin, who sees runaway behavior as a surface manifestation of maladaptive parent transactional modes, suggests counselors need to determine which mode is in operation and gear their interventions accordingly. In case of a severe binding pattern in which runaway episodes would be abortive, the therapeutic task becomes one of helping the adolescent to "unbind" from the family. The expelling mode calls for helping the parents provide the care and concern that is likely to promote the forming of loyalty bonds; this includes limit-setting. In the delegating mode parent-adolescent intrapsychic as well as interpersonal conflicts need to be reconciled and family obligations clarified.

Orten and Soll (1980) similarly operate with a tripartite typology, with first, second, and third degree runners classified according to the degree of alienation between parent and child. Individual and joint family therapy are recommended in various blends and for different purposes depending on whether the adolescent is to return home or move to out-of-home placement or independent living. In all the direct interventive modes, the therapeutic task involves delicate mediation of adolescent and parental interests. If the counselor carries the advocacy on behalf of the adolescent too far, the parents will fail to become engaged in the therapeutic work (Zastrow and Navarre 1975).

Finally, in terms of interventions, comprehensive treatment is strongly advocated by many, for example, Wodarski and Ammons (1981), who have developed a model consisting of child management, family enrichment, and interpersonal enrichment services involving both the runaway and the family.

Prior to direct intervention, prevention is also stressed. Brennan et al., for example, have 12 indices (presented in table 11-1, p. 310) clearly associated with the emergence of runaway behavior. The variables with greatest predictive powers were (p. 311):

Negative labeling by parents

Absence of nurturance in parent-child relations

High delinquent behavior among the youth's peer group

Negative attitudes toward school and teachers

From these variables specific concrete behavior checklists need to be developed to serve as early warning signals, particularly for youths in the 12-to-14 age bracket, which was demonstrated to be a turning point for many.

This section concludes with the summarization by Brennan et al. that their research has demonstrated the fallacy of the assumption that runaways in general have strong tendencies toward psychopathology. Most runaway behavior is not sick but a response to stressful family and social conditions, and even though there is a strong correlation between runaway and delinquent behavior, it is essential to discriminate between those runaways who are highly delinquent and those who are not much more delinquent than the general youth population.

In working with runaways it may also be well to keep in mind the finding that most runaways return home on their own without assistance from police or parents; only 5 percent of the studied runaways utilized runaway-houses, which may be geared toward serving one segment of the runaway population even though they were set up to serve all. Thus, the authors caution against generalizing from samples of runaway-house populations to the overall population of runaway youth. Finally, they point to a critical lack of aftercare and follow-up services after the runaway's return home, and they recommend further study of the possible consequences of this service lack. Other topics recommended for research are: development of early warning behavior checklists; evaluation of different treatment and intervention modes; the temporal process of deterioration of family bonds; runaway

214 ADOLESCENTS: THEORETICAL AND HELPING PERSPECTIVES

behavior in the unstressed "normal" group of adolescents; and further clarification of the runaway/delinquency association. Work is in progress by two of the original researchers, Elliott and Huizinga (1984), in expanding the integrated social psychological model to juvenile delinquent behavior.

A Closing Word

Many other specific problems encountered by youth are brought to the human service professionals than have been considered in this book. There are school problems, learning disabilities, suicide attempts and bereavement of the families of those who completed the act, voluntary starvation in the form of anorexia and bulimia, addictions to alcohol and chemical substances, violent aggression and other delinquent acts, and the psychiatric illnesses. The young, struggling with one or more of these problems, can be helped by the various services and interventive modalities enumerated in the second half of this book. But for some adolescents and for some problems no amount or combination of even the best, empirically tested and most artistically and sensitively delivered counseling will really succeed.

Charlotte Towle (1957) aptly calls adolescence "all ages in one," a stage dependent on childhood experiences and attachments and the arena for emergence of capabilities and behavior patterns that will shape functioning in future adult roles. The outcome depends on many factors, as elaborated in the first part of this book. Among them is the quality of the adolescent's environment. Carol H. Meyer (1984) is right when she states that adolescents cannot be expected to create their own constructive, nurturent environments in families, schools, and community without the help of the adult world. A curious paradox exists between the fascination we have with adolescents and their development and the almost callous, even cruel double messages we are sending to many of our teenagers: Develop your talents, educate yourself, master the four Rs and the knowledge that has exploded during this century, even though we can only give you overcrowded classrooms in much of the public school system. Develop your skills, minds, and a commitment to one chosen vocation or profession, even though we cannot provide you with opportunities and jobs to aid you. A majority of adolescents receive the needed support from their environments, but a sizable number do not, as the large numbers of school drop-outs and unemployed testify. To all of the young, a broad range of direct services and interventions should be available, and there is plenty of room for improvement and strengthening of the empirical foundations of these. Many human service professionals are working diligently to deliver such services, often under restricting circumstances and shrinking budgets. As a social worker one cannot help but wonder if we have run out of energy or have we been overcome by a sense of futility in working with the young. Are our efforts in this regard simply taken for granted? What can explain why adolescents are given only scant attention in recent handbooks of social services and clinical social work practice. Whatever the reason, some hope exists in the attention given to adolescents in the official journal of the National Association of Social Workers in the January–February 1984 issue, where the editor-in-chief, Carol H. Meyer, poses the question: "Adolescents: An Age-Group or a Problem?" She leaves us with the additional and nagging question: Given the constraint that adolescents cannot be expected to create their own environments and do better than adults, "are we not indeed blaming the victim when we reject and demean their social behavior and mores?" (p. 3). It is hard to escape an affirmative answer. And it seems that the only action that provides hope for giving better chances and environments to all of the young lies in respectful collaboration among the adults and the adolescents, between the direct and the indirect service providers across disciplinary and professional lines, across the gender line, and among the peoples of all colors, creeds, and cultures. By that we may help shape a new kind of identity, over and above that of nationality, cultures and time — just *human*, plain and simple.

Additional Readings on Interventions with Physically and Sexually Abused Adolescents and Their Families

The following references are in addition to those referred to in chapters 3 and 8. The references below are not included in the bibliography.

1. Sexual Abuse References

Cohen, T. 1983. "The Incestuous Family Revisited." *Social Casework* 64(3): 154–161.

Dietz, C.A., and Craft, J.L. 1980. "Family Dynamics of Incest: A New Perspective." *Social Casework* 61(10): 602–609.

Goodwin, J. 1982. *Sexual Abuse. Incest Victims and Their Families*. Boston: John Wright, PSG, Inc.

Gordy, P.L. 1983. "Group Work That Supports Adult Victims of Childhood Incest." *Social Casework* 64(5): 300–307.

Herman, J. 1981. *Father-Daughter Incest*. Boston: Harvard University Press.

James, K.L. 1977 "Incest: The Teenager's Perspective." *Psychotherapy: Theory, Research and Practice* 14(2): 146–155.

MacVicar, K. 1979. "Psychotherapeutic Issues in the Treatment of Sexually Abused Girls." *The American Academy of Child Psychiatry* 18(2): 342–353.

McCarty, L.M. 1981. "Investigation of Incest: Opportunity to Motivate Families to Seek Help." *Child Welfare* 60:(10): 679–689.

Rist, K. 1979. "Incest: Theoretical and Clinical Views." *American Journal of Orthopsychiatry* 49(4): 680–691.

Sagatun, I.J. 1982. "Attributional Effects of Therapy with Incestuous Families." *Journal of Marital and Family Therapy* 8(1): 99–104.

Schultz, L.G. 1979. "The Sexual Abuse of Children and Minors: A Bibliography." *Child Welfare* 63(3): 147–163.

Schultz, L.G., and Jones, P. 1983. "Sexual Abuse of Children: Issues for Social Service and Health Professionals." *Child Welfare* 62(2): 99–108.

Sgroi, S.M. 1982. "Family Treatment of Child Sexual Abuse." *Journal of Social Work and Human Sexuality* 1:109–129.

2. References Concerning Physical Violence and Mixed Violent and Sexual Abuse

Guyer, M.J. 1982. "Child Abuse and Neglect Statutes: Legal and Clinical Implications." *American Journal of Orthopsychiatry* 52(1): 73-81.

Kratcoski, P.C. 1982. "Child Abuse and Violence Against the Family." *Child Welfare* 61(7): 435-443.

Laughlin, J., and Weiss, M. 1981. "An Outpatient Milieu Therapy Approach to Treatment of Child Abuse and Neglect Problems." *Social Casework* 62(2): 106-109.

Lewis, D.O.; Shanock, S.S.; Pincus, J.H.; and Glaser, G.H. 1980. "Violent Juvenile Delinquents: Psychiatric Neurological, Psychological, and Abuse Factors." *Journal of the American Academy of Child Psychiatry* 2:507-519.

Rathbone-McCuan, E., and Pierce, R. 1981. "Intergenerational Treatment Approach: An Alternative Model for Working with Abusive/Neglectful and Delinquent Prone Families." In Hunner, R.J., and Walker, Y.E. (Eds.) *Exploring the Relationship Between Child Abuse and Delinquency.* Montclair, N.J.: Allanheld, Osmun & Co.

Turbett, J.P. 1979. "Intervention Strategies and Conceptions of Child Abuse." *Children and Youth Review* 1(2): 205-213.

Watkins, H.D., and Bradbard, M.R. 1982. "Child Maltreatment: An Overview with Suggestions for Intervention and Research." *Family Relations* 31:323-333.

Wolock, I. 1982. "Community Characteristics and Staff Judgments in Child Abuse and Neglect Cases." *Social Work Research & Abstracts* 18(2):9-15.

Bibliography

Abelsohn, D. 1983. "Dealing With The Abdication Dynamic In The Post Divorce Family: A Context For Adolescent Crisis." *Family Process* 22(3): 359–383.

Abramson, M., Ash, M.U., and Nash, W.R. 1979. "Handicapped Adolescents— A Time for Reflection." *Adolescence* 14(55): 557–565.

Achenbach, T.M. 1982. *Developmental Psychopathology*. Second edition. New York: John Wiley and Sons.

Ackerman, N.J. 1980. "The Family With Adolescents." In E.A. Carter and M. McGoldbrick (eds.) *The Family Life Cycle: A Framework For Family Therapy*. New York: Gardner Press.

Ackerman, N.W., and Behrens, M.L. 1974. "Family Diagnosis and Clinical Process." In G. Caplan (ed.) *Child and Adolescent Psychiatry, Sociocultural and Community Psychiatry. American Handbook of Psychiatry*. Second edition. Vol. 2. New York: Basic Books.

Adams, G.R., and Gullotta, T. 1983. *Adolescent Life Experiences*. Monterey: Brooks/Cole Publishing Co.

Adams, G.R., and Montemayor, R. 1983. "Identity Formation During Early Adolescence." *Journal of Early Adolescence* 3(3): 193–202.

Adams, G.R., and Munro, G. 1979. "Portrait of the North American Runaway: A Critical Review." *Journal of Youth and Adolescence* 8(3): 359–373.

Adams, J.E., and Lindemann, E. 1974. "Coping with Long-term Disability." In G.V. Coelho, D.A. Hamburg, and J.E. Adams (eds.) *Coping and Adaptation*. New York: Basic Books, pp. 127–138.

Adelson, J., ed. 1980. *Handbook of Adolescent Psychology*. New York: John Wiley and Sons.

Adelson, J., and Doehrman, M.J. 1980. "The Psychodynamic Approach to Adolescence." In J. Adelson (ed.) *Handbook of Adolescent Psychology*. New York: John Wiley and Sons.

Ahrons, C.R. 1980. "Redefining the Divorced Family: A Conceptual Framework." *Social Work* 25(6): 437–441.

219

Ahrons, C.R. 1983. "Divorce: Before, During, and After." In H.I. McCubbin and C.R. Figley (eds.) *Stress and the Family. Vol. I: Coping With Normative Transitions.* New York: Brunner/Mazel.

Algozzine, B.; Schmid, R.; and Wells, D. 1982. "Characteristics of Teachers of Emotionally Disturbed Adolescents." *Adolescence* 17(65): 167–175.

Ambert, A.-M. 1982. "Differences in Children's Behavior Toward Custodial Mothers and Custodial Fathers." *Journal of Marriage and the Family* 44(1): 73–86.

American Psychiatric Association. 1980. *Diagnostic and Statistical Manual of Mental Disorders.* Third edition. Washington, D.C.: American Psychiatric Association.

Anderson, C.W. 1977. "The Sealed Record in Adoption Controversy." *Social Service Review* 51(1): 141–154.

Anderson, E.M., and Clarke, L. 1982. *Disability in Adolescence.* New York: Methuen.

Anderson, J.E., and Brown, R.A. 1980. "Life History Grid for Adolescents." *Social Work* 25(4): 321–323.

Aponte, H.J. 1976. "Underorganization in the Poor Family." In P.J. Guerin (ed.) *Family Therapy.* New York: Gardner Press, Inc.

Aponte, H.J., and Van Deusen, J. 1981. "Structural Family Therapy." In A.S. Gurman and D.P. Kniskern (eds.) *Handbook of Family Therapy.* New York: Brunner/Mazel.

Ariès, P. 1962. *Centuries of Childhood. A Social History of Family Life.* New York: Alfred A. Knopf.

Aumend, S.A., and Barrett, M.C. 1984. "Self-Concept and Attitudes Toward Adoption: A Comparison of Searching and Nonsearching Adoptees." *Child Welfare* 63(3): 251–259.

Austin, K.B.; Manak, J.J.; and Horwitz, R. 1981. "A Workshop for Introducing Adolescents to Mental Health Services." *Social Casework* 62(6): 368–372.

Ausubel, D.P. 1954. *Theory and Problems of Adolescent Development.* New York: Grune & Stratton.

Ausubel, D.P.; Montemayor, R.; and Svajian, P. 1977. *Theory and Problems of Adolescent Development.* Second edition. New York: Grune & Stratton.

Bandura, A. 1977a. "Self-Efficacy: Toward a Unifying Theory of Behavioral Change." *Psychological Review* 84: 191–215.

————. 1977b. *Social Learning Theory.* Englewood Cliffs, N.J.: Prentice-Hall.

Bandura, A., and Walters, R.H. 1959. *Adolescent Aggression.* New York: Ronald Press.

Bank, S., and Kahn, M. 1975. "Sisterhood-Brotherhood is Powerful: Sibling Subsystems and Family Therapy." *Family Process* 14(3): 311–337.

Barret, R.L., and Robinson, B.E. 1982. "Teenage Fathers: Neglected too Long." *Social Work* 27(6): 484–488.

Barth, R.P.; Blythe, B.J.; Schinke, S.P.; and Schilling, R.F. II. 1983. "Self-Control Training with Maltreating Parents." *Child Welfare* 62(4): 313–324.

Bass, B.A.; Wyatt, G.E.; and Powell, G.J. (eds.) 1982. *The Afro-American Family. Assessment, Treatment, and Research Issues.* New York: Grune & Stratton.

Bass, M. 1977. "Toward A Model Of Treatment For Runaway Girls In Detention." In W.J. Reid and L. Epstein (eds.) *Task-Centered Practice*. New York: Columbia University Press.

Bauer, J.E., and Heinke, W. 1976. "Treatment Family Care Homes for Disturbed Foster Children." *Child Welfare* 55(7): 478–490.

Baumrind, D. 1980. "New Directions in Socialization Research." *American Psychologist* 35(7): 639–652.

Beal, E.W. 1980. "Separation, Divorce, and Single-Parent Families." In E.A. Carter and M. McGoldrick (eds.) *The Family Life Cycle: A Framework for Family Therapy*. New York: Gardner Press.

Beavers, W.R. 1977. *Psychotherapy and Growth. A Family Systems Perspective*. New York: Brunner/Mazel.

Beavers, W.R., and Voeller, M.N. 1983. "Family Models: Comparing and Contrasting the Olson Circumplex Model with the Beavers Systems Model." *Family Process* 22(1): 85–98.

Belsky, J. 1980. "Child Maltreatment: An Ecological Integration." *American Psychologist* 35(4): 320–335.

Benedek, E.P. 1978. "Dilemmas in Research on Female Adolescent Development." In M. Sugar (ed.) *Female Adolescent Development*. New York: Brunner/Mazel, pp. 3–19.

———. 1979. "Female Adolescents and the Law in the United States." In M. Sugar (ed.) *Female Adolescent Development*. New York: Brunner/Mazel.

Berger, M.; Jurkovic, G.J.; and Associates. 1984. *Practicing Family Therapy in Diverse Settings*. San Francisco: Jossey-Bass.

Berkman, I.P., and Rosenblum, L. 1982. "Serving the High School Student in Need: A Look at Restrengthening the Linkage Between the School and Community Referral Sources." *Adolescence* 17(66): 465–470.

Berkovitz, I.H. (ed.). 1972. *Adolescents Grow in Groups. Experiences in Adolescent Group Psychotherapy*. New York: Brunner/Mazel.

Berkovitz, I.H., and Sugar, M. 1975. "Indications and Contraindications for Adolescent Group Psychotherapy." In M. Sugar (ed.) *The Adolescent in Group and Family Therapy*. New York: Brunner/Mazel.

Bienenstock, A., and Epstein, N.B. 1978. "Current Adaptive Challenges Facing Young Females." In M. Sugar (ed.) *Female Adolescent Development*. New York: Brunner/Mazel.

Bilge, B., and Kaufman, G. 1983. "Children of Divorce and One-Parent Families: Cross Cultural Perspectives." *Family Relations* 32:59–71.

Blechman, A.E. 1982. "Are Children with One Parent at Psychological Risk? A Methodological Review." *Journal of Marriage and the Family* 44(1): 179–195.

Block, N.M. 1981. "Toward Reducing Recidivism in Foster Care." *Child Welfare* 60(9): 597–610.

Blood, L., and D'Angelo, R. 1974. "A Progress Research Report On Value Issues In Conflict Between Runaways and Their Parents." *Journal of Marriage And The Family* 36(3): 486–490.

Bloom, M. (ed.) 1980. *Life Span Development. Bases for Preventive and Interventive Helping.* New York: MacMillan.

Bloom, M.V. 1980. *Adolescent-Parental Separation.* New York: Gardner Press, Inc.

Blos, P. 1962. *On Adolescence: A Psychoanalytic Interpretation.* New York: The Free Press, 1962.

――――. 1967. "The Second Individuation Process of Adolescence." In *The Psychoanalytic Study of the Child.* Vol. 22. New York: International University Press, pp. 162–186.

――――. 1979. *The Adolescent Passage: Developmental Issues.* New York: International Universities Press.

――――. 1981. "Modifications in the Traditional Psychoanalytic Theory of Female Adolescent Development." In S.C. Feinstein, P.L. Giovacchini, J.G. Looney, A.Z. Schwartzberg, and A.D. Sorosky (eds.) *Adolescent Psychiatry.* Vol. 8. Chicago: University of Chicago Press.

Blum, R.W., and Runyan, C. 1980. "Adolescent Abuse. The Dimensions of the Problem." *Journal of Adolescent Health Care* 1(2): 121–126.

Boatman, B., and Borkan, E.L. 1981. "Treatment of Child Victims of Incest." *American Journal of Family Therapy* 9(4): 43–51.

Bohman, M., and Sigvardsson, S. 1981. "A Prospective, Longitudinal Study Of Children Registered For Adoption: A 15-Year Follow-Up." *Annual Progress in Child Psychiatry and Development,* pp. 217–237.

Bolen, J.K. 1972. "Easing the Pain of Termination for Adolescents." *Social Casework* 53(9): 519–527.

Bolton, F.G. 1983. *When Bonding Fails. Clinical Assessment of High-Risk Families.* Beverly Hills, Calif.: Sage.

Borgman, R. 1982. "The Consequences Of Open and Closed Adoptions For Older Children." *Child Welfare* 61(4): 217–226.

Bourne, E. 1978a. "The State of Research on Ego Identity: A Review and Appraisal. Part I." *Journal of Youth and Adolescence* 7:223–251.

――――. 1978b. "The State of Research on Ego Identity: A Review and Appraisal. Part II." *Journal of Youth and Adolescence* 7:371–392.

Bowen, M. 1976. "Theory in the Practice of Psychotherapy." In P.J. Guerin (ed.) *Family Therapy: Theory and Practice.* New York: Gardner Press, pp. 42–90.

Bowerman, C.E., and Dobash, R.M. 1974. "Structural Variations in Inter-Sibling Affect." *Journal of Marriage and the Family* 36(1): 48–54.

Boyne, J. 1978. "A Mental Health Note in Adoption of School-age and Teen-age Children." *Child Welfare* 57(3): 196–199.

Brennan, T. 1980. "Mapping The Diversity Among Runaways. A Descriptive Multivariate Analysis of Selected Social Psychological Background Conditions." *Journal of Family Issues* 1(2): 189–210.

Brennan, T.; Huizinga, D.; and Elliot, D.S. 1978. *The Social Psychology of Runaways.* Lexington, Mass.: Lexington Books, D.C. Heath and Co.

Breunlin, C., and Breunlin, D.C. 1979. "The Family Therapy Approach To Adolescent Disturbances: A Review Of The Literature." *Journal of Adolescence* 2:153–169.

Brieland, D., and Lemmon, J. 1977. *Social Work and the Law*. St. Paul: West Publishing Company.

Bronfenbrenner, U. 1958. "Socialization and Social Class through Time and Space." In E.E. Maccoby, et al. (eds.) *Readings in Social Psychology*. New York: Holt, pp. 400–425.

———. 1979. *The Ecology of Human Development. Experiments by Nature and Design*. Cambridge, Mass.: Harvard University Press.

Bronfenbrenner, U., and Crouter, A.C. 1983. "The Evolution of Environmental Models in Developmental Research." In Paul H. Mussen (ed.) *Handbook of Child Psychology* (Formerly Carmichael's Manual of Child Psychology). Fourth edition. Vol. I. History, Theory and Methods, edited by W. Kessen. New York: John Wiley and Sons.

Brown, J.H.; Finch, W.A., Jr.; Northern, H.; Taylor, S.H.; and Weil, M. 1982. *Child/Family/Neighborhood: A Master Plan for Social Service Delivery*. New York: Child Welfare League of America.

Brun, G. 1978. "Conflicted Parents: High and Low Vulnerability of Children to Divorce." In E.J. Anthony, C. Koupernik, and C. Chiland (eds.) *The Child in His Family. Vulnerable Children*. Vol. 4. New York: John Wiley and Sons.

Buktenica, N.A. 1970. "A Multidisciplinary Training Team in the Public Schools." *Journal of School Psychology* 8(3): 220–225.

Burke, R.J., and Weir, T. 1978. "Sex Differences in Adolescent Life Stress, Social Support, and Well-Being." *Journal of Psychology* 98:277–288.

Bybee, R.W. 1979. "Violence Toward Youth: A New Perspective." *Journal of Social Issues* 35(2): 1–14.

Byrne, K.O., and Belucci, M.T. 1982. "Subsidized Adoption: One Country's Program." *Child Welfare* 61(3): 173–180.

Callicutt, J.W., and Lecca, P.J. 1983. *Social Work and Mental Health*. New York: The Free Press.

Carnegie Commission on Policy Studies in Higher Education. 1980. *Giving Youth a Better Chance*. San Francisco: Jossey-Bass.

Carter, E.A., and McGoldrick, M. (eds.). 1980. *The Family Life Cycle: A Framework for Family Therapy*. New York: Gardner Press, Inc.

Carter, W.W. 1968. "Group Counseling for Adolescent Foster Children." *Children* 15(1): 22–27.

Case, P.S. 1976. "A Systems Approach to Modifying Behavior in a Children's Residential Center." *Child Care Quarterly* 5(1): 35–41.

Cashion, B.G. 1982. "Female-Headed Families: Effects on Children and Clinical Implications." *Journal of Marital and Family Therapy* 8(2): 77–85.

Catron, D., and Catron, S. 1983. "Preventing Parent-Adolescent Crises." In D.R. Mace (ed.) *Prevention in Family Services. Approaches to Wellness*. Beverly Hills, Calif.: Sage.

Caulfield, B.A. 1978. *The Legal Aspects of Protective Services for Abused and Neglected Children. A Manual*. Washington, D.C.: U.S. Dept. of Health, Education and Welfare, Office of Human Development Services, Administration for Public Services.

Charnas, J.F. 1983. "Joint Custody Counseling: Divorce 1980's Style." *Social Casework* 64(9): 546–554.

Chase, A.M., et al. 1979. "Treating the Throwaway Child: A Model for Adolescent Service." *Social Casework* 60(9): 538–546.

Chess, S., and Fernandez, P. 1980. "Do Deaf Children Have a Typical Personality?" *Journal of Child Psychiatry* 19(4): 654–664.

Chestang, L.W. 1978. "The Delivery of Child Welfare Services to Minority Group Children and Their Families." In *Child Welfare Strategy in the Coming Years.* U.S. Department of Health, Education and Welfare, Adm. for Children, Youth and Families, Children's Bureau, Washington, D.C., pp. 167–194.

Chestang, L.W., and Heymann, I. 1976. "Preparing Older Children for Adoption." *Public Welfare* 34(1): 35–40.

Child Welfare League of America, Inc. 1975. *Standards for Foster Family Service.* Revised. New York.

———. 1978. *Standards for Adoption Service.* Revised. New York.

———. 1982. *Standards for Residential Centers for Children.* New York.

Chilman, C. 1979. *Adolescent Sexuality in a Changing American Society.* U.S. Department of Health, Education and Welfare, Public Health Service, Pub. No. (NIH) 79-1426.

Chilman, C.S. 1980. "Social and Psychological Research Concerning Adolescent Childbearing: 1970–1980." *Journal of Marriage and the Family* 42(4): 793–805.

Citizens' Committee for Children of New York, Inc. 1980. *Lost and Found and Lost Again: Adolescents in and out of Emergency Temporary Foster Care.* New York, p. 56.

Clapp, D.F., and Raab, R.S. 1978. "Follow-up Of Unmarried Adolescent Mothers." *Social Work* 23(2): 149–153.

Cloward, R.A., and Ohlin, L.E. 1960. *Delinquency and Opportunity.* New York: The Free Press.

Coates, T.J.; Petersen, A.C.; and Perry, C. (eds.). 1982. *Promoting Adolescent Health: A Dialog on Research and Practice.* New York: Academic Press, Inc.

Colca, C., and Colca, L. 1978. "Improving Services to Foster Parents of Delinquent Youth." *Federal Probation* 42(4): 33–37.

Coleman, J.C. 1974. *Relationships in Adolescence.* Boston and London: Routledge & Kegan Paul.

———. 1979. "Current Contradictions in Adolescent Theory." In S. Chess and A. Thomas (eds.) *Annual Progress in Child Psychiatry and Child Development, 1979.* New York: Brunner/Mazel, pp. 623–634. Also in *Journal of Youth and Adolescence* 7(1): 1–11.

———. 1980a. *The Nature of Adolescence.* London: Methuen & Co., Ltd.

———. 1980b. "Friendship and the Peer Group in Adolescence." In J. Adelson (ed.) *Handbook of Adolescent Psychology.* New York: John Wiley and Sons, pp. 408–431.

Coleman, J.S. 1961. *The Adolescent Society.* New York: The Free Press.

Coleman, J.S., et al. 1966. *Equality of Educational Opportunity.* Washington, D.C.: U.S. Government Printing Office.

Colon, F. 1978. "In Search of One's Past: An Identity Trip." *Family Process* 12(4): 429–438.

Compher, J.V. 1982. "Parent-School-Child Systems: Triadic Assessment and Intervention." *Social Casework* 63(7): 415–423.

Compton, B.R. 1983. "Traditional Fields of Practice." In A. Rosenblatt and D. Waldfogel (eds.) *Handbook of Clinical Social Work.* San Francisco: Jossey-Bass.

Corder, B.F.; Whiteside, L.; and Haizlip, T.M. 1981. "A Study of Curative Factors in Group Psychotherapy with Adolescents." *International Journal of Group Psychotherapy* 31(3): 345–354.

Corder, B.F.; Whiteside, R.; Koehne, P.; and Hortman, R. 1981. "Structured Techniques for Handling Loss and Addition of Members in Adolescent Psychotherapy Groups." *Journal of Early Adolescence* 1(4): 413–421.

Costin, L.B. 1981. "School Social Work as Specialized Practice." *Social Work* 26(1): 36–43.

Cullinan. D., and Epstein, M.H. (eds.). 1979. *Special Education for Adolescents.* Columbus, Ohio: Merrill.

Cullinan, D.; Epstein, M.H.; and Lloyd, J.W. 1983. *Behavior Disorders of Children and Adolescents.* Englewood Cliffs, N.J.: Prentice-Hall.

D'Angelo, R. 1974. *Families of Sand: A Report Concerning the Flight of Adolescents From Their Families.* Columbus, Ohio: Ohio State University School of Social Work.

Dahl, G. 1980. "Oligofreni." In Joseph Welner (ed.) *Psykiatri. En Tekstbog.* Copenhagen, Denmark: FADL's Forlag, pp. 510–530.

Daniel, W.A., Jr. 1977. *Adolescents in Health and Disease.* St. Louis: The C.V. Mosby Co.

Davids, A. 1974. *Children in Conflict: A Casebook.* New York: John Wiley and Sons, Inc.

Davis, I.P. 1979. *Troubled Children and Their Families. Before, During and After Placement.* Child Welfare Monograph Number 1. San Diego: San Diego State University.

———. 1980. *Troubled Adolescents and Their Families.* Child Welfare Monograph Number 2. San Diego: San Diego State University.

———. 1982. *Adolescents and the Child Welfare System: Text and Cases.* With contributions from Elsie Herman and Hope Logan. Child Welfare Monograph Number 4. San Diego: San Diego State University.

Day, J.R. 1972-73. "Treatment Models for Adolescents: Residential Treatment Center vs. Hospital." *Journal of the National Association of Private Psychiatric Hospitals* 4(4): 25–29.

de Anda, D., and Beccera, R.M. 1984. "Support Networks for Adolescent Mothers." *Social Casework* 65(3): 172–181.

DeBlassie, R.R. 1978. "Counseling With Culturally Disadvantaged Adolescents." *Adolescence* 13(50): 221–229.

Defrain, J., and Eirick, R. 1981. "Coping as Divorced Single Parents: A Comparative Study of Fathers and Mothers." *Family Relations* 30(2): 265–273.

Delissovoy, V. 1973. "High School Marriages: A Longitudinal Study." *Journal of Marriage and the Family* 35:245-255.

Depp, C.H. 1982. "After Reunion: Perceptions of Adult Adoptees, Adoptive Parents, and Birth Parents." *Child Welfare* 61(2): 113-119.

Derdeyn, A.P., and Scott, E. 1984. "Joint Custody: A Critical Analysis and Appraisal." *American Journal of Orthopsychiatry* 54(2): 199-209.

Devore, W., and Schlesinger, E.G. 1981. *Ethnic-Sensitive Social Work Practice.* St. Louis: The C.V. Mosby Co.

de Young, M. 1981. "Siblings of Oedipus: Brothers and Sisters of Incest Victims." *Child Welfare* 60(8): 561-568.

Dore, M.M.; Young, T.M.; and Pappenfort, D.M. 1984. "Comparison of Basic Data for the National Survey of Residential Group Care Facilities: 1966-1982." *Child Welfare* 63(6): 485-495.

Douvan, E., and Adelson, J. 1966. *The Adolescent Experience.* New York; John Wiley and Sons.

Douvan, E., and Gold, M. 1966. "Modal Patterns in American Adolescence." In *Review of Child Development Research.* Vol. 2. New York: Russell Sage Foundation, pp. 469-528.

Duberman, L. 1975. *The Reconstituted Family.* Chicago: Nelson-Hall.

Dunham, J. 1980. "Conflict and Competence in Inter-Professional Communication in the Services for Adolescents." Chap. 4 in R. Jones and C. Pritchard (eds.) *Social Work with Adolescents.* Boston: Routledge & Kegan Paul.

Dunham, J., and Jones, R. 1980. "Understanding Adolescence." In R. Jones and C. Pritchard (eds.) *Social Work with Adolescents.* London: Routledge & Kegan Paul.

Dunphy, D.C. 1963. "The Social Structure of Urban Adolescent Peer Groups." *Sociometry* 26:50-65.

Durkheim, E. 1951. *Suicide. A Study in Sociology.* New York: The Free Press.

Duvall, E. 1977. *Marriage and Family Development.* Fifth edition. Philadelphia: J.B. Lippincott.

Earls, F., and Siegel, B. 1980. "Precocious Fathers." *American Journal of Orthopsychiatry* 50(3): 469-480.

Edelbrock, C. 1980. "Running Away from Home: Incidence and Correlates among Children and Youth Referred for Mental Health Services." *Journal of Family Issues* 1(2): 210-228.

Edwards, M.P., and Boyd, F.E. 1975. "Adoption of Adolescents." *Child Welfare* 54(4): 298-299.

Ehrlich, M.I. 1980. "Adolescents in Transition: A Look at a Transitional Treatment Center." *Journal of Community Psychology* 8(4): 323-331.

Elder, G.H., Jr. 1980. "Adolescence in Historical Perspective." In J. Adelson (ed.) *Handbook of Adolescent Psychology.* New York: John Wiley and Sons.

Elliott, D.S., and Huizinga, D. 1984. *The Relationship between Delinquent Behavior and ADM Problems.* The National Youth Survey Project Report No. 28. Boulder, Colo.: Behavioral Research Institute.

Elliott, D.C., and Voss, H.L. 1974. *Delinquency and Dropout.* Lexington, Mass.: Lexington Books, D.C. Heath and Co.

Ellis, A.E., and Bernard, M.E. 1983. *Rational-Emotive Approaches to the Problems of Childhood*. New York: Plenum Press.

Ellis, E.H. 1979. "Some Problems in the Study of Adolescent Development." *Adolescence* 14(53): 101-109.

English, C.J. 1973. "Leaving Home—A Typology of Runaways." *Society* 10(5): 22-24.

Enright, R.D.; Lapsley, D.K.; Drivas, A.E.; and Fehr, L.A. 1980. "Parental Influences on the Development of Adolescent Autonomy and Identity." *Journal of Youth and Adolescence* 9(6): 529-545.

Epstein, N.B.; Baldwin, L.M.; and Bishop, D.S. 1983. "The McMaster Family Assessment Device." *Journal of Marital and Family Therapy* 9(2): 171-180.

Epstein, N.B., and Bishop, D.S. 1981. "Problem-Centered Systems Therapy of the Family." In A.S. Gurman and D.P. Kniskern (eds.) *Handbook of Family Therapy*. New York: Brunner/Mazel, pp. 444-482.

Erikson, E.H. 1950. *Childhood and Society*. New York: Norton.

————. 1959a. "Identity and the Life Cycle: Selected Papers." *Psychological Issues Monographic Series I*, No. 1. New York: International Universities Press.

————. 1959b. In D.H. Funkenstein (ed.) *The Student and Mental Health: An International View*. New York: World Federation for Mental Health (as quoted by Finkelstein and Gaier. 1983. *Adolescence* 69:115-129).

————. 1965. *The Challenge of Youth*. Garden City, N.Y.: Doubleday/Anchor Books.

————. 1968. *Identity: Youth and Crisis*. New York: Norton.

————. 1975. (originally publ. 1956). "The Concept of Ego Identity" and "The Problem of Ego Identity." In A.H. Esman (ed.) *The Psychology of Adolescence. Essential Readings*. New York: International Universities Press, pp. 178-195, 318-346.

Esman, A.H. (ed.). 1975. *The Psychology of Adolescence. Essential Readings*. New York: International Universities Press, Inc.

———— (ed.). 1983. *The Psychiatric Treatment of Adolescents*. New York: International Universities Press, Inc.

Euster, S.D.; Ward, V.P.; Varner, J.G.; and Euster, G.L. 1984. "Life Skills Group For Adolescent Foster Children." *Child Welfare* 63(1): 27-36.

Evenshaug, O., and Hallen, D. 1981. *Børne- og Ungdomspsykologi*. Copenhagen: Munksgaard.

Falicov, C.J.; and Karrer, B.M. 1980. "Cultural Variations In The Family Life Cycle: The Mexican-American Family." In E.A. Carter and M. McGoldrick (eds.) *The Family Life Cycle: A Framework For Family Therapy*. New York: Gardner Press.

Faller, K.C. 1981. *Social Work with Abused and Neglected Children*. New York: The Free Press.

Family Service Association of America. 1967. *Casebook on Family Treatment Involving Adolescents*. New York: FSAA.

Fanshel, D. 1966. *Foster Parenthood: A Role Analysis*. Minneapolis: University of Minnesota Press.

————. 1975. "Parental Visiting of Children in Foster Care: Key to Discharge?" *Social Service Review* 49(4): 493-514.

Fanshel, D., and Shinn, E.B. 1978. *Children in Foster Care: A Longitudinal Investigation*. New York: Columbia University Press.

Fein, E.; Maluccio, A.N.; Hamilton, V.J.; and Ward, D.E. 1983. "After Foster Care: Outcomes of Permanency Planning For Children." *Child Welfare* 62(6): 485–558.

Feinstein, S.C. (ed.). 1980. *Adolescence: Perspectives on Psychotherapy*. San Francisco: Jossey-Bass.

Feldman, R.A.; Caplinger, T.E.; and Wodarski, J.S. 1983. *The St. Louis Conundrum: The Effective Treatment of Antisocial Youths*. Englewood Cliffs, N.J.: Prentice-Hall.

Feldman, R.A., and Wodarski, J.S. 1975. *Contemporary Approaches To Group Treatment*. San Francisco: Jossey-Bass.

Felker, E.H. 1978. "Why Are Foster Parents So Hung Up on Values?" *Child Welfare* 57(4): 259–261.

Ferguson, Y.B. 1982. "Improving Intervention Strategies with Minority Group Adolescents." In B.A. Bass, G.E. Wyatt, and G.J. Powell (eds.) *The Afro-American Family. Assessment, Treatment, and Research Issues*. New York: Grune & Stratton.

Festinger, T. 1983. *No One Ever Asked Us . . . A Postscript to Foster Care*. New York: Columbia University Press.

Figley, C.R., and McCubbin, H.I. (eds.). 1983. *Stress and the Family. Vol. II: Coping With Catastrophe*. New York: Brunner/Mazel.

Filsinger, E.E., and Anderson, C.C. 1982. "Social Class and Self-Esteem in Late Adolescence: Dissonant Context or Self-Efficacy?" *Developmental Psychology* 18(3): 380–384.

Fineberg, B.L.; Kettlewell, P.W.; and Sowards, S.K. 1982. "An Evaluation of Adolescent Inpatient Services." *American Journal of Orthopsychiatry* 52(2): 337–345.

Fineberg, B.L.; Sowards, S.K.; and Kettlewell, P.W. 1980. "Adolescent Inpatient Treatment: A Literature Review." *Adolescence* 15(60): 913–925.

Finkelstein, M.J., and Gaier, E.L. 1983. "The Impact of Prolonged Student Status on Late Adolescent Development." *Adolescence* 69:115–129.

Finkelstein, N.E. 1981. "Family-Centered Group Care—The Children's Institution, from a Living Center to a Center for Change." In A. Maluccio and P.A. Sinanoglu (eds.) *The Challenge of Partnership*. New York: Child Welfare League of America.

Fischman, S.M., and Palley, H.A. 1978. "Adolescent Unwed Motherhood: Implication For A National Family Policy." *Health & Social Work* 3(1): 30–46.

Fisher, B., and Berdie, J. 1978. "Adolescent Abuse and Neglect: Issues of Incidence, Intervention and Service Delivery." *Child Abuse and Neglect* 2:173–192.

Fisher, R.A. 1977. *School Social Work in the Literature: A Bibliography*. Washington, D.C.: NASW.

———. 1981. *Update to School Social Work in the Literature: A Bibliography*. Washington, D.C.: NASW.

———. 1983. "The Status of School Social Work as it is Reflected in its Literature." *Social Work in Education* 5(2): 109–118.

Fitzgerald, J.E. 1978. "Rights of Neglected Children and Attempts by the State to Regulate Family Relationships." In *Child Welfare Strategy in the Coming Years.* Washington, D.C., U.S. Dept. of HEW, Children's Bureau.

Foster, R.M. 1962. "Intrapsychic and Environmental Factors In Running Away From Home." *American Journal Of Orthopsychiatry* 32:486–491.

Fox, G.L. 1981. "The Family's Role in Adolescent Sexual Behavior." In T. Ooms (ed.) *Teenage Pregnancy in a Family Context.* Philadelphia: Temple University Press.

Fox, G.L., and Inazu, J.K. 1982. "The Influence of Mother's Marital History on the Mother-Daughter Relationship in Black and White Households." *Journal of Marriage and the Family* 44(1): 143–152.

Frazier, D.J., and DeBlassie, R.R. 1982. "A Comparison of Self-Concept in Mexican American and Non-Mexican American Late Adolescents." *Adolescence* 17(66): 327–334.

Freeman, G.C.; Goldberg, G.; and Sonnega, J.A. 1983. "Cooperation between Public Schools and Mental Health Agencies." *Social Work in Education* 5(3): 178–187.

French, A., and Berlin, I. 1979. *Depression in Children and Adolescents.* New York: Human Sciences Press.

Freud, A. 1946. *The Ego and the Mechanisms of Defense.* New York: International Universities Press, Inc.

————. 1958 (1957). "Adolescence in the Psychoanalytic Theory." In *Research at the Hampstead Child-Therapy Clinic and Other Papers. The Writings of Anna Freud.* Vol. 5. New York: International Universities Press, Inc. (1969).

————. 1965. *Normality and Pathology in Childhood. Assessments of Development.* New York: Internatonial Universities Press, Inc.

————. 1975. "Children Possessed. Anna Freud Looks at a Central Concern of the Children's Bill: The Psychological Needs of Adopted Children." In *Psychoanalytic Psychology of Normal Development. 1970–1980. The Writings of Anna Freud.* Vol. 8. New York: International Universities Press, Inc. (1981).

Furstenberg, F.F., Jr. 1976. *Unplanned Parenthood.* New York: Macmillan.

Gallagher, J.R.; Heald, F.P.; and Garell, D.C. (eds.). 1976. *Medical Care of the Adolescent.* Third Edition. New York: Appleton-Century-Crofts.

Gambrill, E.D., and Stein, T.J. 1981. "Decision Making and Case Management: Achieving Continuity of Care for Children in Out-of-Home Placement." In A. Maluccio and P.A. Sinanoglu (eds.) *The Challenge of Partnership.* New York: Child Welfare League of America.

Garbarino, J. 1979. "The Issue is Human Quality: In Praise of Children." *Children and Youth Services Review* 1(4): 353–377.

————. 1980a. "Some Thoughts on School Size and Its Effects on Adolescent Development." *Journal of Youth and Adolescence* 9(1): 19–31.

————. 1980b. "Meeting the Needs of Mistreated Youth." *Social Work* 25(2): 122–126.

————. 1982. *Children and Families in the Social Environment.* New York: Aldine.

Garell, D.C. 1976. "Health Care Delivery Systems." In J.R. Gallagher, F.P. Heald, and D.C. Garell (eds.) *Medical Care of the Adolescent.* Third Edition. New York: Appleton-Century-Crofts.

Garigue, P. 1956. "French Canadian Kinship and Urban Life." *American Anthropologist* 58:1090–1106, as quoted by Tsukada, G.K. 1979. "Sibling Interaction: A Review of the Literature." *Smith College Studies in Social Work* 49(3): 229–247.

Garvin, C.D. 1977. "Strategies for Group Work with Adolescents." In Reid and Epstein (eds.) *Task-Centered Practice*. New York: Columbia University Press.

Gecas, V. 1979. "The Influence of Social Class on Socialization." In W.R. Burr et al. (eds.) *Contemporary Theories about the Family. Research-Based Theories*. Vol. 1. New York: The Free Press.

Geismar, L.L. 1980. *Family and Community Functioning. A Manual of Measurement for Social-Work Practice and Policy*. Second, revised, and expanded edition. Metuchen, N.J.: The Scarecrow Press, Inc.

Gelles, R.J. 1980. "Violence in the Family: A Review of Research in the Seventies." *Journal of Marriage and the Family* 42(4): 873–885.

———. 1982. "Applying Research on Family Violence to Clinical Practice." *Journal of Marriage and the Family* 44(1): 9–20.

Gelles, R.J., and Straus, M. 1979. "Determinants Of Violence In The Family: Toward A Theoretical Integration." In W.R. Burr et al. (eds.) *Contemporary Theories About The Family. Research-Based Theories*. Vol. 1. New York: The Free Press.

Germain, C.B., and Gitterman, A. 1980. *The Life Model of Social Work Practice*. New York: Columbia University Press.

Gershenson, H.P. 1983. "Redefining Fatherhood in Families with White Adolescent Mothers." *Journal of Marriage and the Family* 45(3): 591–599.

Gilchrist, L.D., and Schinke, S.P. 1983. "Teenage Pregnancy and Public Policy." *Social Service Review* 57(2): 307–322.

Gilchrist, L.; Schinke, S.T.; and Blythe, B.J. 1979. "Primary Prevention Services for Children and Youth." *Children and Youth Services Review* 1(4): 379–391.

Gill, M.M. 1978. "Adoption of Older Children: The Problems Faced." *Social Casework* 59(5): 272–278.

Gilligan, C. 1982. *In a Different Voice. Psychological Theory and Women's Development*. Cambridge, Mass.: Harvard University Press.

Gillis, J.R. 1974. *Youth and History. Tradition and Change in European Age Relations 1770–Present*. New York: Academic Press.

Godenne, G.D. 1982. "The Adolescent Girl and Her Female Therapist." *Adolescence* 17(65): 225–242.

Goertzel, V., and Goertzel, M.G. 1962. *Cradles of Eminence*. Boston: Little, Brown and Co.

Golan, N. 1981. *Passing Through Transitions: A Guide for Practitioners*. New York: The Free Press.

Goldberg, B. 1983. "Psychiatric Aspects of Mental Retardation. Society's Attitude Toward the Mentally Retarded." In P.D. Steinnauer and Q. Rae-Grant (ed.) *Psychological Problems of the Child in the Family*. Second Edition. New York: Basic Books.

Goldberg, L., and Goldberg, W. 1982. "Group Work with Former Cultists." *Social Work* 27(2): 165–170.

Goldmeier, J. 1980. "Intervention in the Continuum from Divorce to Family Reconstitution." *Social Casework* 61(1): 39-47.

Goldmeier, J., and Dean, R.D. 1973. "The Runaway: Person, Problem or Situation?" *Crime & Delinquency* 19(4): 539-544.

Goldstein, H.; Gabay, D.; and Switzer, R.E. 1981. " 'Fail-Safe' Foster Family Care: A Mental Hospital-Child Welfare Agency Program." *Child Welfare* 60(9): 627-636.

Goldstein, J.; Freud, A.; and Solnit, A.J. 1973. *Beyond the Best Interests of the Child.* New York: The Free Press.

————. 1979. *Before the Best Interest of the Child.* New York: The Free Press.

Goodman, J.D., and Magno-Nora, R. 1975. "Adoption and Its Influence During Adolescence." *The Journal of the Medical Society of New Jersey* 72(11): 922-928.

Gordon, J.S. 1976. "Alternative Group Foster Homes. A New Place for Young People to Live." *Psychiatry* 39(4): 339-354.

————. 1979. "Running Away: Reaction or Revolution." In S.C. Feinstein and P.L. Giovacchini (eds.) *Adolescent Psychiatry* Vol. 7. Chicago: University of Chicago Press.

————. 1981. "The Runaway Center as a Community Mental Health Center." In J.S. Gordon and M. Beyer (eds.) *Reaching Troubled Youth. Runaways and Community Mental Health.* Rockville, Md.: National Institute of Mental Health.

Gordon, J.S., and Beyer, M. (eds.). 1981. *Reaching Troubled Youth. Runaways and Community Mental Health.* Rockville, Md.: National Institute of Mental Health.

Gossett, J.T.; Lewis, J.M.; and Barnhart, F.D. 1983. *To Find A Way. The Outcome of Hospital Treatment for Disturbed Adolescents.* New York: Brunner/Mazel.

Gottesman, R. 1981. *The Child And The Law.* St. Paul, Minn.: West Publishing Co.

Gould, M.S.; Wunsch-Hitzig, R.; and Dohrenwend, B. 1981. "Estimating the Prevalence of Childhood Psychopathology." *Journal of the American Academy of Child Psychiatry* 20(3): 462-476.

Green, A.H. 1978. "Psychopathology of Abused Children." *Journal of Child Psychiatry* 17(1): 92-103.

Greenberg, M.T.; Siegel, J.M.; and Leitch, C.J. 1983. "The Nature and Importance of Attachment Relationships to Parents and Peers During Adolescence." *Journal of Youth and Adolescence* 12(5): 373-386.

Greenberger, E.; Steinberg, L.D.; and Vaux, A. 1981. "Adolescents Who Work: Health and Behavioral Consequences of Job Stress." *Developmental Psychology* 17:691-703.

Gresham, F.M. 1983. "Social Skills Assessment as a Component of Mainstreaming Placement Decisions." *Exceptional Children* 49(4): 331-336.

Grotevant, H.D. 1983. "The Contribution of the Family to the Facilitation of Identity Formation in Early Adolescence." *Journal of Early Adolescence* 3(3): 225-237.

Grotevant, H.D., and Cooper, C.R. (eds.). 1983. *Adolescent Development in the Family.* New Directions for Child Development, Number 22. San Francisco: Jossey-Bass.

Grotevant, H.D., and Thorbecke, W.L. 1982. "Sex Differences in Styles of Occupational Identity Formation in Late Adolescence." *Developmental Psychology* 18:396–405.

Grotevant, H.D.; Thorbecke, W.; and Meyer, M.L. 1982. "An Extension of Marcia's Identity Status Interview into the Interpersonal Domain." *Journal of Youth and Adolescence* 11:33–47.

Group for the Advancement of Psychiatry. 1968. *Normal Adolescence: Its Dynamics and Impact*. Formulated by the Committee on Adolescence. New York: Group for the Advancement of Psychiatry, GAP Report No. 68, pp. 745–858.

Group for the Advancement of Psychiatry. Committee on the Family. 1981. *Divorce, Child Custody and the Family*. San Francisco: Jossey-Bass.

Guldner, C. 1983. "Growth-Promoting Family Therapy." In D.R. Mace (ed.) *Prevention in Family Service. Approaches to Wellness*. Beverly Hills, Calif.: Sage.

Gullotta, T.P. 1978. "Runaway: Reality Or Myth." *Adolescence* 13(52): 543–549.

———. 1979. "Leaving Home: Family Relationships Of The Runaway Child." *Social Casework* 60(2): 111–114.

Gurman, A.S., and Kniskern, D.P. 1978. "Research on Marital and Family Therapy —Progress, Perspective and Prospect." In S.L. Garfield and A.E. Bergin (eds.) *Handbook of Psychotherapy and Behavior Change: An Empirical Analysis*. Second edition. New York: John Wiley and Sons.

Gurman, A.S., and Kniskern, D.P. (eds.). 1981. *Handbook of Family Therapy*. New York: Brunner/Mazel.

Haley, J. 1973. *Uncommon Therapy. The Psychiatric Techniques of Milton H. Erickson, M.D.* New York: W.W. Norton & Co.

———. 1980. *Leaving Home. The Therapy of Disturbed Young People*. New York: McGraw-Hill.

Hall, G.S. 1904. *Adolescence: Its Psychology and Relations to Physiology, Anthropology, Sociology, Sex, Crime, Religion, and Education*. New York: Appleton.

Hall, J. 1982. "Adolescence: Life Cycle Needs of Adolescents with Handicapping Conditions." In L. Riehman and B. Reichert (eds.) *Social Work Practice: Meeting the Life Cycle Needs of Children and Youth with Handicapping Conditions*. San Diego: San Diego State University, pp. 175–186.

Hall, J.A. 1984. "Empirically Based Treatment for Parent-Adolescent Conflict." *Social Casework* 65(8): 487–495.

Hampson, R.B., and Tavormina, J.P. 1980. "Feedback from the Experts: A Study of Foster Mothers." *Social Work* 25(2): 108–113.

Hancock, B.L. 1982. *School Social Work*. Englewood Cliffs, N.J.: Prentice-Hall.

Hartman, A. 1981. "Bowen Family Systems: Theory and Practice." In E.R. Tolson and W.J. Reid (eds.) *Models of Family Treatment*. New York: Columbia University Press.

Hartman, A., and Laird, J. 1983. *Family-Centered Social Work Practice*. New York: The Free Press.

Havighurst, R.J. 1972. *Developmental Tasks and Education*. Third edition. New York: David McKay Co.

Hepworth, D.H., and Larsen, J.A. 1982. *Direct Social Work Practice. Theory and Skills.* Homewood, Ill.: The Dorsey Press.

Herrenkohl, E.C., and Herrenkohl, R.C. 1979. "A Comparison of Abused Children and Their Nonabused Siblings." *Journal of the American Academy of Child Psychiatry* 18(2): 260-269.

Herzog, E., and Sudia, C.E. 1973. "Children in Fatherless Families." In B.M. Caldwell and H.N. Ricciuti (eds.) *Review of Child Development Research* Vol. 3. Chicago: University of Chicago Press.

Hess, P., and Howard, T. 1981. "An Ecological Model for Assessing Psychosocial Difficulties in Children." *Child Welfare* 60(8): 499-518.

Hill, J.H. 1981. "Social Relations: Peers and Families." In U.S. Dept. of HHS, Public Health Service. *Adolescence And Stress. Report of an NIMH Conference* Science Reports, DHHS Publ. No. 81-1098, Washington, D.C.

Hill, J.P. 1980. *Understanding Early Adolescence—A Framework.* Chapel Hill, N.C.: Center for Early Adolescence.

Hill, R. 1970. *Family Development in Three Generations.* Cambridge, Mass.: Schenkman.

Hirschi, T. 1969. *Causes for Delinquency.* Berkeley: University of California.

Hoffman, L. 1980. "The Family Life Cycle and Discontinuous Change." In E.A. Carter and M. McGoldrick (eds.) *The Family Life Cycle: A Framework For Family Therapy.* New York: Gardner Press.

————. 1981. *Foundations of Family Therapy. A Conceptual Framework for Systems Change.* New York: Basic Books.

Hoffman, M.L. 1980. "Moral Development in Adolescence." In J. Adelson (ed.) *Handbook of Adolescent Psychology.* New York: John Wiley and Sons.

Hofmann, A.D. (M.D.). 1976. "Consent and Confidentiality and Their Legal and Ethical Implications for Adolescent Medicine." In J.R. Gallagher, F.P. Heald, and D.C. Garell (eds.) *Medical Care of the Adolescent* Third edition. New York: Appleton-Century-Crofts.

Hofstad, M.O. 1977. "Treatment in a Juvenile Court Setting." In Reid and Epstein (eds.) *Task-Centered Practice.* New York: Columbia University Press.

Hogan, M.J.: Buehler, C.; and Robinson, B. 1983. "Single Parenting: Transitioning Alone." In H.I. McCubbin and C.R. Figley (eds.) *Stress and the Family. Volume I: Coping With Normative Transitions.* New York: Brunner/Mazel.

Hogan, R. 1980. "The Gifted Adolescent." In J. Adelson (ed.) *Handbook of Adolescent Psychology.* New York: John Wiley and Sons, pp. 536-559.

Hollis, F., and Woods, M.E. 1981. *Casework: A Psychosocial Therapy.* New York: Random House.

Holman, A.M. 1983. *Family Assessment. Tools for Understanding and Intervention.* Beverly Hills, Calif.: Sage.

Homer, L.E. 1973. "Community-Based Resource For Runaway Girls." *Social Casework* 54(8): 473-479.

Hoorwitz, A.N. 1983. "Guidelines For Treating Father-Daughter Incest." *Social Casework* 64(9): 515-524.

Hornby, H., and Collins, M.I. 1981. "Teenagers in Foster Care: The Forgotten Majority." *Children and Youth Services Review* 3:7-20.

Howard, M. 1978. "Young Parent Families." *Child Welfare Strategy In The Coming Years.* Washington, D.C.: DHEW Publication No (OHDS) 78-30158: 197-226.

Hudson, W.W. 1982. *The Clinical Measurement Package. A Field Manual.* Homewood, Ill.: The Dorsey Press.

Hunner, R.J., and Walker, Y.E. (eds.). 1981. *Exploring the Relationship Between Child Abuse and Delinquency.* Montclair, N.J.: Allanheld, Osmun & Co.

Hunter, F.T., and Youniss, J. 1982. "Changes in Functions of Three Relations During Adolescence." *Developmental Psychology* 18(6): 806-811.

Hunter, L.W. 1964. "Foster Homes For Teenagers." *Children* 11(6): 234-243.

Hunter, W.B.; Hackney, N.; and Kingdon, M.L. 1978. "Family Intervention In A Treatment Program For The Hospitalized Adolescent." *International Journal of Family Counseling* 6(1): 45-51. [now entitled *American Journal of Family Therapy*]

Ingersoll, G.M. 1982. *Adolescents in School and Society.* Lexington, Mass.: D.C. Heath and Co.

Jacobson, D.S. 1979. "Stepfamilies: Myths and Realities." *Social Work* 24(3): 202-207.

Jaffe, E.D. 1969. "Effects of Institutionalization on Adolescent, Dependent Children." *Child Welfare* 48(2): 64-71, 111.

Janchill, M.P. 1983. "Services for Special Populations of Children." In B.G. McGowan and N. Meezan (eds.) *Child Welfare.* Itasca, Ill.: F.E. Peacock.

Jencks, C.; Smith, M.; Acland, H.; Bane, M.J.; Cohen, D.; Gintis, H.; Heyns, B.; and Michelson, S. 1972. *Inequality: A Reassessment of the Family and Schooling in America.* New York: Basic Books.

Jenkins, S. 1981a. "The Tie That Bonds." In A. Maluccio and P.A. Sinanoglu (eds.) *The Challenge of Partnership: Working with Parents of Children in Foster Care.* New York: Child Welfare League of America.

——— . 1981b. *The Ethnic Dilemma in Social Services.* New York: The Free Press.

Jenkins, S., and Norman, E. 1972. *Filial Deprivation and Foster Care.* New York: Columbia University Press.

Joe, B. 1978. "In Defense of Intercountry Adoption." *Social Service Review* 52(1): 1-20.

Johnson, H.C. 1980. "Working with Stepfamilies: Principles of Practice." *Social Work* 25(4): 304-308.

Johnson, S.B. 1981. "Psychosocial Factors in Juvenile Diabetes: A Review." In S. Chess and A. Thomas (eds.) *Annual Progress in Child Psychiatry and Development 1981.* New York: Brunner/Mazel, pp. 271-294.

Johnston, R.L. 1979. "Adolescent Growth and Development." In W.T. Hall and C.L. Young (eds.) *Health and Social Needs of the Adolescent: Professional Responsibilities.* Pittsburgh: University of Pittsburgh, Graduate School of Public Health, pp. 8-12.

Jones, E.E. 1979. "Personality Characteristics of Black Youth: A Cross-Cultural Investigation." *Journal of Youth and Adolescence* 8(2): 149-159.

Jones, M.A.; Magura, S.; and Shyne, A.W. 1981. "Effective Practice with Families in Protective and Preventive Services: What Works?" *Child Welfare* 60(2): 67-80.

Jones, M.L. 1979. "Preparing the School-Age Child for Adoption." *Child Welfare* 58(1): 27-34.

Jones, R., and Pritchard, C. (eds.). 1980. *Social Work with Adolescents*. London: Routledge & Kegan Paul.

Joseph, B.W. 1971. "Group Therapy with Adolescent Girls in Foster Care." *Adolescence* 6(23): 299-316.

Josselyn, I.M. 1952. *The Adolescent and His World*. New York: Family Service Association of America.

————. 1971. *The Adolescent*. New York: Harper and Row.

————. 1972. "Prelude: Adolescent Group Therapy: Why, When, and a Caution." In I.H. Berkowitz (ed.) *Adolescents Grow in Groups* New York: Brunner/Mazel.

Jurich, A.P. 1979. "Coping With Moral Problems of Adolescents in Foster Care." *Child Welfare* 58(3): 187-195.

Kadushin, A. *Child Welfare Services*. 1980. Third edition. New York: Macmillan.

Kagan, J. 1972. "A Conception of Early Adolescence." In J. Kagan and R. Coles. 1972. *Twelve to Sixteen: Early Adolescence*. New York: Norton.

Kandel, D., and Lesser, G.S. 1969. "Parent-Adolescent Relationships and Adolescent Independence in the United States and Denmark." *Journal of Marriage and the Family* 31(2): 348-358.

————. 1972. *Youth in Two Worlds*. San Francisco: Jossey-Bass.

Kandler, H.O. 1979. "Comprehensive Mental Health Consultation in High Schools." S.C. Feinstein and P.L. Giovacchini (eds.) *Adolescent Psychiatry. Developmental and Clinical Studies*. Vol. 7. Chicago: The University of Chicago Press.

Kaplan, S.L. 1977. "Structural Family Therapy for Children of Divorce: Case Reports." *Family Process* 16(1): 75-83.

Kashani, J.H., and Cantwell, D.P. 1983. "Characteristics Of Children Admitted To Inpatient Community Mental Health Center." *Archives of General Psychiatry* 40:397-400.

Kaslow, F.W. (ed.). 1982. *The International Book Of Family Therapy*. New York: Brunner/Mazel.

Katz, L. 1977. "Older Child Adoptive Placement: A Time for Family Crisis." *Child Welfare* 56(3): 165-171.

Kaufman, D.R., and Richardson, B.L. 1982. *Achievement and Women: Challenging the Assumptions*. New York: The Free Press.

Keating, D.P. 1980. "Thinking Processes in Adolescence." In J. Adelson (ed.) *Handbook of Adolescent Psychology*. New York: John Wiley and Sons.

Kellam, S.G. et al. 1981. "Why Teenagers Come for Treatment." *American Academy of Child Psychiatry* 20(3): 477-495.

Kessler, E.S. 1979. "Individual Psychotherapy with Adolescents." In J.R. Novello (ed.) *The Short Course in Adolescent Psychiatry*. New York: Brunner/Mazel.

Kidwell, J.S. 1981. "Number of Siblings, Sibling Spacing, Sex, and Birth Order: Their Effects on Perceived Parent-Adolescent Relationships." *Journal of Marriage and the Family* 43(2): 315-332.

Kim, D.S. 1978. "Issues in Transracial and Transcultural Adoption." *Social Case-work* 59(8): 477–486.

Kline, D., and Overstreet, H.M.F. 1972. *Foster Care of Children. Nurture and Treat-ment.* New York: Columbia University Press.

Klumpner, G.H. 1978. "A Review of Freud's Writings on Adolescence." In S.F. Fein-stein and P.L. Giovacchini (eds.) *Adolescent Psychiatry. Developmental and Clinical Studies.* Vol. 6. Chicago: University of Chicago Press.

Knitzer, J. 1982a. "Children's Rights In the Family and Society: Dilemmas and Realities." *American Journal of Orthopsychiatry* 53(3): 481–495.

——— . 1982b. *Unclaimed Children. The Failure of Public Responsibility to Chil-dren and Adolescents in Need of Mental Health Services.* Washington, D.C.: Children's Defense Fund.

Konopka, G. 1976a. "The Needs, Rights and Responsibilities of Youth." *Child Welfare* 55(3): 173–182.

——— . 1976b. *Young Girls: A Portrait of Adolescence.* Englewood Cliffs, N.J.: Prentice-Hall.

Korbin, J.E. (ed.). 1981. *Child Abuse and Neglect: Cross-Cultural Perspectives.* Berkeley: University of California Press.

Kraemer, S. 1982. "Leaving Home, and the Adolescent Family Therapist." *Journal of Adolescence* 5:51–62.

Kraus, J. 1971. "Predicting Success of Foster Placements for School-Age Chil-dren." *Social Work* 16(1): 63–72.

Lahti, J., et al. 1978. *A Follow-Up Study of the Oregon Project: A Summary.* Port-land, Oregon: Regional Research Institute for Human Services, Portland State University: U.S. Children's Bureau, Department of H.E.W.

Lahti, J., and Dvorak, J. 1981. "Coming Home From Foster Care." In A. Maluccio and P.A. Sinanoglu (eds.) *The Challenge of Partnership.* New York: Child Wel-fare League of America.

Laird, J. 1979. "An Ecological Approach to Child Welfare: Issues of Family Iden-tity and Continuity." Chap. 6 in C.B. Germain (ed.) *Social Work Practice: Peo-ple and Environments.* New York: Columbia University Press.

Lamb, D. 1978. *Psychotherapy with Adolescent Girls.* San Francisco: Jossey-Bass.

Lambert, B.G.; Rothschild, B.F.; Altland, R.; and Green, L.B. 1978. *Adolescence. Transition from Childhood to Maturity.* Second edition. Monterey, Calif.: Brooks/Cole.

Larsen, J.A., and Mitchell, C.T. 1980. "Task-Centered, Strength-Oriented Group Work with Delinquents." *Social Casework* 61(3): 154–163.

Larson, R.W. 1983. "Adolescents' Daily Experience with Family and Friends: Contrasting Opportunity Systems." *Journal of Marriage and the Family* 45(4): 739–750.

Lecca, P.L. 1983. "Current Trends in Mental Health Services and Legislation." Chap. 2 in Callicut and Lecca (eds.) *Social Work and Mental Health.* New York: The Free Press.

LeCroy, C.W. (Guest ed.). 1982. "Social Skills Training For Children And Youth." *Child & Youth Services* 5(3/4): 1–152.

Lee, J.A. 1977. "Group Work With Mentally Retarded Foster Adolescents." *Social Casework* 58(3): 164–173.

Lee, J.A., and Park, D.N. 1978. "A Group Approach to the Depressed Adolescent Girl in Foster Care." *American Journal of Orthopsychiatry* 48(3): 516–527.

Lefebvre, A. 1983. "The Child with Handicaps." In P.D. Steinhauer and Q. Rae-Grant (eds.) *Psychological Problems of the Child in the Family*. Second edition. New York: Basic Books, pp. 478–508.

Lerman, P. 1982. *Deinstitutionalization and the Welfare State*. New Brunswick, N.J.: Rutgers University Press.

Leveton, E. 1984. *Adolescent Crisis. Family Counseling Approaches*. New York: Springer.

Levinson, H. 1973. "Communication with an Adolescent in Psychotherapy." *Social Casework* 54(8): 480–488.

Lewin, K. 1936. (reprinted 1966) *Principles of Topological Psychology*. New York: McGraw-Hill.

———. 1939. "Field Theory and Experiment in Social Psychology: Concepts and Methods." *American Journal of Sociology* 44:868–896.

Lewis, J.M.; Beavers, W.R.; Gossett, J.T.; and Phillips, V.A. 1976. *No Single Thread. Psychological Health in Family Systems*. New York: Brunner/Mazel.

Lewis, J.M., and Looney, J.G. 1983. *The Long Struggle. Well-Functioning Working-Class Black Families*. New York: Brunner/Mazel.

Libbey, P., and Bybee, R. 1979. "The Physical Abuse of Adolescents." *Journal of Social Issues* 35(2): 101–126.

Liberman, F. 1982. "The Mixed-Age Group as an Adolescent Transitional Family." In F. Lieberman (ed.) *Clinical Social Workers as Psychotherapists*. New York: Gardner Press.

Libertoff, K. 1980. "The Runaway Child in America: A Social History." *Journal of Family Issues* 1(2): 151–164.

Lieberman, F. 1979. *Social Work With Children*. New York: Human Sciences Press.

Lipsitz, J. 1977. *Growing Up Forgotten*. Lexington, Mass.: Lexington Books, D.C. Heath and Co.

Livson, N., and Peskin, H. 1980. "Perspectives on Adolescence from Longitudinal Research." In J. Adelson (ed.) *Handbook of Adolescent Psychology*. New York: John Wiley and Sons, chap. 2, pp. 47–98.

Loevinger, J., and Knoll, E. 1983. "Personality: Stages, Traits, and the Self." *Annual Review of Psychology* 34:195–222.

Lordi, W.M. 1979. "Hospital and Residential Treatment of Adolescents." In J. Novello (ed.) *The Short Course In Adolescent Psychiatry*. New York: Brunner/Mazel.

Lourie, I.S. 1979. "Family Dynamics And The Abuse Of Adolescents: A Case For A Developmental Phase Specific Model Of Child Abuse." *Child Abuse and Neglect* 3(4): 967–974.

Lutz, P. 1983. "The Stepfamily: An Adolescent Perspective." *Family Relations* 32:367–375.

Mace, D.R. (ed.). 1983. *Prevention in Family Services. Approaches to Wellness*. Beverly Hills, Calif.: Sage.

MacGregor, R.; Ritchie, A.M.; Serrano, A.C.; and Schuster, F.P. 1964. *Multiple Impact Therapy with Families*. New York: McGraw-Hill.

MacIntyre, J.M. 1970. "Adolescence, Identity & Foster Family Care." *Children* 17(6): 213–217.

MacLennan, B.W., and Felsenfeld, N. 1968. *Group Counseling and Psychotherapy with Adolescents*. New York: Columbia University Press.

Madanes, C. 1981. *Strategic Family Therapy*. San Francisco: Jossey-Bass.

Magazino, C.J. 1983. "Service to Children and Families at Risk of Separation." In B.G. McGowan and W. Meezan (eds.) *Child Welfare*. Itasca, Ill.: F.E. Peacock.

Magura, S. 1981. "Are Services to Prevent Foster Care Effective?" *Children and Youth Services Review* 3(3): 193–212.

——— . 1982. "Clients View Outcomes Of Child Protective Services." *Social Casework* 63(9): 522–531.

Magura, S., and Moses, B.S. 1984. "Clients as Evaluators in Child Protective Services." *Child Welfare* 63(2): 99–112.

Malin, N.R. 1981. "Pathways to Placement of Adolescent Children." *Social Work* 26(6): 482–487.

Maloney, D.M. 1980. "The Teaching-Family Model: Working With Runaways." *Journal of Family Issues* 1(2): 304–307.

Maloney, D.M.; Timbers, G.D.; Maloney, K.B. 1977. "BIABH Project: Regional Adaptation of the Teaching-Family Model Group Home for Adolescents." *Child Welfare* 56(1): 787–796.

Maluccio, A.N. 1981a. "An Ecological Perspective on Practice with Parents of Children in Foster Care." In A. Maluccio and P.A. Sinanoglu (eds.) *The Challenge of Partnership: Working with Parents of Children in Foster Care*. New York: Child Welfare League of America.

——— (ed.). 1981b. *Promoting Competence in Clients. A New/Old Approach to Social Work Practice*. New York: The Free Press.

Maluccio, A.N., and Fein, E. 1983. "Permanency Planning: A Redefinition." *Child Welfare* 62(3): 195–201.

Maluccio, A., and Sinanoglu, P.A. (eds.). 1981. *The Challenge of Partnership: Working with Parents of Children in Foster Care*. New York: Child Welfare League of America.

Malyon, A.K. 1981. "The Homosexual Adolescent: Developmental Issues and Social Bias." *Child Welfare* 60(5): 321–330.

Manuel, D.C. 1981. "Plight of the Older Adoptees." *Los Angeles Times*, 12-4-1981.

Marcia, J.E. 1980. "Identity in Adolescence." In J. Adelson (ed.) *Handbook of Adolescent Psychology*. New York: John Wiley and Sons.

——— . 1983. "Some Directions for the Investigation of Ego Development in Early Adolescence." *Journal of Early Adolescence* 3(3): 215–223.

Margolin, C.R. 1978. "Salvation versus Liberation: The Movement for Children's Rights in a Historical Context." *Social Problems* 25(4): 441–452.

Martin, M.J., and Walters, J. 1982. "Familial Correlates Of Selected Types Of Child Abuse and Neglect." *Journal of Marriage and the Family* 44(2): 267–276.

Masterson, J. 1967. "The Symptomatic Adolescent Five Years Later: He Didn't Grow Out of It." *American Journal of Psychiatry* 123:1338–1345.
————. 1967. *The Psychiatric Dilemma of Adolescence.* Boston: Little, Brown.
————. 1968. "The Psychiatric Significance of Adolescent Turmoil." *American Journal of Psychiatry* 124:1549.
————. 1972. *Treatment of the Borderline Adolescent: A Developmental Approach* New York: Wiley-Interscience.
Masterson, J.R., and Washburne, A. 1966. "The Symptomatic Adolescent: Psychiatric Illness or Adolescent Turmoil?" *American Journal of Psychiatry* 122 (part 3): 1240–1248.
Matteson, D.R. 1977. "Exploration and Commitment. Sex Differences and Methodological Problems in the Use of Identity Status Categories." *Journal of Youth and Adolescence* 6:353–374.
Mayer, G., and Pearson, J.C. 1975. "Social Control in the Treatment of Adolescents in Residential Care: A Dilemma." *Child Welfare* 44(4): 246–256.
Mayer, M.F.; Richman, L.H.; and Balcerzak, E.A. 1978. *Group Care Of Children: Crossroads and Transitions.* New York: Child Welfare League of America.
McAdoo, H.P. (ed.). 1981. *Black Families.* Beverly Hills, Calif.: Sage.
————. 1983. "Societal Stress: The Black Family." In H.I. McCubbin and C.R. Figley (eds.) *Stress and the Family.* Vol. 1. New York: Brunner/Mazel.
McCubbin, H.I., and Figley, C.R. (eds.). 1983. *Stress and the Family. Vol. I: Coping With Normative Transitions.* New York: Brunner/Mazel.
McGoldrick, M., and Carter, E.A. 1980. "Forming a Remarried Family." In E.A. Carter and M. McGoldrick (eds.) *The Family Life Cycle: A Framework for Family Therapy.* New York: Gardner Press.
McGoldrick, M.; Pearce, J.K.; and Giordano, J. (eds.). 1982. *Ethnicity and Family Therapy.* New York: The Guilford Press.
McGowan, B.G., and Meezan, W. (eds.). 1983. *Child Welfare.* Itasca, Ill.: F.E. Peacock.
McKenry, P.C., et al. 1979. "Adolescent Pregnancy: A Review of the Literature." *The Family Coordinator* 28(1): 17–28.
McNeely, R.L., and Badami, M.K. 1984. "Interracial Communication in School Social Work." *Social Work* 29(1): 22–26.
McNeil, J.S., and Wright, R. 1983. "Special Populations: Black, Hispanic, and Native American. In Callicut and Lecca (eds.) *Social Work and Mental Health.* New York: The Free Press, Chap. 9.
McRoy, R.G.; Zurcher, L.A.; Lauderdale, M.L.; and Anderson, R.N. 1982. "Self-Esteem and Racial Identity in Transracial and Inracial Adoptees." *Social Work* 27(6): 522–526.
————. 1984. "The Identity of Transracial Adoptees." *Social Casework* 65(1): 34–39.
McWhinnie, A.M. 1969. "The Adopted Child In Adolescence." In G. Caplan and S. Lebovici (eds.) *Adolescence: Psychosocial Perspectives.* New York: Basic Books.
Mead, M. 1928. *Coming of Age in Samoa.* New York: Morrow.

Mech, E.V. 1983. "Out-Of-Home Placement Rates." *Social Service Review* 57(4): 659–667.

Meeks, J.E. 1980. *The Fragile Alliance. An Orientation to the Outpatient Psychotherapy of the Adolescent.* Second edition. Malabar, Florida: Robert E. Krieger.

Meezan, W. 1980. *Adoption Service in the States.* U.S. Department of Health and Human Services, Children's Bureau. DHHS Publication No. (OHDS) 80-30288. Washington, D.C.

———. 1983. "Toward an Expanded Role For Adoption Services." In B.G. McGowan and W. Meezan (eds.) *Child Welfare.* Itasca, Ill.: F.E. Peacock.

Meezan, W., and Shireman, J.F. 1982. "Foster Parent Adoption: A Literature Review." *Child Welfare* 61(8): 525–535.

Menken, J. 1980. "The Health and Social Consequences of Teenage Childbearing." In M. Bloom (ed.) *Life Span Development.* New York: Macmillan, pp. 226–246.

Merton, R.K. 1957. *Social Theory and Social Structure.* Revised edition. New York: The Free Press.

Meyer, C.H. 1984. "Adolescents: An Age-Group or a Problem." *Social Work* 29(1): 3.

Meyer, J.H., and Zegans, L.S. 1975. "Adolescents Perceive Their Psychotherapy." *Psychiatry* 38:11–22.

Minuchin, S. 1979. *Families & Family Therapy.* Cambridge, Mass.: Harvard University Press.

———. 1981. "Structural Family Therapy." In R.J. Green and J.L. Framo (eds.) *Family Therapy.* New York: International Universities Press, Inc.

Minuchin, S., and Fishman, C. 1981. *Family Therapy Techniques.* Cambridge, Mass.: Harvard University Press.

Moore, C.D. (ed.). 1981. *Adolescence and Stress. Report of an NIMH Conference.* Rockville, Md.: U.S. Department of Health and Human Services, Public Health Service. Alcohol, Drug Abuse, and Mental Health Administration.

Moos, R.H., and Fuhr, R. 1982. "The Clinical Use of Social-Ecological Concepts: The Case of an Adolescent Girl." *American Journal of Orthopsychiatry* 52(1): 111–122.

Morgan, E., and Farber, B.A. 1982. "Toward a Reformulation of the Eriksonian Model of Female Identity Development." *Adolescence* 17(65): 199–211.

Moses, A.B. 1978. "The Runaway Youth Act: Paradoxes Of Reform." *Social Service Review* 52(2): 227–243.

Moss, J.A. 1982. "Unemployment among Black Youths: A Policy Dilemma." *Social Work* 27:47–52.

Mouzakitis, C.M. 1984. "Characteristics of Abused Adolescents and Guidelines for Intervention." *Child Welfare* 63(2): 149–157.

Munro, G., and Adams, G.R. 1977. "Ego Identity Formation in College Students and Working Youth." *Developmental Psychology*, 13:523–524.

Muuss, R.E. 1982. *Theories of Adolescence.* Fourth edition. New York: Random House.

Myers, B.A.; Friedman, S.B.; and Weiner, I.B. 1970. "Coping with a Chronic Disability: Psychosocial Observations of Girls with Scoliosis Treated with the Milwaukee Brace." *American Journal of Diseases of Children* 120(3): 175–181.

The National Association of Attorneys General. 1976. *Legal Issues in Foster Care.* Raleigh, N.C.: Committee on the Office of Attorney General.

National Commission on Youth. 1980. *The Transition of Youth to Adulthood: A Bridge too Long.* Boulder, Colorado: Westview Press.

National Panel on High School and Adolescent Education. 1976. *The Education of Adolescents.* Washington, D.C.: U.S. Government Printing Office.

Nettler, G. 1974. *Explaining Crime.* New York: McGraw-Hill.

Norman, J.S. 1980. "Short-Term Treatment with the Adolescent Client." *Social Casework* 61(2): 74–82.

Northen, H. 1982. *Clinical Social Work.* New York: Columbia University Press.

Norvell, M., and Guy, R.F. 1977. "A Comparison Of Self-Concept In Adopted And Non-Adopted Adolescents." *Adolescence* 12(47): 443–448.

Novello, J.R. (ed.). 1979. *The Short Course in Adolescent Psychiatry.* New York: Brunner/Mazel.

Nye, F.I., and Edelbrock, C. (eds.). 1980. "Runaways." *Journal of Family Issues* 1(2): 147–312.

Offer, D. 1967. "Normal Adolescents." *Archives of General Psychiatry* 17:285–290.

———. 1969. *The Psychological World of the Teenager.* New York: Basic Books.

———. 1978. Foreword. In D. Lamb *Psychotherapy with Adolescent Girls.* San Francisco: Jossey-Bass.

Offer, D.; Marohn, R.C.; and Ostrov, E. 1979. *The Psychological World of the Juvenile Delinquent.* New York: Basic Books.

Offer, D.; Ostrov, E.; and Howard, K.I. 1981. *The Adolescent. A Psychological Self-Portrait.* New York: Basic Books.

Offer, D.; Sabshin, M.; and Marcus, D. 1965. "Clinical Evaluation of Normal Adolescents." *American Journal of Psychiatry* 121 (part 2): 864–872.

Offer, D., and VanderStoep, E. 1975. "Indicators and Contraindicators for Family Therapy." In M. Sugar (ed.) *The Adolescent in Group and Family Therapy.* New York: Brunner/Mazel, chap. 9.

Ogbu, J. 1981. "Roundtable Comments." In Department of Health and Human Services, Public Health Service, *Adolescence and Stress Science Reports*, Publ. No. 81-1098. Washington, D.C.

Oldham, D.G. 1978. "Adolescent Turmoil: A Myth Revisited." *Journal of Continuing Education in Psychiatry* 39(3): 23–32. Reprinted in Martin Bloom (ed.) *Life Span Development. Bases for Preventive and Interventive Helping.* New York: Macmillan, 1980, pp. 270–285.

Oldham, D.G.; Looney, J.G.; and Blotcky, M. 1980. "Clinical Assessment of Symptoms in Adolescents." *American Journal of Orthopsychiatry* 50(4): 697–703.

Olson, D.H., et al. 1982. *Family Inventories. Inventories Used in a National Survey of Families Across the Family Life Cycle.* St. Paul, Minn.: Family Social Science, University of Minnesota.

Olson, D.H., and McCubbin, H.I. 1983. *Families. What Makes Them Work.* Beverly Hills, Calif.: Sage.

Olson, D.H.; Russell, C.S.; and Sprenkle, D.H. 1980. "Marital and Family Therapy: A Decade Review." *Journal of Marriage and the Family* 42(4): 973–993.

Olson, L.; Liebow, E.; Mannino, F.V.; and Shore, M.F. 1980. "Runaway Children Twelve Years Later. A Follow-Up." *Journal of Family Issues* 1(2): 165–188.

Ooms, T. (ed.). 1981. *Teenage Pregnancy in a Family Context.* Philadelphia: Temple University Press.

Orten, J.D.; and Soll, S.K. 1980. "Runaway Children and Their Families. A Treatment Typology." *Journal of Family Issues* 1(2): 249–262.

Ostensen, K.W. 1981. "The Runaway Crisis: Is Family Therapy The Answer." *The American Journal of Family Therapy* 9(3): 3–11.

Pannor, R., and Nerlove, A.E. 1977. "Fostering Understanding Between Adolescents and Adoptive Parents Through Group Experiences." *Child Welfare* 56(8): 537–545.

Papp, P. (ed.). 1977. *Family Therapy. Full Length Case Studies.* New York: Gardner Press.

Pappenfort, D.; Kilpatrick, D.; and Roberts R. (eds.). 1973. *Child Caring: Social Policy and the Institution.* Chicago: Aldine.

Parish, T. 1981. "The Impact of Divorce on the Family." *Adolescence* 16(63): 577–580.

Parish, T.S., and Taylor, J.C. 1979. "The Impact of Divorce and Subsequent Father Absence on Children's and Adolescent's Self-concepts." *Journal of Youth and Adolescence* 8(4): 427–432.

Parke, R.D.; Power, T.G.; and Fisher, T. 1980. "The Adolescent Father's Impact on the Mother and Child." *Journal of Social Issues* 36(1): 88–106.

Paull, J.E. 1956. "The Runaway Foster Child." *Child Welfare* 35:21–26.

Perlman, H.H. 1957. *Social Casework. A Problem-solving Process.* Chicago: University of Chicago Press.

———. 1970. "The Problem-Solving Model in Social Casework." In R.W. Roberts and R.H. Nee (eds.) *Theories of Social Casework.* Chicago: University of Chicago Press.

Petersen, A.C. 1983. "Menarche: Meaning of Measures and Measuring Meaning." In S. Golu (ed.) *Menarche: The Transition from Girl to Woman.* Lexington, Mass.: D.C. Heath and Co.

Petersen, A.C., and Taylor, B. 1980. "The Biological Approach to Adolescence: Biological Change and Psychological Adaptation." In J. Adelson (ed.) *Handbook of Adolescent Psychology.* New York: John Wiley and Sons.

Petersen, A.C.; Tobin-Richards, M.; and Boxer, A. 1983. "Puberty: Its Measurement and Its Meaning." *Journal of Early Adolescence* 3(1–2): 47–62.

Petersen, A.C, and Wittig, M.A. 1979. "Differential Cognitive Deveopment in Adolescent Girls." In M. Sugar (ed.) *Female Adolescent Development.* New York: Brunner/Mazel.

Phipps-Yonas, S. 1980. "Teenage Pregnancy and Motherhood: A Review of the Literature." *American Journal of Ortho-Psychiatry* 50(3): 403–431.

Piaget, J. 1975. "The Intellectual Development of the Adolescent." In A.H. Esman (ed.) *The Psychology of Adolescence.* New York: International Universities Press, Inc., pp. 104–108.

Pool, M.L., and Frazier, J.R. 1973. "Family Therapy: A Review Of The Literature Pertinent To Children And Adolescents." *Psychotherapy, Theory, Research And Practice* 10(3): 256–260.

Porter, B.R., and Chatelain, R.S. 1981. "Family Life Education For Single Parent Families." *Family Relations* 30(4): 517–525.

Porter, J.B. 1984. "Juvenile Law." In R.H. Woody (ed.) *The Law And The Practice of Human Services*. San Francisco: Jossey-Bass.

Powell, G.J. (ed.). 1983. *The Psychosocial Development of Minority Group Children*. New York: Brunner/Mazel.

Powers, D. (Guest editor). 1983. "Adoption For Troubled Children." *Residential Group Care & Treatment* 2(1/2): 1–201.

The President's Commission on Mental Health. 1978. *Report of the Task Panel on Mental Health and American Families: Sub-Task Panel on Infants, Children, and Adolescents*. Washington, D.C.: U.S. Government Printing Office.

Proch, K. 1982. "Differences Between Foster Care And Adoptive Foster Parents." *Child Welfare* 61(5): 259–268.

Rabichow, H.G., and Sklansky, M.A. 1980. *Effective Counseling of Adolescents*. Chicago: Association Press, Follett.

Radin, N., and Welsh, B.L. 1984. "Social Work, Psychology, and Counseling in the Schools." *Social Work* 29(1): 28–33.

Ralston, N.C., and Thomas, G.P. 1974. *The Adolescent. Case Studies for Analysis*. New York: Harper & Row.

Raschke, H.J., and Raschke, V.J. 1979. "Family Conflict and Children's Self-Concepts: A Comparison of Intact and Single-Parent Families." *Journal of Marriage and the Family* 41(2): 367–374.

Raubolt, R.R. 1983. "Brief, Problem-Focused Group Psychotherapy with Adolescents." *American Journal of Orthopsychiatry* 53(1): 157–165.

Rawlings, S.W. 1984. *Household and Family Characteristics: March 1983*. Population Characteristics. Series P-20, No. 388. Washington, D.C.: U.S. Department of Commerce. Bureau of the Census.

Redmore, C.D., and Loevinger, J. 1979. "Ego Development in Adolescence: Longitudinal Studies." *Journal of Youth and Adolescence* 8(1): 1–19.

Regeringens Ungdomsudvalg. 1983. *Salomons unge. Analyse og vurdering af den sektoropdelte ungdomspolitik*. Rapport Nr. 3. København (Copenhagen, Denmark).

Reid, W.J. 1978. *The Task-Centered System*. New York: Columbia University Press.

———. 1981. "Family Treatment Within a Task-Centered Framework." In E.R. Tolson and W.J. Reid (eds.) *Models of Family Treatment*. New York: Columbia University Press.

———. (in press). *Family Problem Solving*. New York: Columbia University Press.

———. "Work with Families." In A. Fortune (ed.) *Task-Centered Practice with Families and Groups*. New York: Springer.

Reid, W.J., and Epstein, L. (eds.). 1977. *Task-Centered Practice*. New York: Columbia University Press.

Reiss, A.I., Jr. 1951. "Delinquency as the Failure of Personal and Social Controls." *American Sociological Review* 16: 196–207.

Reiss, D.; Oliveri, M.E.; and Curd, K. 1983. "Family Paradigm and Adolescent Behavior." In H.D. Grotevant and C.R. Cooper (eds.) *Adolescent Development in the Family*. San Francisco: Jossey-Bass, pp. 77–92.

Rhodes, S.L. 1977. "A Developmental Approach to the Life Cycle of the Family."
Social Casework 58(5): 301-311.

Rice, F.P. 1981. *The Adolescent Development, Relationships, and Culture.* Thir
edition. Boston: Allyn and Bacon.

Richter, P.E. 1977. "A Group Home Program in a Family Agency." *Social Case
work* 58(5): 259-267.

Riehman, L., and Reichert, B. (eds.). 1982. *Social Work Practice: Meeting the Li*
Cycle Needs of Children and Youth with Handicapping Conditions. San Diego
San Diego State University.

Rinsley, D.B. 1980. *Treatment of the Severely Disturbed Adolescent.* New York
Jason Aronson, Inc.

Robey, A.; Rosenwald, R.J.; and Snell, J.E. 1964. "The Runaway Girl: A Reactio
To Family Stress." *American Journal of Orthopsychiatry* 34:762-767.

Robison, D. 1980. "The Youth Unemployment Problem: Facts and Figures." I
A Review of Youth Employment Problems, Programs, and Policies: Vol. I. Th
Youth Employment Problem: Causes and Dimensions. Washington, D.C.: Vic
President's Task Force on Youth Employment, U.S. Department of Labor.

Rogow, A.M.; Marcia, J.E.; and Slugoski, B.R. 1983. "The Relative Importanc
of Identity Status Interview Components." *Journal of Youth and Adolescenc*
12(5): 387-400.

Rooney, R. 1977. "Adolescent Groups in Public Schools." In Reid and Epstei
(eds.) *Task-Centered Practice.* New York: Columbia University Press.

————. 1981. "A Task-Centered Reunification Model for Foster Care." In A
Maluccio and P.A. Sinanoglu (eds.) *The Challenge of Partnership.* New York
Child Welfare League of America.

Rose, Carol M. 1978. *Some Emerging Issues in Legal Liability of Children's Agen*
cies. New York: Child Welfare League of America.

Rosen, P.M.; Petersen, L.E.; and Walsh, B.W. 1980. "A Community Residence fo
Severely Disturbed Adolescents: A Cognitive-Behavioral Approach." *Chil*
Welfare 59(1): 15-25.

Rosen, R.H.; Benson, T.; and Stack, J.M. 1982. "Help or Hindrance: Parenta
Impact on Pregnant Teenagers' Resolution Decisions." *Family Relations* 31(2)
271-280.

Rosenberg, M., and Pearlin, L.I. 1978. "Social Class and Self-Esteem among Chi
dren and Adults." *American Journal of Sociology* 84(1): 53-77.

Rosenblatt, A., and Waldfogel, D. (eds.). 1983. *Handbook of Clinical Social Wor*
San Francisco: Jossey-Bass.

Rosenheim, M.K. (ed.). 1976. *Pursuing Justice for the Child.* Chicago: The Un
versity of Chicago Press.

Rosenwald, R.J., and Mayer, J. 1976. "Runaway Girls From Suburbia." *America*
Journal Of Orthopsychiatry 37(2): 402-403.

Ruback, R.B. 1984. "Family Law." In R.H. Woody (ed.) *The Law And The Prac*
tice of Human Services. San Francisco: Jossey-Bass.

Ruggiero, M.; Greenberger, E.; and Steinberg, L.D. 1982. "Occupational Devianc
among Adolescent Workers." *Youth & Society* 13:423-448.

Rutter, B.A. 1978. *The Parents' Guide to Foster Family Care*. New York: Child Welfare League of America.

Rutter, M. 1980. *Changing Youth in a Changing Society*. Cambridge, Mass.: Harvard University Press.

Rutter, M., and Giller, H. 1984. *Juvenile Delinquency. Trends and Perspectives*. New York: The Guilford Press.

Sager, C.J.; Brown, H.S.; Crohn, H.; Engel, T.; Rodstein, E.; and Walker, L. 1983. *Treating the Remarried Family*. New York: Brunner/Mazel.

Saluter, A.F. 1983. *Marital Status and Living Arrangements: March 1983*. Population Characteristics. Series P-20, No. 389. Washington, D.C.: U.S. Department of Commerce. Bureau of the Census.

Sarri, R.C. 1974. *Under Lock and Key: Juveniles in Jails and Detention*. Ann Arbor: University of Michigan.

Schachter, B. 1978. "Treatment of Older Adolescents in Transitional Programs Rapproachement Crisis Revisited." *Clinical Social Work Journal* 6(4): 293–304.

Schaefer, C.E.; Briesmeister, J.M.; and Fitton, M.E. 1984. *Family Therapy Techniques for Problem Behaviors of Children and Teenagers*. San Francisco: Jossey-Bass.

Scheiner, L.C.; Musetto, A.P.; and Cordier, D.C. 1982. "Custody and Visitation Counseling: A Report of an Innovative Program." *Family Relations* 31:99–107.

Scherz, F.H. 1967. "The Crisis of Adolescence in Family Life." *Social Casework* 48:209–215.

———. 1971. "Maturational Crisis and Parent-Child Interaction." *Social Casework* 52(6): 362–369.

Schinke, S.P., and Gilchrist, L.D. 1984. *Life Skills Counseling with Adolescents*. Baltimore: University Park Press.

Schoettle, U.C., and Cantwell, D.P. 1980. "Children of Divorce." *Journal of Child Psychiatry* 19(3): 453–475.

Schvaneveldt, J.D, and Ihinger, M. 1979. "Sibling Relationships in the Family." In W.R. Burr, R. Hill, F.I. Nye, and I.L. Reiss (eds.) *Contemporary Theories About the Family. Research-Based Theories*. Vol. 1. New York: The Free Press, pp. 453–467.

Schwartz, A. 1983. "Behavioral Principles and Approaches." In A. Rosenblatt and D. Waldfogel (eds.) *Handbook of Clinical Social Work*. San Francisco: Jossey-Bass.

Schwartzberg, A.Z. 1980. "Adolescent Reactions to Divorce." In S.C. Feinstein, et al. (eds.) *Adolescent Psychiatry Developmental and Clinical Studies*. Vol. 8. Chicago: University of Chicago Press, pp. 379–392.

Sears, R.R. 1975. "Your Ancients Revisited: A History of Child Development." In E.M. Hetherington (ed.) *Review of Child Development Research*. Vol. 5. Chicago: University of Chicago Press, pp. 1–73.

Segal, S.P. 1981. "Community Mental Health." In N. Gilbert and H. Specht (eds.) *Handbook of the Social Services*. Englewood Cliffs, N.J.: Prentice-Hall, chap. 8.

The Select Panel for the Promotion of Child Health. See U.S. Department of Health and Human Services, Public Health Service. 1981.

Seltzer, V.C. 1982. *Adolescent Social Development: Dynamic Functional Interaction.* Lexington, Mass.: Lexington Books, D.C. Heath and Co.

Serrano, A.C.; Zuelzer, M.B.; Howe, D.D.; and Reposa, R.E. 1979. "Ecology of Abusive and Nonabusive Families." *Journal of the American Academy of Child Psychiatry* 18(1): 67-75.

Server, J.C., and Janzen, C. 1982. "Contraindications to Reconstitution of Sexually Abusive Families." *Child Welfare* 61(5): 279-288.

Shapiro, C.H., and Seeber, B.C. 1983. "Sex Education and The Adoptive Family." *Social Work* 28(4): 291-296.

Shearin, R.B., and Jones, R.L. 1979. "Puberty and Associated Medical Disorders of Adolescence." In J.R. Novello (ed.) *The Short Course in Adolescent Psychiatry.* New York: Brunner/Mazel, chap. 3.

Shostack, A.L. 1978. "Staffing Patterns in Group Homes for Teenagers." *Child Welfare* 57(5): 309-319.

Shyne, A.W., and Schroeder, A.G. 1978. *National Study of Social Services to Children and Their Families.* Washington, D.C.: U.S. Department of Health, Education and Welfare. Administration for Children, Youth, and Families.

Silbert, M.H., and Pines, A.M. 1983. "Early Sexual Exploitation As An Influence In Prostitution." *Social Work* 28(4): 285-289.

Simmons, R.G.; Brown, L.; Bush, D.M.; and Blyth, D.A. 1978. "Self-Esteem and Achievement of Black and White Adolescents." *Social Problems* 26(1): 86-96.

Simon, R.M. 1980. "Family Life Cycle Issues In The Therapy System." In E.A. Carter and M. McGoldrick (eds.) *The Family Life Cycle: A Framework For Family Therapy.* New York: Gardner Press.

Simpson, M.; Timm, H.; and McCubbin, H.L. 1981. "Adoptees in Search of Their Past: Policy Induced Strain on Adoptive Families and Birth Parents." *Family Relations* 30(3): 427-434.

Slater, E.J.; Stewart, K.J.; and Linn, M.W. 1983. "The Effect of Family Disruption on Adolescent Males and Females." *Adolescence* 18(72): 931-942.

Smith, E.J. 1982. "The Black Female Adolescent: A Review of the Educational, Career and Psychologial Literature." *Psychology of Women Quarterly* 6(3): 261-288.

Sobol, M.P., and Cardiff, J. 1983. "A Sociopsychological Investigation of Adult Adoptees' Search For Birth Parents." *Family Relations* 32(4): 477-483.

Social Service Review. 1973. "The Rights of Children." *Notes and Comments* 47(4): 607-609, December.

Sommerville, J. 1982. *The Rise and Fall of Childhood.* Beverly Hills, Calif.: Sage. Vol. 140. Sage Library of Social Research.

Sorosky, A.; Baran, A.; and Pannor, R. 1975. "Identify Conflicts in Adoptees." *American Journal of Orthopsychiatry* 45(1): 18-27.

——. 1978. *The Adoption Triangle — The Effects of the Sealed Record on Adoptees, Birth Parents and Adoptive Parents.* Garden City, N.Y.: Anchor Books.

Sprenkle, D.H., and Cyrus, C.L. 1983. "Abandonment: The Stress of Sudden Divorce." In C.R. Figley and H.I. McCubbin (eds.) *Stress and the Family. Vol. II: Coping With Catastrophe* New York: Brunner/Mazel.

Stafford-Clark, D. 1966. *What Freud Really Said.* New York: Schocken Books.

Stanton, D.M. 1981. "Strategic Approaches to Family Therapy." In A.S. Gurman and D.P. Kniskern (eds.) *Handbook of Family Therapy.* New York: Brunner/Mazel.

Staples, R., and Mirandé, A. 1980. "Racial and Cultural Variations among American Families: A Decennial Review of the Literature on Minority Families." *Journal of Marriage and the Family* 42(4): 887–903.

Stein, J.M., and Derdeyn, A.P. 1980. "The Child in Group Foster Care. Issues of Separation and Loss." *Journal of Child Psychiatry* 19(1): 90–100.

Stein, M.D., and Davis, J.K. 1982. *Therapies for Adolescents. Current Treatments for Problem Behaviors.* San Francisco: Jossey-Bass.

Stein, T.J., and Rzepnicki, T.L. 1984. *Decision Making in Child Welfare Services. Intake and Planning.* Boston: Kluwer-Nijhoff.

Steinberg, L.D.; Greenberger, E.; Vaux, A.; and Ruggiero, M. 1981. "Early Work Experience. Effects on Adolescent Occupational Socialization." *Youth & Society* 12:403–422.

Steinberg, L.D.; Greenberger, E.; Garduque, L.; Ruggiero, M.; and Vaux, A. 1982. "Effects of Working on Adolescent Development." *Developmental Psychology* 18:385–395.

Steinhauer, P.D., and Rae-Grant, Q. (eds.). 1983. *Psychological Problems of the Child in the Family.* Second edition. New York: Basic Books.

Stewart, M.W. 1981. "Adolescent Pregnancy: Status Convergence for the Well-Socialized Adolescent Female." *Youth & Society* 12(4): 423–464.

Stheno, S.M. 1982. "Differential Treatment Of Minority Children In Service Systems." *Social Work* 27(1): 39–45.

Stick, R.S. 1984. "Rights of Handicapped Children to an Education." In R.H. Woody (ed.) *The Law And The Practice of Human Services* San Francisco: Jossey-Bass.

Stierlin, H. 1973. "A Family Perspective on Adolescent Runaways." *Archives of General Psychiatry* 29(1): 56–62.

————. 1977. "Treatment Perspectives on Adolescent Runaways." *Adolescent Psychiatry* 5:413–421. Chicago: University of Chicago Press.

————. 1981. *Separating Parents and Adolescents. Individuation in the Family.* Second edition. New York: Jason Aronson.

Stierlin, H.; Rucker-Embden, I.; Wetzel, N.; and Wirsching, M. 1980. *The First Interview with the Family.* New York: Brunner/Mazel.

Sugar, M. (ed.). 1975. *The Adolescent in Group and Family Therapy.* New York: Brunner/Mazel.

————. 1978. *Female Adolescent Development.* New York: Brunner/Mazel.

————. 1979. "Integration of Therapeutic Modalities in the Treatment of an Adolescent." *International Journal of Group Psychotherapy* 29(4): 509–522.

Swire, M.R., and Kavaler, F. 1977. "The Health Status of Foster Children." *Child Welfare,* Extended Issue, 56(10): 635–653.

————. 1978. "Health Supervision of Children in Foster Care." *Child Welfare* 57(9): 563–569.

Taggart, R., and Linder, B. (eds.). 1980. *A Review of Youth Employment Problems, Programs, and Policies: Vol. I. The Youth Employment Problem: Causes and Dimensions*. Washington, D.C.: Vice President's Task Force on Youth Employment, U.S. Department of Labor.

Tanner, J.M. 1980. "Sequence, Tempo, and Individual Variation in the Growth and Development of Boys and Girls Aged 12 to 16." In S.I. Harrison and J.F. McDermott, Jr. (eds.) *New Directions in Childhood Psychopathology*. Vol. 1: Developmental Considerations. New York: International Universities Press, Inc., pp. 182-202.

Taylor, D.A., and Alpert, S.W. 1973. *Continuity and Support Following Residential Treatment*. New York: Child Welfare League of America.

Taylor, J.L., et al. 1976. *A Group Home For Adolescent Girls: Practice and Research*. New York: Child Welfare League of America.

Terkelsen, K.G. 1980. "Toward A Theory Of The Family Life Cycle." In E.A. Carter and M. McGoldrick (eds.) *The Family Life Cycle: A Framework For Family Therapy*. New York: Gardner Press.

Teyber, E. 1983. "Effects of the Parental Coalition on Adolescent Emancipation from the Family." *Journal of Marital and Family Therapy* 9(3): 305-310.

Thomas, A., and Chess, S. 1977. *Temperament and Development*. New York: Raven Press.

Timberlake, E.M. 1979. "Aggression and Depression among Abused and Non-Abused Children in Foster Care." *Children and Youth Services Review* 1(3): 279-291.

Timberlake, E.M., and Hamlin, E.R., II. 1982. "The Sibling Group: A Neglected Dimension of Placement." *Child Welfare* 61(8): 545-552.

Toews, J.; Martin, R.; and Prosen, H. 1981. "The Life Cycle of the Family: Perspectives on Psychotherapy with Adolescents." In S.C. Feinstein; J.G. Looney; A.Z. Schwartzberg; and A.D. Sorosky (eds.) *Adolescent Psychiatry. Developmental and Clinical Studies*. Vol. 9. Chicago: University of Chicago Press.

Tolson, E.R., and Reid, W.J. (eds.). 1981. *Models of Family Treatment*. New York: Columbia University Press.

Tomlinson, R., and Peters, P. 1981. "An Alternative to Placing Children: Intensive and Extensive Therapy with 'Disengaged' Families." *Child Welfare* 55(2): 95-103.

Towle, C. 1957. *Common Human Needs*. Revised edition. New York: National Association of Social Workers.

Tramontana, M.G., 1980. "Critical Review of Research on Psychotherapy Outcome with Adolescents: 1967-1977." *Psychological Bulletin* 88(2): 429-450.

Triseliotis, J. 1973. *In Search of Origins: The Experience of Adopted People*. London: Routledge & Kegan Paul.

Tsukada, G.K. 1979. "Sibling Interaction: A Review of the Literature." *Smith College Studies in Social Work* 49(3): 229-247.

Tyler, F.B., and Gatz, M. 1977. "Development of Individual Psychosocial Competence in a High School Setting." *Journal of Consulting and Clinical Psychology* 45(3): 441-448.

Ulrici, D.K. 1983. "The Effects of Behavioral and Family Interventions on Juvenile Recidivism." *Family Therapy* 10(1): 25-36.

United Nations Department of International Economic and Social Affairs, Statistical Office. 1983. *Demographic Yearbook 1981*. Thirty-third Issue. New York: United Nations.

U.S. Department of Commerce, Bureau of the Census. 1982. *1980 Census of Population and Housing*. Provisional Estimates of Social, Economic, and Housing Characteristics. Washington, D.C.

U.S. Department of Health and Human Services, Public Health Service. 1981. *The Report of the Select Panel for the Promotion of Child Health. Vol. 1. Major Findings and Recommendations. Vol. 2. Analysis and Recommendations for Selected Federal Programs. Vol. 3. A Statistical Profile*. Washington, D.C., DHHS (PHS) Publication No. 79-55071.

U.S. Department of Health and Human Services, Public Health Service. Alcohol, Drug Abuse, and Mental Health Administration. 1981. *Adolescence and Stress. Report of an NIMH Conference*. Edited by C.D. Moore. Rockville, Md.

U.S. Department of Health, Education and Welfare, Health Care Financing Administration. 1980. *A Guide to Adolescent Health Care EPSDT*. Washington, D.C., pp. 26-27.

Vanderkooi, L., and Pearson, J. 1983. "Mediating Court Disputes: Mediation Behaviors, Styles, and Roles." *Family Relations* 32(4): 557-566.

Vils, U. 1982. "Options House: For Throwaway Youths." *Los Angeles Times* (7-7-82).

Visher, E., and Visher, J. 1979. *Stepfamilies: A Guide to Working with Stepparents and Stepchildren*. New York: Brunner/Mazel.

————. 1983. "Stepparenting: Blending Families." In H.I. McCubbin and C.R. Figley (eds.) *Stress and the Family. Volume I: Coping With Normative Transitions*. New York: Brunner/Mazel.

Wald, E. 1981. *The Remarried Family: Challenge and Promise*. New York: Family Service Association of America.

Wald, M. 1976. "State Intervention on Behalf of 'Neglected' Children: Standards for Removal of Children from Their Homes, Monitoring the Status of Children in Foster Care, and Termination of Parental Rights." *Stanford Law Review* 28:623-706.

Wald, P. 1976. "Making Sense Out of the Rights of Youth." *Child Welfare* 55(6): 379-393.

Wald, P.M. 1976. "Pretrial Detention for Juveniles." In M.K. Rosenheim (ed.) *Pursuing Justice for the Child*. Chicago: University of Chicago Press.

Waldinger, G. 1982. "Subsidized Adoption: How Paid Parents View It." *Social Work* 27(6): 516-521.

Walker, C.W. 1971. "Persistence of Mourning in the Foster Child as Related to the Foster Mother's Level of Maturity." *Smith College Studies in Social Work* 41(3): 173-246.

Walker, D.K. 1975. *Runaway Youth: An Annotated Bibliography and Literature Overview*. Washington, D.C.: Department of Health, Education and Welfare.

Wallerstein, J.S, and Kelly, J.B. 1974. "The Effects of Parental Divorce: The Adolescent Experience." In E.J. Anthony and C. Koupernik (eds.) *The Child In His Family: Children at Psychiatric Risk*. Vol. 3. New York: John Wiley and Sons.

———. 1979. "Children and Divorce: A Review." *Social Work* 24(6): 468–475.

———. 1980. *Surviving the Break-Up: How Parents and Children Cope with Divorce*. New York: Basic Books.

Walsh, B., and Rosen, P. 1979. "A Network of Services for Severely Disturbed Adolescents." *Child Welfare* 58(2): 115–125.

Walters, J., and Stinnett, N. 1971. "Parent-Child Relationships: A Decade Review of Research." *Journal of Marriage and the Family* 33(1): 70–111.

Walters, J., and Walters, L.H. 1980. "Parent-Child Relationships: A Review, 1970–1979." *Journal of Marriage and the Family* 42(4): 807–822.

Ward, M. 1979. "The Relationship Between Parents and Caseworker in Adoption." *Social Casework* 60(2): 96–103.

———. 1981. "Parental Bonding in Older Child Adoptions." *Child Welfare* 60(1): 24–34.

Waterman, A.S. 1982. "Identity Development From Adolescence to Adulthood: An Extension of Theory and a Review of Research," *Developmental Psychology* 18(3): 341–358.

Watson, M.A. 1981. "Custody Alternatives: Defining the Best Interests of the Children." *Family Relations* 30(3): 474–479.

Watson, R.I., and Lindgren, H.C. 1979. *Psychology of the Child and the Adolescent*. Fourth edition. New York: Macmillan.

Weiner, I. 1982. *Child and Adolescent Psychopathology*. New York: John Wiley and Sons.

Weinstein, E.A. 1960. *The Self-Image of the Foster Child*. New York: Russell Sage Foundation.

Weisberg, P.S. 1979. "Group Therapy with Adolescents." In J.R. Novello, (ed.) *The Short Course in Adolescent Psychiatry*. New York: Brunner/Mazel.

Weiss, R.S. 1979. "Growing Up a Little Faster: The Experience of Growing Up in a Single-Parent Household." *The Journal of Social Issues* 35(4): 97–111.

Wellisch, D.K.; Vincent, J.; and Ro-Trock, G.K. 1976. "Family Therapy versus Individual Therapy: A Study of Adolescents and Their Parents." In D.H.L. Olson (ed.) *Treating Relationships*. Lake Mills, Iowa: Graphic Book Co.

Wells, S.J. 1981. "A Model of Therapy with Abusive and Neglectful Families." *Social Work* 26(2): 113–118.

Welner, J. (ed.). 1980. *Psykiatri. En Tekstbog*. Copenhagen, Denmark: FADL's Forlag.

Westley, W.A., and Epstein, N.B. 1969. *The Silent Majority*. San Francisco: Jossey-Bass.

Westman, Jack C. 1973. "The Legal Rights of Adolescents from a Developmental Perspective." In Joseph C. Schoolar (ed.) *Current Issues in Adolescent Psychiatry*. New York: Brunner/Mazel.

Whiteside, M.F. 1982. "Remarriage: A Family Developmental Process." *Journal of Marital and Family Therapy* 8(2): 59–68.

Whittaker, J.K. 1981. "Family Involvement in Residential Treatment: A Support System for Parents." In A. Maluccio and P.A. Sinanoglu (eds.) *The Challenge of Partnership*. New York: Child Welfare League of America.

Whittaker, J.K., and Small, R.W. 1977. "Differential Approaches to Group Treatment of Children and Adolescents." *Child & Youth Services* 1(1): 5–13.

Whittaker, Y. 1979. *Caring for Troubled Children: Residential Treatment in a Community Context*. San Francisco: Jossey-Bass.

Wiehe, V.R. 1982. "Differential Personality Types of Foster Parents." *Social Work Research & Abstracts* 18(2): 16–20.

Wilgus, A., and Epstein, I. 1978. "Group Homes for Adolescents: A Comparative Case Study." *Social Work* 23(6): 486–491.

Williams, J.B.W. 1981. "DSM-III: A Comprehensive Approach to Diagnosis." *Social Work* 26(2): 101–106.

Wodarski, J.S., and Ammons, P.W. 1981. "Comprehensive Treatment of Runaway Children and Their Parents." *Family Therapy* 8:229–240.

Woody, R.H. (ed.). 1984. *The Law And The Practice of Human Services*. San Francisco: Jossey-Bass.

Wright, B. 1981. "In Search of the Problem: A Needs Assessment for Adolescents." *Health and Social Work* 6(4): 47–54.

Yalom, I.D. 1975. *The Theory and Practice of Group Psychotherapy*. Second edition. New York: Basic Books.

Young, R.L.; Godfrey, W.; Matthews, B.; and Adams, G.R. 1983. "Runaways: A Review of Negative Consequences." *Family Relations* (32):275–281.

Young, T.M., and Pappenfort, D.M. 1977. *Secure Detention of Juveniles and Alternatives to Its Use*. Washington, D.C.: U.S. Government Printing Office.

Youniss, J. 1983. "Social Construction of Adolescence by Adolescents and Parents." In H.D. Grotevant and C.R. Cooper (eds.) *Adolescent Development in the Family*. San Francisco: Jossey-Bass.

Yu, K.H., and Kim, L.I.C. 1983. "The Growth and Development of Korean-American Children." In G.J. Powell (ed.) *The Psychosocial Development of Minority Children*. New York: Brunner/Mazel.

Zastrow, C., and Navarre, R. 1975. "Help For Runaways And Their Parents." *Social Casework* 56(2): 74–78.

Zelnik, M.; Kantner, J.F.; and Ford, K. 1981. *Sex and Pregnancy in Adolescence*. Vol. 133, Sage Library of Social Research. Beverly Hills and London: Sage.

Ziefert, M. 1981. "Abuse and Neglect: The Adolescent as Hidden Victim." In K.C. Faller (ed.) *Social Work with Abused and Neglected Children*. New York: The Free Press.

Zimmerman, R.B. 1982. *Foster Care in Retrospect*. New Orleans: Tulane University.

Zimring, F.E. 1982. *The Changing Legal World of Adolescence*. New York: The Free Press.

Zitner, P., and Miller, S.H. 1980. *Our Youngest Parents. A Study of the Use of Support Services by Adolescent Mothers*. New York: Child Welfare League of America, Inc.

NAME INDEX

SUBJECT INDEX

Abortions, 83–85, 120
Abuse and neglect. *See also* Sexual abuse
abuse by foster parents, 141–42
abused/neglected in foster care, 140, 198, 199
case example: foster home abuse, 149–50
discharge from care to bio-family, 199
legal issues, 132
protective services, 129
reporting by school social workers, 118
residential care, 147
runaways, 209
siblings, 182–83
treatment of abusive families, 200
treatment of incestuous families, 199–200
Accidents, 120
Adaptability in families (Circumplex Model), 54
Adolescence. *See also* Historical trends
as family life cycle stage, 1
as labor force, 15
defined, 11
Adolescent developmental theories, 25–40
Ausubel's Integrated Psychology, 27
behavior theory, 34–36
ecological theory, 38–40
field theory, 36–38
Hall's biogenetic recapitulation theory, 25
neo-freudianism (Blos, Erikson), 28–34
psychoanalytic theory, 25
social psychology, 36–38
Adolescent fathers. *See* Teenage fathers
Adolescent Health Services, Pregnancy Prevention, and Care Act of 1978, 121

Adolescent medicine, 19–20, 120–22
confidentiality, 132
international symposia, 20
Adolescent mothers. *See* Teenage mothers
Adolescent population,
size of in the U.S. and world populations, 2
Adolescent Psychopathology Scale, 174
Adolescent-sibling relations. *See* Sibling relations
Adoption, 90, 155–65. *See also* Genealogical searches; Sealed record controversy; Transracial adoptions
Child Welfare League Standards, 165
disrupted, 164
distinguished from foster care, 157
follow-up study (Sweden), 165
geneological search, 39, 158–64
identity achievement of adoptees, 158–64
legal rights of adoptees, 162
"open" adoptions, 165
postplacement services, 203
reunion with biological parents, 162–63
sealed record controversy, 158, 161–64
search, 39, 158–64
services to adoptive families, 202–03
statistics, 155
subsidized adoptions, 157
transracial adoptions, 160–61
views of Anna Freud, 159
Adoption failures, 164
Adoptive families,
special services to, 202–03
Adoption Assistance and Child Welfare Act of 1980 (Public Law 96–272), 113
Aggression, 35